KT-434-692

Analysing Organisations

ANALYSING ORGANISATIONS

Second Edition

Sandra Dawson
Professor, The Management School
Imperial College, University of London

M

© Sandra Dawson 1986, 1992

All rights reserved. No reproduction, copy or transmission of this publication may be made without written permission.

No paragraph of this publication may be reproduced, copied or transmitted save with written permission or in accordance with the provisions of the Copyright, Designs and Patents Act 1988, or under the terms of any licence permitting limited copying issued by the Copyright Licensing Agency, 90 Tottenham Court Road, London W1P 9HE.

Any person who does any unauthorised act in relation to this publication may be liable to criminal prosecution and civil claims for damages.

First edition 1986
Reprinted 1988, 1989
Second edition 1992

Published by
THE MACMILLAN PRESS LTD
Houndmills, Basingstoke, Hampshire RG21 2XS
and London
Companies and representatives
throughout the world

ISBN 0–333–57645–4 hardcover
ISBN 0–333–57646–2 paperback

A catalogue record for this book is available
from the British Library

Printed in Great Britain by
Billing & Sons Ltd
Worcester

To Henry, Hannah, Rebecca and Tom

Acknowledgements

The author and publishers wish to thank the following who have kindly given permission for the use of copyright material:

Jossey Bass for material from *Managing Organizational Performance* by Michael Nash, published by Jossey Bass 1983.

Administrative Science Quarterly for a diagram from 'An Empirical Taxonomy of Structures of Work Organizations' by D. S. Pugh, D. J. Hickson and C. R. Hinings, published in *Administrative Science Quarterly*, Vol. 14 (1) (March 1969) p. 123.

Every effort has been made to trace all the copyright-holders, but if any have been inadvertently overlooked the publishers will be pleased to make the necessary arrangement at the first opportunity.

Contents

List of Figures

List of Tables

Preface to the First Edition

This book began as a series of lectures given at Imperial College to first-year students who were among the pioneers on the 'Dainton' four-year enhanced engineering courses. Each cohort of students, through their occasionally sharp and frequently thought-provoking injections of inspiration, questions and scepticism, has had an unwitting hand in the formation of the text. Its form and content have also been much influenced by contact, through research, consultancy and short courses, with managers and specialists who have proffered a different range of interests and criticisms to my analysis of organisations. The final product is intended for the successors of both these groups of people, that is, for those men and women who are now, or are intending to become, managers or specialists in organisations and who want, or are required, to become more expert in their analysis. I hope that the text will also be of interest to those who wish to make a more academic study of organisations. It may provide them with a different perspective on literature with which they are already familiar, and in particular the discussions in the last five chapters may introduce them to some new ideas. Its main attraction to students who wish to specialise in the study of organisations must, however, be that it attempts to bridge the gap between theory and practice in such a way as not to trivialise the former while establishing a framework for the latter.

This is an introductory text; it assumes no prior knowledge of organisational analysis. However, once the initial introduction is effected, the maintenance of the relationship between text and reader will demand careful thought and reflection from the latter. These demands derive, I hope, not from academic pretentiousness, which the reader may be assured is given little quarter by either the engineering students of Imperial College or young managers preoccupied with their immediate problems. In writing primarily for these audiences I hope I have fulfilled my side of the bargain and met the demands which the exercise has placed on me. I have certainly tried to avoid the unnecessary use of 'jargon' and to provide a readable yet stimulating and rigorous guide to the nature of organisations and their analysis, drawing on illustrations and examples which I have encountered in the course of my industrial research and consultancy. The demands placed on the reader have not therefore been artificially created; they derive directly from the nature of the subject.

Organisations are highly complex, as are the people who inhabit them, and they should not, I believe, be oversimplified to the point where the impression is gained that they are easy systems to understand. To adopt a too simple approach is to trivialise the subject and to open the way for instantly appealing but ultimately misleading advice. I hope I have avoided the dangers of both trivialisation and of unnecessary complexity. If I have, it is certainly in part due to the encouragement and constructive criticism I have received from my colleagues, friends and family to write, rewrite and often rewrite again. If I have failed, I regret that it is essentially my fault.

Many people have contributed significantly to my endeavours in writing this book. Thanks are due to Karen Legge, with whom I've worked closely in teaching this subject at Imperial College, to my other colleagues, my students and those in industry who have invited my consultancy and teaching or facilitated my research. The burden of typing the manuscript and coping with my idiosyncratic use of pen, paper, scissors and sellotape has fallen to several people, notably Kay Barnes, Joan Wright and, above all, Patricia Burge. My thanks to them all for their perseverance and kindness. I am also grateful for the help I have received from the staff at the publisher, particularly Jennifer Pegg.

Last, but certainly not least, I must record my debts to those at home. During the time in which this book has taken shape I have been the fortunate recipient of help and friendship from many people, particularly Elizabeth, Monika, Veronika, Petra, Giovanna and Lydia, and the staff of the Imperial College Nursery. In many different ways they have contributed to the creation of a home life in which a 'dual career' family with young children has, to give or take the odd crisis, flourished. My thanks to them all. My husband Henry, himself a manager, has in a sense acted as both target and inspiration for the book. He has responded to the challenge of my preoccupation with this text with a quiet generosity of ideas, comment and love which would be difficult to match. Perhaps I should also thank our children Hannah, Rebecca and Tom for the introductions they have given me to yet more organisations. For example, they have moved from nursery to school, they have joined drama and swimming clubs and together we have been reluctant but extensive explorers of a range of health service provision from routine outpatient clinics to intensive care units with almost all possible stops in between. But these incidental insights into organisations are of course nothing compared to living with those one loves. I can't claim they have always been patient with me, nor I with them, but I can be sure that we are all greatly relieved and not a little proud that 'the book' which has so often seemed to come before a trip to the swimming pool, the cinema or the zoo or a walk in the country has now really left my desk for the bookshop. Needless to say, though, another has already insinuated itself into the desk-top position!

November 1985   SANDRA DAWSON

Preface to the Second Edition

This new edition of *Analysing Organisations* incorporates a large amount of new material while remaining true to its original purpose to be a rigorous guide to the nature of organisations and thereby to reveal things which are intellectually stimulating and practically relevant. There are two completely new chapters on culture and managing change and the sections on performance, structure and strategy have been substantially rewritten. These changes reflect significant developments in the theory and practice of organisational analysis and the interests and questions of the groups of MBA students whom I have been privileged to teach since the foundation of The Management School at Imperial College in 1987. Among the many to whom thanks are due are Karen Legge and Michael Brocklehurst, with whom I have worked closely in course design and all the managers, friends, colleagues and students who have shared in discussions which find reflection in the present text.

Lastly, and most importantly, there is the home team, Henry, Hannah, Rebecca and Tom, and all our friends who have joined our family in the five years that have elapsed between these two editions. The theme of managing conflict and paradox introduced in 1986 is further developed here. In rededicating this book to those I love, I remember with gratitude our shared efforts to balance the conflicting demands of work and play.

March 1992   SANDRA DAWSON

Introduction

Large-scale organisations play an important part in all our lives. They are the means by which goods and services are provided beyond the boundaries of an individual's or small group's capacity for self-sufficiency. Such provision may be made for profit through the framework of markets, or through some other more controlled framework of commercial or social provision. We are in contact with organisations, as employees, as customers, as clients and claimants, as suppliers, and as regulators. Organisations specialise in education, health care, the collection of rubbish, broadcasting radio and television programmes, supplying food and household requirements, and providing a range of other goods and services which are used by individuals, families, groups and other organisations. To understand how organisations have grown, how they function and the sources of stress and strain as well as efficiency within them, is an important area of knowledge. The aim of this book is to provide the reader with a framework for the analysis and understanding of organisations. The framework can be applied from different people's viewpoints but, as the choice of examples will show, the book has been written particularly with one large group of people in mind; its target is those who are, or who are likely to become, managers or technical specialists, who are as yet novices in the analysis of organisations, but who share an intellectual as well as a practical curiosity in discovering more about the subject.

In coming to the subject of organisation people often hope to be given instant recipes for personal and organisational success, and quickly become disillusioned when simple and specific answers and advice are not forthcoming. Therefore, let no such hopes be raised. This book will not prescribe particular actions or decisions, but it will offer something far more fundamental: understanding through analysis. Organisations are highly complex dynamic systems which emerge, develop or decline in diverse and changing technological, economic and social contexts. What is appropriate in one context will be totally inappropriate in another. What is advantageous to one person may be disadvantageous to another. The aim of this book is not to say categorically what actions should be taken but to describe and explain the interacting characteristics and processes that are found in organisations. On this basis readers will be better equipped to make their own decisions and play their own parts, which ultimately is what everyone has to do. The reader's curiosity and understanding will be fed more through illustrated examples and fairly simple forms of explanation than through detailed theoretical debates, although a number of theoretical alternatives will be introduced along the way.

Definition and Characteristics

Organisations are defined as collections of people joining together in some formal association in order to achieve group or individual objectives. At least one set of objectives for any organisation will relate to the production and output of specified goods and services to individuals, groups and other organisations.

The book is written in two parts. Part 1 deals with the nature and interrelationships between six key characteristics of any organisation. These are:

1. The *people* who are associated with it, their attitudes and values, their aspirations and experience of different types of work. The extent to which values, experience and objectives are shared varies, and is reflected in the formation of a variety of *interest groups*.
2. The *strategies* and tactics which together constitute the plans and policies for such areas as product range, price structure, personnel and technical innovation and change.
3. The *technology* or hardware of production processes, plant, machinery, materals and products.
4. The *environment* to which an organisation's goods and services are supplied, from which its resources are obtained and which also provides the source of attempts to regulate its activities. This environment is constituted of individuals, groups, and most importantly other organisations, which have their own internal complexities and sources of stress and strength.
5. The *structure* of roles and relationships, which is partially revealed in organisation charts and job descriptions, but extends to the content and form of control systems and administrative procedures.
6. The *culture* of the organisation, which is the shared values and beliefs which create distinctive patterns of thinking and feeling within organisations.

Part 1 provides the building blocks of the analysis through a discussion of these six characteristics and their interrelationships which are represented in the cover design of the book. As the reader becomes acquainted with the blocks it becomes clear that a static snapshot of characteristics is not sufficient and that change must be considered. This is the subject of Part 2, which deals with social processes in organisation with particular reference to the acquisition and exercise of power and influence, communication, decision-making and implementation, with a focus on the management of change, innovation and learning. The concluding chapter draws the threads together by revisiting the subject of understanding and managing performance, since this is the ultimate objective for the practitioner.

One of the first lessons which may be taken from this book is that it is foolish to accept the definition of problems which arise in organisations at their face value. The nature of the problem should be explored, it will be argued, using the analytical framework presented. The need to gain a realistic diagnosis of problems as a basis for deciding upon solutions and their implementation can be demonstrated through the example of Elco, an electrical engineering firm.

The Elco Case

Elco had reached an established and still growing position in the light electronics market through manufacturing fairly standard electrical equipment, which was largely sold as components to manufacturers of other products. On the retirement of the production director, his successor, Tom Wilson, was promoted from within the company on the basis of a good track record. He had started with the firm twelve years earlier as a graduate process engineer and had completed seven years' experience as a production manager. During his career with the firm he had been noted as conscientious and clever, someone who kept abreast of technical developments even when they were not directly relevant to his patch, who was 'fair' but not 'soft' in his dealings with people, and who was well able to stand the stresses associated with having to find short-term solutions to problems arising from the competing priorities of cost, quality and delivery. He also appeared well able to command respect from his subordinates and maintain good relations with his colleagues in other departments. And yet it seemed promotion went instantly to his head. No sooner did he sit in the production director's chair than he was reported to be unco-operative with all other departments and to be unable to delegate within his own department. The only person with whom he had a good working relationship was his personal assistant, Bill, whom he had appointed himself. Bill, a young graduate engineer with three years' industrial experience in another company, had taken his degree at the production director's own university.

Everyone's attention became focused on the problem of 'what to do about Tom'. The fact that he got on well with Bill only served to convince his critics that as well as being a megalomaniac he was also given to nepotism. Various suggestions were made about how to improve the situation and they all revolved around ways of 'changing' the impact that Tom was having on the company. One group of senior executives led by the Finance and Managing Directors, reluctant to throw away what had promised to be good board material, were thinking in terms of trying to change him through training. Their idea was to send him on a senior executive development programme which would be liberally peppered with hints on managing personal relations as well as some good solid material on delegation and co-operation. Another group, led by the Sales Director, was less charitable. They said they had always had reservations about his appointment and that now he had been revealed in his true colours, which were clearly not up to the calibre expected of a director, the board should cut their losses and 'let him go'. They proposed to offer Tom favourable terms if he left the company, but said that if he stayed, he would have to make a sideways move which they knew he would find unattractive. Fortunately, before either of these courses of action was undertaken the lone voice of the Technical Director suggested that as well as looking at the personal qualities of Tom, the board should also consider the context in which the company was now working.

Standing back from their immediate crisis and from their preoccupations with cash flow and market share, they began to realise where their piecemeal approach to process and product development had taken them. A paper from the Technical Director showed that recent technical and market developments meant that the fastest growing and certainly most profitable sectors of the company's production were no longer concerned with easy-to-make items which were hard to sell, but with hard-to-make items which were relatively easy to sell providing that the quality was up to specification. The newly appointed Production Director was in fact behaving perfectly rationally in the face of an inappropriate structure in which sales dictated delivery dates irrespective of production's views. Such a situation had been appropriate in the past since sales, facing a difficult task, had secured orders by promises of very quick deliveries which production had usually managed to meet. Now, however, quick delivery was not as important as high quality. Tom and Bill both appreciated this but were too impatient and preoccupied with their problems to discuss the implications with others. They also feared that discussions would be thwarted by the defence of vested interests which had derived strength and power, particularly for sales, from the 'old' situation. Rather than quarrel over every order, particularly as entrenched positions and interests were involved, Tom and Bill merely worked as a close-knit team, keeping all the information to themselves and 'fobbing off' sales with inaccurate predictions whenever they were tackled about delivery. They also began dealing directly with customers, cutting out sales and thus adding further fuel to the quarrel. As the crisis became acute, Tom and Bill became more distant from the rest of the organisation. There were still considerable technical teething problems with the new production processes and these were having an adverse effect on quality, the one thing which Tom and Bill knew the company could not afford. They were increasingly found at every hour of the day and night on the shop-floor, firefighting the problems as they arose.

One reason for the quality problems was inadequate training for the production and maintenance teams in the new technology. Both Tom and Bill were highly competent process engineers and so they became personally involved in solving the problems rather than developing an appropriate group of supervisors, operatives and craftsmen to handle day-to-day issues. Tom and Bill were so bound up with managing their hectic working hours on a short-term basis that they had not yet begun to consider how the production and maintenance workforce could be trained; indeed, they had not even raised the problem with the personnel and training department.

What appeared at first sight to be a problem with the personality and behaviour of one or two individuals subsequently showed itself to be a problem of far-reaching implications for the organisation. Had Tom been replaced, one can predict with confidence that his successor, who at the selection board appeared to be 'just the man', would probably soon have begun exhibiting similar behaviour. Alternatively, had he conformed to the expectations of the Sales Director, they would together have presided over a fall in market position, even if they had remained friends in the face of this adversity. This is not to say that Tom could not have behaved differently; he could. Had he voiced his concerns earlier, had he lobbied for support for a programme of organisational change, had he called upon other specialist functions earlier, then he could have helped to overcome the crisis sooner.

The particular problems manifest in Elco were a result of a combination of individual and organisational developments. Changes in the technology and markets inevitably created strains and stresses. Neither the changes themselves, nor their implications for marketing, personnel and production policy, were properly considered. Once the board began to appreciate that their problems were not simply ones of difficult personalities, they instituted a number of immediate developments.

The Technical Director chaired a strategic working party to plan the journey upon which they had already embarked, almost as a result of 'automatic pilot'. The group considered the extent to which they should try to boost their specialist markets and whether their old markets for 'easy-to-make' items had gone for ever. The Production and Personnel Directors gave careful consideration to recent process innovation and drew up a programme for training, manpower planning and an appropriate industrial relations structure. The whole board vowed that they would never let such changes 'creep up' on them again. What was wrong with their internal communications? Why did functions not speak to each other? Why did they not receive good intelligence information from their environment?

All these questions became subjects for serious discussion and resulted in a wealth of ideas and explicit proposals. But far from solving their problems these ideas and proposals seemed only to exacerbate them. Several pulled in conflicting directions, others appeared to have extremely difficult industrial relations implications, and yet others attacked vested interests. To make the diagnosis is clearly not enough to secure effective change. Decisions must be made in the context of different interests and the pursuit of associated short-and long-term objectives, or else they emerge from compromise or by default. Once made, decisions have to be implemented and evaluated.

The diagnosis of problems through an understanding of structure and process in organisations and the selection of solutions is the subject matter of this book. Put simply, it aims to help people to know their organisation, to appreciate why particular characteristics and behaviours are exhibited, and to choose from a range of possible actions within the opportunities and constraints they have identified.

Main Themes of Analysis

As the analysis unfolds, the reader's attention will be drawn to a number of key themes, which have already been introduced in the Elco example. These will be stated here by way of introduction; the rationale for their inclusion will become clearer as they are elaborated in the book.

1. *Interactive open systems.* Organisations are interactive open systems. One can picture them as both generating and reacting to streams of interactive outcomes for each of their main parts: people, structure, culture, technology and strategy within the context of their environment. Change in one aspect inevitably means changes in others, and some of these changes will be unanticipated, and may be uncontrollable. Some of the changes will be internally generated; others will flow from interactions across boundaries with the environment. Openness to the environment means that organisations are both influenced by, and yet can have an influence on, their environment.
2. *Uncertainty.* Organisations are highly complex systems in which there is often a great deal of uncertainty. A lot of resources are always likely to be devoted to reducing and coping with uncertainties. Information, even if generated, will often not be shared between different parts of the organisation. Different participants operate with varying pictures of reality, and nearly all of them are incomplete.
3. *An appropriate path through paradox.* There is no one best way to act in organisations. The aim must always be to find an appropriate fit between a variety of elements such as technology, markets, history and the power and interests of the people involved. One must beware of jumping to unsubstantiated conclusions and always seek to examine assumptions both

in diagnosis and prescription. But, even then, there are no simple solutions to problems; paradoxes are continually encountered and the reader will often be urged to heed two apparently contradictory pieces of advice: for example, to take advantage of specialisation and yet benefit from integration; to reap the benefits of giving subordinates discretion and yet maintain control; to consider the advantages of having clear lines of responsibility while also facilitating consultation and decision-making in cross-functional groups. Coping with uncertainty and contradiction are not things one does just once 'to get them out of the way'. They are an integral part of life in organisations, and individuals need to learn both how to deal with them and how they, as actors, contribute to their creation.

The creation of an appropriate balance or, as Pascale (1990) says, of 'managing on the edge' and not allowing strength on one side of a contradiction (e.g., specialisation) to reduce the other side (e.g., co-ordination) to insignificance, is an extremely important art in managing organisations.

4. *Scarce resources.* Resources are always more or less scarce, and none of the strategies chosen is likely to be without financial or social costs. The crucial question is to appreciate the value of the 'trade-offs' being made between costs and benefits, both in the short and the long term: 'there is no such thing as a free lunch'. It is always important to try to understand the menu and to attempt to estimate the full costs of benefits using both financial and non-financial indicators. In this way one is less likely to be surprised and to be faced with unanticipated consequences.

5. *Conflicts and consensus between interest groups.* People become involved with organisations in a variety of ways. The only common factor is that the organisation is seen as likely to provide things of value. What is of value to one group may be a subject of indifference or even hostility for another. Organisations are arenas in which different interest groups operate. Some degree of co-operation is usual; but so is an element of conflict. Emergent patterns of conflict and consensus not only reflect different interests but also the relative power and influence of groups to pursue those interests.

6. *Opportunity, choice and constraint.* People in organisations face varying degrees of constraints within which they have an element of choice. The relative balance between constraint and choice varies between groups and individuals and over time. What is seen as a constraint by one person may be seen as an opportunity by others. Moreover, today's constraints are largely the result of yesterday's choices. The juxtaposition of constraint and choice relates to an underlying issue of the relationship between an individual's freedom to act and think and her subjection to the influence of social structure and culture. This book takes a middle position in which everyone is more than an amalgamated reflection of the social influences to which they are exposed; but at the same time social influences are critically important in generating individual attitudes, values and actions.

Technologies, environments, and indeed social structures and cultures are both the creators and creatures of people in organisations.

7. *Levels and modes of analysis.* A concern with the individual and social levels of analysis suggests one last general introductory comment. The activities which constitute life in organisations and the outcomes that arise can be analysed in terms of the different levels of the individual, group, organisation and society. For example, the introduction of a new payment system for maintenance workers in an oil refinery can be considered at the individual level in terms of its impact on a craftsman's motivation to stay in the job or his weekly spending habits. At a group level, the activities of the branch of the craft trade union in negotiating the deal are relevant, as is the effect of the new payment system on patterns of co-operation in working practices within and between groups. At an organisational level the impact of the new scheme on levels of refinery productivity is relevant, as are the changes in supervisory practices that accompany the new payment system. At a societal level one might consider the employment or redundancy effects of the new system and its relationship with trends in trade unionism generally. A further variation in styles of the analysis is between a static view based upon a cross-sectional snapshot, or a dynamic view based upon concepts of change. Rather than just looking at craft workers' responses to the new system at one time, their attitudes and behaviour in connection with payment systems before and after the change could be examined. Similarly, productivity could be considered over an extended time period.

This book is mainly concerned with analysis at the individual and organisational levels, although some consideration is given to the group. The treatment of the societal level is one-sided; considerable emphasis is given to prior social influences on individual attitudes, values and behaviour and to the economic and social context in which organisations operate. Less consideration is given to the reverse set of influences: that is, to the way the activities of individuals and the operations of organisations profoundly affect and indeed continually create conditions in the wider society and economy.

Even though the analysis is concentrated at the individual and organisational level, it is nonetheless important to recall the interrelationships between all four levels. The image of a set of Russian dolls in which the outer casing encapsulates dolls of decreasing size is a useful metaphor. Each doll is individually crafted but bears the shape of both the larger and the smaller ones; so, too, with individuals, groups, organisations and society.

Part One

A Framework for Organisational Analysis

People: Attitudes, Motivation and Performance 1

People are always important in employing organisations. Even in the most highly automated electrical assembly plant or oil refinery the intervention of craftspeople and operators is crucially important on a day-to-day basis in securing the yields, quality, etc., required. Within a longer-term perspective it was people who designed, built and commissioned the plant and it will be people who redesign and modify the plant to meet the demands posed by changes made by others in the market which may in turn lead other people to question the technical and commercial feasibility of new capital expenditure. Other people – such as politicians, civil servants, institutional investors – are also likely to influence the company's operations and to have a part in making and implementiing the strategic decisions designed to secure survival and growth.

However automated and capital-intensive manufactuuring and service industries become, whatever the developments in robotics and information systems, one will never be able to neglect the importance of people. A concern with individual attitudes and behaviour is relevant to this book from three points of view. For all employees there is the very important question of what they expect to get from work and whether their expectations of different sorts of reward are satisfied. For their 'bosses' there is a concern with motivation; how can they motivate their people to work harder, work at different jobs, stay with the firm, etc.? And for specialists there is the issue of the implications of their design and control activities for the attitudes and behaviour of those who will work within the systems they create and maintain.

It is not possible in a general text to provide a summary of all the main findings of occupational psychologists and industrial sociologists about people at work. This chapter is deliberately selective and concentrates on just three areas: attitudes to work, motivation and performance. These have been chosen because there is a high level of popular mythology about them which often blurs any analysis of organisations. Many people hold strong views on the content and consequences of the attitudes and motivation of those groups, whether trade unionists, merchant bankers or engineers, whom they either praise or blame for industrial performance. Often, as the Elco case suggested in the Introduction, such an approach may rely on analysis at an inappropriate level. Problems often concern organisation structure or changing technologies or markets rather than being simply to do with the actors involved. To be able to appreciate the importance of analysis at the different levels of the individual group, organisation and society, one needs to have an introductory understanding of how attitudes are formed and motivation is developed. The chapter concludes by commenting on one of the more widely held myths, namely that a happy worker is always a more productive worker. In this way the subjects of attitudes and motivation will be related to performance.

1.1   The Formation of Attitudes to Work

'The attitudes of workers', 'the attitudes of managers', 'the attitudes of customers' are always being cited as reasons for the failure or success of industrial enterprises. Attitudes are said to be entrenched, unco-operative, favourable, encouraging or whatever, and are applauded or deplored according to their sentiment and the views of the commentators. This section deals with how attitudes at work are formed, both in terms of individual experience and social context. An attitude is a predisposition to perceive, evaluate and act in a particular way which is relatively enduring. It has three elements: feelings (of like and dislike, etc.), beliefs and values (of truth and falsehood, good and bad, etc.) and a predisposition to act. However, the predisposition to act is not always carried into actual behaviour, not least because some predispositions may be in conflict, as well as being of varying salience to the individual.

   Let us start with a proposition: individuals are not just crude tape recordings of their surroundings, but neither are attitudes randomly held. To appreciate the derivation of attitudes to work, one has to keep in mind the interaction between individuality, born of uniqueness in terms of genetic structure (except for identical twins) and social experience derived from mass media and associations with family, community, work and other groups. The interaction between individuality and social influences is overlaid by an interaction between the characteristics of an individual's experiences outside and inside the workplace. Figure 1.1 illustrates important general facets of these interactions in so far as they are relevant to an understanding of individual attitudes to work. The outer ring of this figure represents the important influence of the social, economic and political scene, which includes industrial and employment structures, forms of government, national policies relating to industry and employment, and dominant belief systems among different national, regional and social class groupings. All these wider factors will have influence within the workplace on such characteristics as culture, strategy, technology, products, structure and size. These in turn will influence the particular nature of an individual's work, which will both be affected by and affect her attitudes to work. Outside the workplace an individual is much influenced by her particular family, community and social class location and experience, which will clearly also be embedded in the wider social context and, together with individuality, account for an individual's abilities and experiences. These in turn will interact with perceptions of work and employment and so influence the attitudes that are held towards employment within particular organisations.

The word 'socialisation' is used in Figure 1.1. This refers to the process of becoming and continuing to be a social human being, as opposed to an

FIGURE 1.1
The Formation of Attitudes to Work

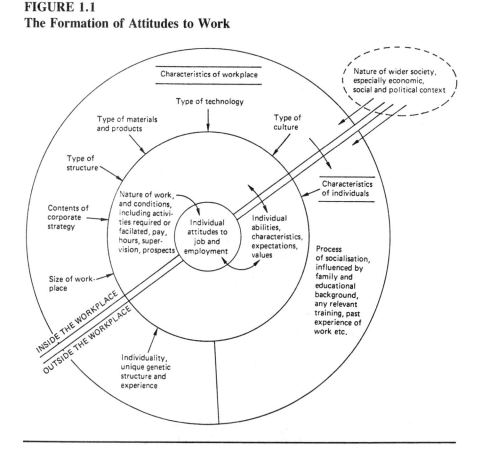

isolated hermit. Behaviour and attitudes are modified by what is learned from and expected by other significant people. The modification can be in terms of either conformity or nonconformity, depending on whether or not the significant people are abhorred or valued. Attitudes are thus 'built up' through more or less integrated layers of experience, with a tendency for people to select those parts of experience and value which conform to present views.

Sources of variation and change in attitudes

Whatever the strength of social pressures, individuals still retain some quintessential individuality. This will come as no surprise to parents who, in battling with their children, begin to doubt the efficacy of social pressure, even supported by rewards and punishment, in persuading their children to adopt particular forms of behaviour and attitudes. Individuality is always an important source of variation within groups.

Further variation derives from the fact that individuals have more than one set of significant social relations, even at any one time and certainly over time. In this way, the process of socialisation itself offers the opportunity for change and variation. It is at its most intense in the early years of 'primary socialisation' in childhood and adolescence, but it continues through life. 'Secondary socialisation' becomes important in the broader context of educational, leisure and work organisations, when attitudes and values are no longer learned just in the bosom of the family and with close friends. Secondary socialisation occurs whether one is training to be a terrorist or a stockbroker, a safe-breaker or an engineer. All these vocations are learned within organised social settings which provide models for attitudes and behaviour as well as sources of support and control.

Moreover, people do not always just react to given situations; they can also precipitate change and begin of their own volition to adapt their attitudes and behaviour so that they are appropriate for a situation they expect to join. Having learned the rules of the game for one situation, people often realise that they can 'anticipate' requirements for conformity or deviancy in other contexts. This form of modification is known as 'anticipatory socialisation', which develops in the context of formal and informal organisations which individuals either hope to join or to escape. The term 'reference group' is given to the groups to which we aspire for membership. These are often particular occupations, firms, leisure associations and friendship groups. Aspiring recruits will try to gather information, through books, conversation and observation about membership of these groups, so that they can 'easily fit in' once entry is gained.

Organisations build on anticipatory socialisation immediately a recruit enters their door. Formal training and induction schemes are often as concerned with generating appropriate attitudes and manners of speech, dress and interaction as they are with imparting specific skills. Induction (or, as some might say, indoctrination) into a first job is a critical piece of secondary socialisation, which may then be reinforced, modified or even rejected when a person actually does the job. To read for a chemical engineering degree which is fairly scientific and theoretical, to read the Institution of Chemical Engineering booklets on what life will be like as a chemical engineer, to go through an elaborate selection procedure of a large multinational company, may all set up grand expectations on the part of a young graduate. However, these expectations may not appear totally justified if our new graduate recruit finds himself the process engineer of a fairly standardised and relatively out-of-date fibre plant. Happily the opposite can also happen, and a disenchanted twenty-year-old, taking the only job she has ever been offered, may find it much more exciting than she had previously expected.

Once a view of the world of employment, of particular companies and particular jobs is created, it forms the basis of a 'common sense' approach to work which is often difficult to change. 'Common sense' views, however, are usually anything but 'common'. What is sensible to a trade unionist may be idiocy to a manager; what is beautiful to a young student may be ugly to a middle-aged critic; what is important to a research scientist may be of no significance to a finance director. People sometimes get very upset when others cannot see the world as they do. Figure 1.1 suggests that such an assumption of consensus is ill-founded, since the context in which attitudes and values develop is subject to considerable variation: by social class, by industrial sector, by educational and training experience, by position in the labour market and by regional location.

Industrial psychologists have investigated the conditions under which individuals may be persuaded to change their views. One approach, developed by Festinger (1957), focused attention on the relationship between an individual's attitudes and behaviour. It is assumed that people prefer consistency and congruence between and within attitudes and behaviour, and that inconsistency or 'cognitive dissonance' makes them feel uncomfortable. They will therefore change either their attitudes or their behaviour, depending on where their greatest commitment lies. For example, a white man who is racially prejudiced may change his attitudes if circumstances lead him to work co-operatively with a black person, particularly if he sees his co-operative behaviour as being 'voluntary'. If, on the other hand, he is only working with a black person because he has been ordered to do so or because he is being paid a large amount of money, he may retain his private attitudes intact and justify his behaviour to himself in terms of 'It wasn't my choice, I was forced to do it', or 'I'm only doing it for the money.'

A second strategy to secure changes in attitudes is to try to use one's powers of persuasion. This may be done by powerful people pushing out information to others who may be persuaded to change their views. Evidence suggests that such change is less likely to be accomplished by the message itself than by the context of authority, fear or charisma in which it is received.

This can be a fairly high-risk strategy in that it may generate entrenched resistance or reluctant acceptance and so need constant reinforcement. Alternatively the information may be 'pulled' from the audience by raising awareness, seeking information, building up trust and understanding. This can secure higher commitment and be self-reinforcing, but it consumes a lot of time. Both these strategies of persuasion can be applied at the individual or group level. In many ways the group level is stronger simply because peer-group pressures are strong influences on individual behaviour. However, just as it is better for protagonists of change to secure the support of groups rather than individuals, it is, on the other hand, worse to meet the resistance of groups rather than that of individuals.

A persuasive approach is often combined with a form of participation or consultation, which Lewin (1948) argued facilitated the three phases necessary in attitude change. First there is 'unfreezing', which requires a recognition of the need to change and a removal of rewards for current behaviour. Second there is the 'moving' stage, in which new behaviour is introduced and reinforced by initial appropriate rewards. Third there is a 'refreezing' stage, which requires continued practice of the new behaviour and establishes a new reward structure. A cynic might say that this model is fine except that change in organisations is rarely so programmatic. Indeed, what is often required at managerial level is the generation of behaviour that is adaptive to changing circumstances. It is a different matter for repetitive jobs closely geared to technology, and this model is probably more appropriate for adaptations at this level.

Coch and French (1948) used participatory persuasive techniques successfully to facilitate changes in methods of work and payment in a sewing machine factory. Similarly, successful attitude change was recorded by Lewin (1948) in persuading wartime American housewives to use liver, kidneys and other offal, and by Jaques (1951) in his attempts to improve understanding between different levels in a London engineering works. Others have drawn attention, as every evangelist knows, to the importance of getting participants to register a conscious decision to 'change attitudes', thereby setting the seal on new views. Besides using the vehicles of participation and consultation to commit people to changed attitudes, an individual may be particularly susceptible to attitude change if an important mentor (for example, a parent or managing director) falls out of favour and other influential people are ready to take that place.

With organisational development there is a school which emphasises the part that can be played by 'sensitivity' or 'T group training' (Argyris, 1962; Bradford, Gibb and Bennie, 1964). This is designed to increase individuals' understanding of their own motives and interdependencies and to create a greater awareness of group processes and group culture so that the group can then determine changes in values and practices which they consider appropriate. As a technique it has created considerable controversy. Its proponents regard it as an essential adjunct to good management, particularly if change is likely. Its opponents, on the other hand, variously criticise it for invading individual privacy, raising expectations which are not satisfied, creating hostilities which are never resolved and being culturally appropriate only in those societies where it is accepted that the psychological well-being of individuals is tied to their capacity to develop or to display strong self-awareness. It and other approaches to change through individual and group characteristics can also be criticised for adhering to the assumption that resistance and hostility are primarily the result of characteristics and neuroses of individuals, and not the result of characteristics of the organisational and social context.

In summary one can say that attitude change is brought about through exposure to additional information, changes in group affiliations, and en-forced changes in behaviour which create dissonance. The complexities suggested in Figure 1.1, together with the enduring characteristics of many attitudes, mean that it is often difficult to predict from limited information about people and social contexts where attitude change will occur.

1.2   Motivation

Motivation refers to the mainspring of behaviour; it explains why individuals choose to expend a degree of effort towards achieving particular goals. Understanding more about attitudes to work provides a partial context for understanding motivation. But this context needs to be expanded beyond individual attitudes and group pressures to include non-attitudinal factors like present life style, material commitments and assumed capabilities. These affect a person's choice of goals as well as the more or less rational processes which underlie their decisions to expend effort in particular ways. Motivation theory has developed in two ways, one focusing on the content and the other on the process of motivation.

Content theories of motivation

The earliest modern attempts to develop a theory of motivation have concentrated attention on the individual's choice of goals; what they are and why they are important. Briefly this question has been answered in terms of the selection of goals associated with the reduction of physiological drives (for satisfaction of hunger, thirst, shelter) or socially acquired needs (for love and friendship, self-esteem, status).

Money as a motivator

Early work on this subject suggested single sources of motivation. F. W. Taylor, famous for the development of the school of 'scientific management', identified money as the single most important goal for workers and thus the key to their motivation (Taylor, 1911). There are substantial difficulties with Taylor's analysis (see Rose, 1975, and Littler, 1982, for a further discussion). One is that money is not the sole motivator, and another, more problematic one is that whilst it may affect motivation, the effects may not be those intended by managers (see, e.g., White, 1981; Smith, 1983). One common response is for workers voluntarily to resist the lure of more money for fear that if they seize the bait they will suffer job losses, since fewer people will be required to do 'faster' work. Alternatively they may fear that the performance targets, once met, will become the 'norm' and they will eventually have to work even harder in order to achieve additional money.

Furthermore, managers use payment systems to achieve three distinct and sometimes conflicting aims. One is indeed to motivate, to increase productivity, but others are to recruit and retain staff and to control costs. In a survey on the effects of incentive payment systems in the United Kingdom in 1977–8, Bowey *et al.* (1982) found that very few of the sixty-three organisations they studied had in fact reduced their costs per unit as result of introducing incentive schemes, and less than half of them had increased their output. In fact it transpired that one of the main reasons for introducing the schemes during this period was to find a way of giving workers pay increases at a time of national pay restraint. Managers, it seemed, had moved a long way from the model Taylor had promulgated, at least as far as money was concerned. When the labour market is tight, one finds managers less concerned to secure pay increases for those workers who are easily replaceable; but they are still concerned to maintain competitive high rates for the valued specialists who are a scarce commodity.

Few would dispute that pay is important to all employees; it provides access to valued goods and services and can also be a mark of success and status. The analytical problem is that everyone does not react to the same payment package in the same way: there are variations with social class, position in the labour market, age, industrial sector, and so on. For example, White (1981), and before him Daniel (1970) and Lupton and Gowler (1969), have shown that payment systems do not always achieve or sustain the objectives which lay behind their foundation. Indeed, sometimes they positively act against them. The art for managers is to choose a system that is likely to sustain the behaviours they identify as most important.

Social relations and motivation

One reason why incentive schemes fail to affect productivity is that workers wish to assert their independence from management. It was the discovery that groups of workers acted collectively in the face of management initiatives to control working conditions that led to another view about motivation. It was the famous 'Hawthorne experiments' which showed that cohesive work groups could work either 'for' or 'against' management initiatives in such matters as payment systems and alterations to the working environment (Roethlisberger and Dickson, 1939). Thus it became fashionable to talk of workers' needs for social relations at work as a predominant source of motivation.

Interest extended beyond the work group to the role of supervision in facilitating 'good' social relations and higher productivity at work. Work at Ohio State University and Michigan's Institute of Social Relations on groups as various as airforce bomber crews (Halpin and Winer, 1957) and clerical and manual workers (Katz and Kahn, 1966) reported that supervisors in high- as opposed to low-producing groups treated their workers with more consideration. They were supportive and helpful rather than punishing in the face of work problems, they generated mutual trust and yet retained some distance from their work groups and continued to plan, regulate and co-ordinate their work. The term 'human relations' is often used to describe the approach of those who emphasise the primary work group and the importance of supervisory styles in influencing workers' attitudes and behaviour (see, e.g., Likert, 1961).

However, these human relations arguments, just as those which identified pay as the key variable, could not be supported by conclusive evidence. For example, Vroom (1964) found that social relationships were important for some work groups but not for others. Other people wondered whether the performance of subordinates was the result or cause of supervisory practice. It seemed likely that non-supportive punitive supervisory practices could be the result rather than the cause of low productivity. Whether the feedback between the two is positive or negative, it is certainly influenced by the position of the work group and supervisor within the wider organisational context, as well as by the expectations of the people involved (Tannenbaum, 1966, p. 77).

A hierarchy of needs

Against this background of a search for single explanations of worker motivation, the work of Maslow (1943, 1954) was particularly important. Rather than emphasising a single source of motivation, he suggested a hierarchy of needs in which individuals sought outcomes which satisfied needs in an ascending hierarchy. He argued that the lower-order needs of physical survival, then security and then affiliation had to be satisfied before the higher ones of self-esteem and then self-actualisation became important. Only the term self-actualisation needs further amplification. It refers to the desire for self-fulfilment, to become everything that one is capable of becoming. Alderfer (1972) revised Maslow's hierarchy into three groups of basic needs, relating to Existence, Relatedness and Growth. In this ERG model, all three sorts of need are always there, but as the more basic ones are satisfied so the individual can be freed to seek satisfaction of higher ones.

Maslow was important in opening up the motivation debate to include more than one goal, and to identify self-esteem and self-actualisation as potentially important goals. However, there has been little empirical support for his view of a universal hierarchy, as the evidence once again points to the fact that people's motivation profiles vary with individual characteristics and with social context.

The kernel of Maslow's ideas was largely presented to the business world by McGregor (1960), who was also important for the stress he gave to the idea that, regardless of the actual motivation profile of workers, their managers' assumptions about their motivation had a profound effect upon the behaviour and attitudes of both managers and workers. McGregor suggested two polar examples of managerial thought: theory X and Y. Theory X managers, rather in the manner of F. W. Taylor, believed workers were lazy, resistant to change and lacking in ambition. Managers therefore needed to control them tightly, to limit their discretion and to manipulate them with incentive schemes. Theory Y managers, on the other hand, followed Maslow. Their view was that employees could be motivated by the goals of achievement, self-esteem and self-actualisation, and hence it was the manager's job to lead them to these rich pastures and help them to develop, to the mutual benefit of themselves and their employers.

In a similar vein, Herzberg's 'two factor theory' states that people will be motivated by things they value, and these, he affirms, are likely to be achievement, responsibility and recognition; in other words, self-actualisation. Such factors he called 'motivators', and he distinguished them from 'hygienic' factors which as aspects of physical working conditions like pay, security, and other conditions, only served as sources of dissatisfaction. Once satisfied to a certain level, they did not motivate people to a higher performance in their work (Herzberg, 1966). Herzberg's work, like that of McGregor, captured the imagination of many managers and influenced their approach to work. However, there is little conclusive evidence to support it as a universal truth. Indeed as we shall see, the links he postulated between satisfaction, motivation and performance are the subject of considerable criticism (Vroom, 1964).

Herzberg's distinction between hygienic factors and motivating factors derives from work done with colleagues which identified two types of reward: extrinsic and intrinsic (Herzberg, Mausner and Snyderman, 1959). Extrinsic rewards are those which derive from the work situation but are not inherently bound up with it. In this sense work is a means to ends which are valued, although the nature of the work itself may be unrewarding. Examples of some important extrinsic rewards are money, security, social status, the opportunity to develop friendships and career development. All these can be achieved through work, but do not necessarily relate to the nature of the work. Intrinsic rewards, on the other hand, are those which are derived through the activities of working: for example, a sense of achievement, fulfilment and autonomy. The general pattern of employment is such that jobs lower down an organisation's hierarchy are those which are more likely to satisfy extrinsic rewards, but as one moves up the organisational hierarchy so the possibility of acquiring additionally satisfying intrinsic rewards increases. There are a few idiosyncratic examples of people, like priests or volunteers working overseas, who may derive high intrinsic rewards but low extrinsic rewards from their work, but these are exceptions, not real challenges to the general rule. There are many jobs which offer only extrinsic rewards, and this is not simply a distinction between manual and managerial or professional work. Many people working in fairly senior positions in large corporations derive a high level of extrinsic reward in terms of pay, social status and career advancement, but nonetheless find their jobs intrinsically unfulfilling; such dissatisfaction may not, however, lead them to seek to change their conditions of employment.

Different expectations from work

Different combinations of extrinsic and intrinsic rewards were documented by Goldthorpe and colleagues in a study of workers in Luton. This work was significant, among other reasons, for establishing the importance of 'prior orientations to work', which was the term given to the way a worker perceives, evaluates and gives meaning to his job in terms of his particular order of wants and expectations. This study, based on workers in a Vauxhall car plant, a ball-bearing factory and a chemical plant, laid the basis for developing a typology of three different orientations to work. These are reflected in variations in patterns of rewards, the centrality of work to the rest of an employee's life and the social groups to which employees typically turn for social support and to whom they give most loyalty (Goldthorpe *et al.*, 1968, pp. 38–42).

An instrumental approach is characteristic of workers who derive the fairly basic extrinsic rewards of money and security from their work. Work is simply a means to an end; workers have a low level of involvement with their employer and will change jobs if a better package of extrinsic rewards is available. Work has no emotional or social significance for them and local social groupings outside the factory are their sources of social identification and claim their loyalties. Typically this approach is characteristic of large sections of manual and clerical workers. A second approach, termed 'solidaristic' by Goldthorpe *et al.*, is characteristic of many craft workers who value money as an important extrinsic reward, but who also value work as a group activity and the sense of achievement and possibly autonomy they may derive from their work, although these intrinsic rewards were often not found to be forthcoming. Fellow workers, as well as local family and community groups, are likely to be important social reference points for 'solidaristic' workers. This may lead them to act cohesively either in support of, or against, management initiatives. Work is a central life interest, and their lives in and out of the workplace are intimately related.

The third, 'bureaucratic' approach characterises many white-collar workers in positions of medium and high seniority. Like the instrumental workers, they do not expect to derive intrinsic rewards from their work, but they not only have high expectations for money and security but also for career advancement and increasing status in the organisation. Work plays an important part in life and their position and prospects are significant sources of social identity. Not surprisingly, their employing organisation is an important focus for their loyalty and a significant social reference point for their behaviour and attitudes.

Goldthorpe *et al.*'s identification of a bureaucratic approach to work is similar to Gouldner's (1957) definition of a 'local', whom he contrasts with a 'cosmopolitan'. Locals display strong allegiance to their employing company and are less likely to be mobile, whereas cosmopolitans have greater allegiance to their professional group and are more likely to be mobile. This suggests that one could expand Goldthorpe's typology to include a fourth 'cosmopolitan' approach which is characteristic of people expecting to achieve significant extrinsic and intrinsic rewards from their work and who refer to their professional colleagues, both within and outside their employing organisation, for support and identification. It should be noted, however, that not all professionally trained people necessarily adopt a cosmopolitan approach to work; they may in fact have jobs which fit directly into a 'bureaucratic', 'local' mode and adjust their motivation accordingly. This is a point we will return to in the discussion of interest groups in the next chapter.

The view that there are significant variations in the place and meaning of work in people's lives makes an important contribution to our consideration of motivation, since it suggests that different people are likely to be motivated by different things. What is more, it is likely that as individual circumstances change, so too will an individual's motivation profile. Age is obviously likely to be a key variable, with certain points in the life-cycle involving heavier financial commitments than others: for example, a high mortgage, a spouse stopping work because of unemployment or maternity, school fees or exotic holidays abroad. As people get older they may review their past activities and achievements and decide they would rather direct their efforts elsewhere. Changes in the motivation profile will not be independent of what are perceived to be available opportunities. Someone who, all other things being equal, would rather change from an instrumental to a professional or craft approach may not find an opportunity to do so, and thus after a brief flirtation with the idea of an alternative may retreat to the old pattern.

Changes in motivation not only occur with changes outside the workplace. Internal changes can also be important. W. W. Daniel, in *The Right to Manage?* (1972), pointed out that the emphasis that people give to different rewards changes with events in the cycle of negotiation and settlement over pay and conditions. When negotiations about productivity are in progress he found that workers expressed themselves to be especially keen to get the best financial deal, with little or no expressed interest in intrinsic rewards. Once the deal was settled, however, the workers said they valued the increased variety and responsibility which came with the changes in working practices that were an integral part of the deal.

Process theories of motivation

Research and assertion covering nearly a century have resulted in a catalogue of goals and rewards but no conclusions about the conditions which would predict an individual's motivational profile. This is partly because, from a practical as well as a theoretical point of view, motivation and goals are both constructs which are too general. Although they talk frequently of motivation, it is rare for executives to want to secure just one definable piece of behaviour. Even the most ordinary job will probably have cost, quality and time elements. Thus to 'discover' the way to motivate an employee to perform so as to reduce costs may be successfully achieved at a cost which is to the detriment of quality. The work of the process theorists has become increasingly important in revealing the complexities which need to be unravelled if we are to understand more about motivation at work.

Process theorists offer a more sophisticated approach by turning their attention to identifying the factors and processes that are important in determining the behaviours which an individual will choose to follow in order to obtain desired goals. A start in this direction was made with *equity theory* (Pritchard, 1969), which suggests that people compare the ratio of their inputs to their job to the outputs which they receive from it. If an individual sees the ratio as 'unfair' or 'inequitable', he is likely to behave so as to try to correct the balance. It is thus perceptions of fairness that are important. The argument is that if people perceive they are not paid enough they will reduce their output, and vice versa. Elliot Jaques (1967), after much work in this area, lays great stress on the importance of fairness. Whilst perceptions of equity are no doubt important in affecting motivation, there are bound to be difficulties in trying to 'measure' and 'balance' inputs and outputs to and from a job. Furthermore, other factors are likely to be important as well.

Expectancy theory

This theory appears to be more promising, at least in terms of acknowledging complexity. Broadly this approach predicts that behaviours that are followed will reflect an individual's selection of goals and what she has learned and believes will produce the rewards she is looking for (Vroom, 1964; Porter and Lawler, 1968). For example, take an individual who has a strong need for financial security and social status. If he is given a task to do and promised a high salary and promotion, then he will expend effort on doing the work to the extent that he believes:

1. good performance in his job will be noted and will lead to increased salary and promotion;
2. increased salary and promotion will satisfy his needs for financial security and social status.

In these terms we are motivated by our expectations about the likelihood of a particular set of behaviours leading to certain outcomes. The key points of motivation are not therefore simply the nature of goals but how they can be best achieved. How much effort, and in what direction, should be expended? As needs are satisfied, so our motivational drive towards them lessens, and vice versa.

Expectancy theory can be useful in illuminating some of the things which mystify people in industry. For example, managers complain that they cannot understand why their employees persist in a practice which results in poor quality work. However, if they were to analyse the situation with the benefit of expectancy theory, they might find that while it was in the managers' interest to have better quality, there were sound reasons why their employees were not similarly motivated. One possibility is that the employees do not see that their extra effort can achieve better quality; another is that even if this is the case, they doubt whether this relationship will be acknowledged and rewarded. A third problem is that any rewards that are forthcoming may not be ones that the employees particularly value. If this string of events is not complete, motivation to improve quality will be low or non-existent. This approach puts the emphasis on managers establishing schemes to motivate the behaviours they want and to discourage those they do not want. It also provides an explanation of the cynical distrust and suspicions which some-times greet managerial schemes for incentive payments. If employees doubt the sincerity of managerial pledges to fulfil their side of the employment contract and to give them promised rewards, then it is rational for them to control and restrict their performance.

A serious problem can arise when some aspects of performance which are very important cannot be clearly identified and measured. For example, creativity in artwork is the output which most managers would expect from their graphic designers. However, precise criteria for its assessment are difficult to identify. On the other hand, it is easy to monitor the number of hours a designer works. But it would be shortsighted to reward hours worked simply because they are easily measurable if they are of relatively little interest to management. In this case the answer might be to give the designers as full and speedy a feedback as possible on the success of their designs in terms of promotional or advertising criteria, but to be very careful about distorting performance by an inappropriate motivational device.

This is sometimes a problem in schemes for management by objectives (MBO) or incentive payments, where superiors are in danger of rewarding easily measurable short-term performance while neglecting longer-term and more important criteria. For example, social workers in social services departments are strongly sanctioned if they keep a child with its family and the child is subsequently battered. In contrast, they may get little positive feedback or rewards regarding the countless children whom they do support in their family homes with success. Not surprisingly social workers in this situation are likely to be overinclined to take children into care at possibly untold cost to the people involved, and considerable economic costs to the community.

One drawback of expectancy theory is that it makes unwarranted assumptions about the extent to which people always proceed on the basis of strong, rational, logical thought. Conditioning theory compliments expectancy theory in this respect. Whereas the latter emphasises human responses to rewards in terms of the rational cognitive processes of calculation of expected efforts and rewards, the former stresses animal 'stimulus-response' behaviour patterns in respect of rewards and punishments. This sounds fairly reasonable as a set of working assumptions, but there is little real-life evidence of the effects of conditioning on humans at work. Thus, although insightful and certainly descriptive of many sequences, not everyone behaves exactly as expectancy theory or conditioning theory predicts. Chance, serendipity, creativity, intuition and whim are also important, and these will be discussed further in Chapter 8.

1.3 Individual Performance

Expectancy and equity theories allow us to scrutinise an unproved but nevertheless widely held assumption, given publiciity by Herzberg (among others), that a satisfied employee is always a 'better' worker than a dissatisfied one. Sufficient has been said already to cause us immediately to raise questions about the object and strength of the satisfaction, particularly in respect of expectations. It now seems likely that any links between effort, performance and satisfaction are circular, as has been suggested in two different schemes by March and Simon (1958) and Porter and Lawler (1968). Both of these are summarised and discussed in Schwab and Cummings (1970).

March and Simon (1958) suggest that if someone is dissatisfied and perceives that he can reduce dissatisfaction by improved performance at work, then performance and satisfaction will be linked. They also identify several conditions where this relationship will not hold: for example, if there are other sources of satisfaction.

Porter and Lawler's scheme suggests that the effort an individual expends reflects the extent to which she values the rewards that may be forthcoming and her assessment of the likelihood that the rewards will be forthcoming as a result of expending effort. The translation of effort into performance will reflect her abilities and her perception of what is required of her. As a result of performance (doing the job over given timescales) a package of rewards will be forthcoming. The extent to which these meet her expectations will profoundly affect her satisfaction, which will then feed back into her continuous assessment of effort and rewards. It is feasible for low satisfaction (i.e. disappointment with rewards) to feed back to increased effort in the hope of securing the rewards expected. Alternatively it may lead to the termination of the job contract, particularly if there are alternative sources of employment. Another possibility, if there are few alternatives, accords with the popular view that disappointment will lead to alienation and less effort.

A manager seeking to improve the work performance of others needs not only to understand the complexities of motivation but also to appreciate the relationships indicated in Figure 1.2. This shows that an individual's performance in a job is a reflection of three things. One is motivation, which can now be seen as the result of complex processes involving expectations, cognition and experience. The second is the individual's abilities as revealed through skills and knowledge. Just as in Figure 1.1 attitudes were shown to reflect both individual characteristics and social experience, so too with ability. The 'raw material' of individual intelligence and aptitudes can be discerned and developed through such managerial processes as selection, training and promotion. The third element of Figure 1.2 is a collection of contextual characteristics which reflect the way the job is defined and resourced within the organisation. This includes not only the provision of tools, equipment and physical facilities to enable jobs to be satisfactorily undertaken, but also the social dimensions of job design. This subject of job requirements and job design will thus provide the last piece in the jigsaw which is entitled 'understanding individual performance at work'.

FIGURE 1.2
Understanding Individual Job Performance

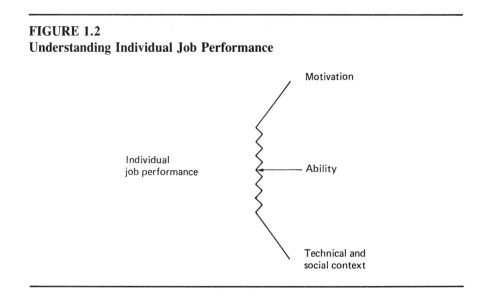

Job requirements

Jobs can be analysed in terms of the basic requirements shown in Table 1.1. These encompass the activities, interactions and decisions which make up the 'why', 'what' and 'how' for any job-holder. The second part of the table illustrates the way the three different jobs (accounts clerk, maintenance electrician and software engineer) vary in terms of the requirements placed upon them. Given the social context of work, the fact that different individuals and groups have different interests means that there are often conflicting interpretations about what is really expected of an employee. For example, in a factory a quality standard may be set by the supervisor and yet be undermined by peer pressure from within the workforce. Similarly, in a hospital a treatment protocol may be developed for a particular medical condition, but a clinician may elect to try another form of treatment. An individual's interpretation of job requirements will also be subject to pressure and influence from significant people outside the workplace: for example, one's spouse or fellow members on a committee of a voluntary organisation. A common area of conflict concerns the attendance time requirements associated with jobs. The employer expects commitment to overtime when necessary, whereas family and friends may think this requirement is unreasonable and seek to influence it.

Table 1.1
Job Requirements: Basic Elements of any Job   *cont. overleaf*

1.	Task:	objective(s) of activity(ies)
2.	Method:	how job is done (nature of activities)
3.	Technology:	plant, equipment, machinery involved
4.	Variety:	how many activities included
5.	Sequencing:	order in which activities undertaken
6.	Timing	time for completion of sequence(s) of activities
7.	Pace:	pace of work
8.	Quality:	standards required
9.	Specialisation:	degree of specialisation in division of labour
10.	Interdependence:	relation of activities to those undertaken by others
11.	Partialness:	relation of activities to completion of overall product
12.	Performance:	how is performance measured?
13.	Monitoring:	who decides action in light of performance information?
14.	Accountability:	what happens if performance information shows good/bad performance?

Table 1.1 *cont.*

Examples of these requirements in three jobs

Requirement	Accounts clerk	Maintenance engineer	Software engineer
1. Task	Record financial transactions	Maintain electrical equipment in good order	Write programmes for in-house users
2. Method	Writing, reading and filing	Diagnosing and rectifying faults	Thinking, writing
3. Technology	Typewriter, computer	Craft tools	Computer
4. Variety	Very few	Moderate	Moderate
5. Sequence	Predetermined	Some leeway	Great leeway
6. Timing	5 minutes	5–200 minutes	Open
7. Pace	Set by input	Self-determined but output monitored	Self-determined but output monitored
8. Quality	Specified	Specified	Open
9. Specialisation	Medium	Medium	Low
10. Interdependence	High	Medium	Low
11. Partialness	Very small part	Whole part	Whole part
12. Performance	Number of records made, accuracy of records	Supervisor's/user's assessment Success of work	Long-term success of programmes
13. Monitoring	Supervisor	Supervisor	Self/Manager
14. Accountability	Supervisor intervenes	Supervisor intervenes	Self/Manager intervenes

Discretion and control

Underlying much of this discussion about job requirements has been the extent to which, for each job element, the job-holder has discretion and, conversely, the extent to which he/she is subject to external control. Some jobs (e.g. operators in some manufacturing industry) are subject to highly specific controls which leave little room for manoeuvre. Others (e.g. community relations officers) may be subject to loose guidelines which leave room for a lot of discretion. Alan Fox (1974) argues that if autonomy and discretion are low and external control is high, then a low 'trust' relationship between levels in the hierarchy can arise. This in turn may create a vicious circle in which increasing external control is seen as necessary. Conditions for nurturing motivation amongst the workforce decrease as they see less opportunity for influencing the delivery of valued rewards. The strength of motivation decreases, performance is increasingly the subject of control and it becomes increasingly difficult to introduce innovation in a co-operative way. This is a theme which will be revisited in Chapter 9 in the discussion on managing change.

Thus far control has been discussed as if it were a single variable. This is too simplistic. Figure 1.3 identifies six different types of control which may be experienced by a job-holder. Each type of control is associated with a different experience of discretion for job-holders. At a minimum, control over jobs with a high degree of autonomy and discretion is usually exercised unobtrusively through the educational and industrial institutions which trained and recruited the job-holder. This means that control has been built into job performance through socialisation. The term 'cultural' instead of 'unobtrusive' is sometimes used for this aspect of control. The craftsman potter learns creative techniques and business practice either formally or informally from colleagues and institutions as well as teaching himself a great deal through original thought and private reading. Once learned, from whatever source, these techniques, values and motivations will exercise control in an unobtrusive way over aspects of job performance. The large Japanese corporations, with their employment policies which appear to generate high loyalty and commitment, are strongly dependent on these unobtrusive, cultural controls in what Ouchi and Price (1978) call the 'industrial clan'. Professionals, like doctors and solicitors, are the archetypal occupational groups whose jobs are often predominantly controlled in this unobtrusive way in the UK.

As individuals become more aware of controls on their activity, so they assume greater formality, and it is possible to talk of personal rather than unobtrusive control. In setting himself a deadline of completing ten pots a week, or in rejecting some pots because he thinks on reflection that their handles are too large, the potter is conscious of exercising personal control over his work.

Third, there is control through the specification of output criteria. Superiors here are less interested in how work is done, so long as goods and services of the required quality, quantity and sequence are produced. There is often little discretion for the job-holder over the specification of these targets, but once specified she may have a great deal of discretion in how to achieve them. The growth of home working, not simply for routine assembly or sewing but also for computer programmers and others who can work 'at a distance' from their superiors, is a reflection on an increase in the use of output controls (Brocklehurst, 1989). 'Responsibility accounting' (Flamholtz,

FIGURE 1.3
Types of Control on a Job-holder

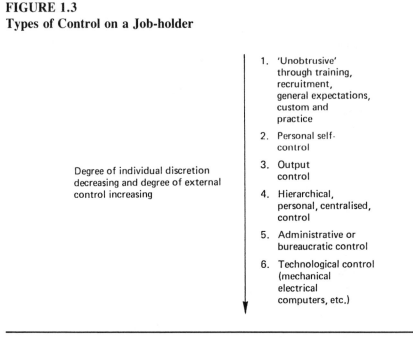

Degree of individual discretion
decreasing and degree of external
control increasing

1. 'Unobtrusive' through training, recruitment, general expectations, custom and practice

2. Personal self-control

3. Output control

4. Hierarchical, personal, centralised, control

5. Administrative or bureaucratic control

6. Technological control (mechanical electrical computers, etc.)

1979), as opposed to tighter systems of budgetary control, is another example; managers are given overall targets for their activities and are then left to their own devices over how to meet them. Output control appears to provide management with an opportunity to facilitate discretion and delegation while maintaining overall (and particularly financial) control. However, there can be managerial problems in that the semi-autonomous centres so created may be resistant to change, and, of course, there are some situations where the output cannot be simply and easily measured and specified. As the earlier discussion of incentive payment systems suggested, to overemphasise one easily measurable aspect of performance may well incline the job-holder to neglect other more important, but less easily measurable, aspects.

At the fourth level there is hierarchical control which is exercised personally by superiors. For example, a supervisor gives instructions to a laboratory technician about how to carry out blood tests; a quality control engineer tells a lathe operator that his products are not of sufficiently high standard; or a headmaster advises his head of modern languages on the need to make greater use of the school's language laboratory. At this fourth level discretion and autonomy are being curtailed in a direct fashion by superiors in a centralised hierarchy.

Stricter and less negotiable controls are examined at the fifth and sixth levels, where modern technology plays an important part. Administrative systems of formalised, written rules and procedures increasingly supported by sophisticated office automation and information technology can effectively control all the aspects of work listed in Table 1.1, as the example of the accounts clerk suggests. Administrative controls include formal job descriptions and promotion procedures. They also extend to budgetary and standard accounting controls, where tight control is exercised through the establishment of financial targets and limits for fairly small areas of work and organisation. Similarly, at the sixth level, manufacturing technology can lead to extensive standardisation and control, so that in fact all the job requirements are outside the individual's discretion and there can be little delegation (see, e.g., Edwards, 1979).

There is a strong relationship between the specificity of job requirements and types of control. If activities are carefully defined and prescribed, then administrative and technological controls, backed up by hierarchical control, are usually important aspects of the job. Hence clerical workers who have routinely to type, fill in and file pro formas, or manufacturing operatives who have routinely to operate or mind repetitive machines, have their activities externally defined and controlled. Sometimes, however, it is not administratively or technologically possible to programme exactly how something is to be done, or else such measures are felt to be unacceptable to those involved. In such cases output control becomes the norm and role-holders exercise discretion, within specified limits, about how to reach the specified quantity, quality or timescale of production. The type and degree of specification and standardisation is not always feasible, however, either because of uncertainty about the definition of appropriate output or because of strong expectations on the part of the job-holder that discretion in both the 'what' and 'how' of her job is important. A last option then is to rely on standardised skills and control exercised personally and unobtrusively through professional, vocational and in-house training. Greatest discretion is available to those people – like professional solicitors, doctors, development engineers, research scientists and social workers – who are recruited for particular skills or experience which are believed to be important.

Job design

Jobs can be analysed to reveal the extent and area of discretion and the extent, type and area of control. Pragmatic and moral arguments have been advanced to suggest where and how the balance should be drawn when the job requirements identified in Table 1.1 are being specified. The process of specifying job requirements is called job design. Where managers are responsible for the achievement of specific goals for production, distribution, service, etc., the more they can specify, standardise and measure job performance, the clearer can be their view on progress and on reasons for underachievement. They may also be attracted by the arguments that highly standardised and specialised jobs allow workers to concentrate their energies on doing limited jobs well, so that proficiency and uniformity will be enhanced by practice. Learning time for the job may also be reduced, and consequently people can be more easily replaced and generally more cheaply. Furthermore, time may be saved because people do not have to solve problems, make decisions, or change jobs or machines. Last but not least, managerial control can be increased. The only problem remaining may be that people do not like the jobs that result, and will only put in a minimum effort and will be reluctant to co-operate with change.

Pragmatic and moral issues feature in counter-arguments. Humanitarian concerns to improve the quality of working life (see, e.g., Davis and Cherns, 1975) find support from those who argue they have a more realistic and longer-term concern for efficiency and effectiveness than those who seek to control as much as possible. Increased specialisation requires increased co-ordination and increased costs. Inflexibility and rigidity lead employees to focus on their own sub-group goals, to pay little attention to objectives of others and to make the organisation extremely resistant to change. The unnecessary simplification of tasks is said to lose the opportunities offered in the array of resources and ideals held by employees, while monotony and boredom lead to dissatisfaction, which in turn may (if expectations are disappointed) lead to absenteeism, lateness, a drop in productivity, etc. Those who espouse the arguments against excessive simplification, standardi-sation and external control of job requirements have supported developments in job enrichment, job enlargement and job rotation, which they hope will help to reverse the trend.

The aim of *job enrichment* is to demand more of an individual's capabilities and talents and to provide workers with the opportunity of working as complete a sequence as possible, resulting in an identifiable product. This enrichment is sometimes extended to involving workers in the decision-making associated with the work processes. Gregory (1978) includes several papers describing Swedish experiments (e.g. at Volvo, where teams of workers were made responsible for producing major sections of a car, including the inspection of completed units; many of the planning and control functions were also vested in the group). Similarly, in another company fifteen workers who had previously completed one or two separate work assignments in the assembly of car radios were reorganised into five separate groups of three who collectively completed the whole task, including inspec-tion.

The aim of *job rotation* is to give employees the opportunity to take turns to do a variety of jobs, although the essential boredom of specialised, routine tasks remains. Job enlargement is an alternative strategy which involves increasing the number of tasks which any individual will do so that she has sight of a clear finished product as well as some discretion in the sequencing of actions.

The research findings on job redesign are inconclusive, on both efficiency and humanitarian grounds. In general it seems that the schemes are most successful in 'efficiency' terms when managements are highly committed to them, when employees positively favour and desire their introduction, when workers have been involved in discussions prior to their introduction (Englestad, 1972) and when workers are given clear goals, clear feedback on performance and control over their performancee. Otherwise they do not have the magical effect some might claim (Fein, 1974). Furthermore, it is always possible that the 'good effects' are in part a reflection of a so-called 'Hawthorne effect', in which it is the fact that a group of workers have become a focus for interest, apart from the nature of the change itself, that is an important determining factor in the outcome of the experiment.

Hackman and Oldham (1980) offer two possible paths for the design of jobs and work systems. Route one, which they favour, involves 'fitting jobs to people' and designing work so that people can be internally motivated to better performance: for example, through greater autonomy or group self-management. Route two, which they fear but which is already well established, represents many an engineer's dream. It involves 'fitting people to jobs' and designing work systems for maximum technological efficiency; here the management task is to help people adapt to the technological requirements through careful systems for monitoring and control. Hackman and Oldham suggest such systems generate negative responses with management and workforce becoming locked into a spiral of increasing control and resistance. But the problem, as they see it, is that the spiral has already begun and will be difficult to reverse, except through powerful political pressure or dramatic changes in social or economic climate so that present policies are no longer tenable.

Kelly (1980) noted that much of the discussion about job redesign was in terms of the economic benefits to employers and the psychological benefits to employees. What, he wondered, were the economic costs to each side? Accordingly he reviewed nearly 200 studies of job redesign, which he defined as 'a relatively enduring change in job content in one or more directions of increased variety, autonomy, responsibility and task identity'. The studies were taken from fourteen different countries, had been reported in thirty-nine journals and covered the period 1950–78. Kelly evaluated their effects and looked at the costs to both management and workers. From the workers' side his review showed that there were job losses both for the workers involved and those in ancillary jobs. However, in general workers who remained employed benefited from pay increases as productivity rose, although there were some exceptions to this rule. Job redesign was generally associated with increases in labour intensity: that is, the proportion of the working day consumed in working or the rate of working. Although workers generally got more autonomy over immediate aspects of production like work pace and methods, they nonetheless were often subject to increased managerial control and accountability for their overall job performance, since this was now more easily identified. Any management costs, in terms of training bills, consultancy fees and increased wages, were hard to estimate and in any case appeared to be easily offset by the economic benefits of improvements in productivity. In discussing these findings Kelly points out the difficulties of generalising from them since he was essentially studying schemes which management thought were successful. He concluded nonetheless that job redesign schemes did involve economic costs for workers directly affected and for workers in associated jobs, but he found the costs to management to be relatively small. In conclusion Kelly stresses that costs, and indeed any psychological benefits accruing, are subject to change because of their relationship to workers' expectations, the strength of trade unions, and the tightness of local labour markets.

Ideas about the enrichment, rotation and enlargement of jobs were received with particular interest in the late 1960s and early 1970s, when tight labour markets and high employment created concern among senior managers that they would not be able to recruit and retain a loyal workforce to undertake repetitive, highly specialised and low discretion work. A focus for this concern was the strike at the American Chevrolet Vega car plant in Lordstown, Ohio, in the early 1970s, where the main issue was not pay but the unsatisfactory nature of assembly line work. In 'the age of Lordstown' there was much talk about work humanisation and the quality of working life. Job enrichment schemes in the USA in AT & T (Ford, 1973) and Philips (reported in Daniel and McIntosh, 1972) were the subject of great discussion, as were the developments in semi-autonomous group working at the Saab Scania petrol engine plant and Volvo's Kalmar plant (both discussed in Gregory, 1978). With a dramatic reversal of economic fortunes, the significant growth of unemployment and a marked weakening of trade union strength in the 1980s, there is now much less talk about how to enrich jobs. Even looking at the heyday of such schemes it is interesting to note that most developments left managerial control unchallenged, being directed more at increasing complexity and decreasing specialisation, and less at increasing discretion.

Designers and managers effectively make frequent, although often implicit, decisions about the advantages and disadvantges of standardisation and control as against flexibility and discretion as a basis for structure. Given the lack of conclusive evidence, they always face a problem of assessing the accuracy and validity of different viewpoints and the weights to be assigned to the various interest groups involved. Yet it is vital to assess the appropriateness of present job requirements and the directions for future developments. The importance of such analysis is underlined by examples of inappropriate or neglected diagnosis. Blackler and Brown (1980) described a participation experiment in a Shell wax plant, where it was assumed that more flexibility and discretion could be introduced into plant operations than was in fact technically feasible. For a short time job-holders' expectations of greater discretion were satisfied to the detriment of the plant's operating efficiency, since operating elements which were not in fact negotiable were taken to be capable of variation. Other examples tell the reverse story of attempts to fix standard procedures on essentially high discretion tasks. Blau (1955) relates how employment agency clerks, when given 'output' targets in terms of the number of applicants whom they saw rather than whom they placed, naturally increased the number of clients seen, while the numbers actually placed decreased.

1.4   Concluding Remarks

This chapter has been concerned to reveal the way in which individual attitudes and behaviour at work are shaped. Interest in this subject is often prompted by a desire to improve individual performance at work: for example, to secure a 'better', 'cheaper' or 'quicker delivered' product. So preoccupied are some people with individual attitudes and behaviour at work that they forget that in some work situations individual effort or commitment may have little impact, at least in the short term, on corporate performance, this being much more influenced by fiscal policy and patterns of international trade than by employee attitudes and behaviour. This warning noted, we can conclude on the subject of this chapter with a reminder of Figure 1.2. This figure is crucial to securing an adequate understanding of the multiple factors which underlie an individual's performance at work. It is essential to appreciate ability, motivation and the physical and social context in which the job is to be undertaken. A mismatch between these elements creates problems for people and their employing organisation. For example, a highly qualified software engineer commanding scarce intellectual resources, highly motivated by money and promotion, would be totally misplaced in a routine programmer's job. He would be much more appropriately placed in an internal consultancy position where he could put his resources to good use, in a context where his motivation to work hard and with inspiration was high. At the other extreme considerations of seniority may lead to the promotion of someone who does not possess appropriate resources and has little chance of acquiring them. This person's initial motivation may be high but, if he does not achieve the expected rewards, he is likely to become very dissatisfied.

Individual characteristics and social context are interdependent. Individuals bear the imprint of social influences and some, especially those with strong power bases, also leave their mark on the organisational context. For example, the software engineer, commanding scarce intellectual resources, can significantly alter his job requirements and possibly fundamentally affect strategic developments in the firm. This is unlikely to be an option for the routine accounts clerk who may feel capable of doing a more advanced job but who is unable to prove this by reference to external sources and so will probably fail to get promotion when placed in competition with someone else with proven qualifications and experience. Job requirements reflect the technical and administrative controls that have been developed in the organisation, but are also subject to individual interpretation. Furthermore, characteristics of relevant occupational and industrial structures are often important in influencing people's attitudes and behaviour at work. The prevailing labour markets, the number and type of job vacancies in the company, in the industry and in the region, will have a bearing on individual expectations and motivation. When there are no vacancies, many people live for long periods with their disappointments. Indeed their motivation in the first place will be heavily influenced by their judgements about the sorts of reward which they may realistically expect. Labour market considerations are also important in influencing a company's decisions about the level and direction of investment in training, and hence will have an effect on the pool of individual resources upon which it can call.

The lack of simple answers to the issues raised by the discussion of attitudes, motivation and performance is an important lesson. The complexities of the relationship between social and economic structures and individual action are so great that at best a framework can be abstracted which will help to diagnose the variables and the linkages involved. Taking people's expectations, present job requirements, and industrial and organisational context, it should be possible to hazard a good guess about their attitudes and expectations. This information can be used by subordinates of seniors, as well as vice versa, and is also relevant to dealings across functional boundaries with people of different departments.

Interest Groups, Objectives and Strategy 2

2.1 Interest Groups

People are recruited into work organisations as individuals, but they bring with them an amalgam of attitudes and values which, together with the nature of their job and position in the organisation, makes it likely that they will become members of one or more interest groups. The term 'interest group' is used to describe a collection of people who believe they share common objectives and viewpoints in work-related matters. Not all their work-related objectives and viewpoints will be identical, but those that are different will not normally be in obvious conflict. Members of interest groups within the workplace will not necessarily share political, educational and other social values outside the workplace. Although members of interest groups may not formally acknowledge their 'groupness', they nonetheless must feel some communality of interest. The term should not be applied from outside to a collection of disparate individuals who 'objectively' may appear to have interests in common but who are subjectively unaware that this is so.

Members of different groups are likely to share similar views on some of the following issues:

- the division of profits between different groups associated with a firm
- the way to secure pay increases
- how to avoid redundancy and to gain job security
- how present bosses 'treat' employees
- what is a 'good' job
- how to 'get on' in the company
- the relative importance of different functions and how they should be linked
- 'discretion' versus 'control' for different jobs
- future directions for the organisation

27

The mixing of views about what is best for individuals and group members and what is best for 'the organisation' is important, since although individuals and groups are concerned with self-interest, growth and defence, these issues cannot be separated from those of the strategies and tactics which they consider appropriate for the corporate organisation to pursue. This is not to say that all groups automatically push for the adoption of plans which will always give them greatest benefit, but rather that, even if they adopt an altruistic posture for the 'greater good', they are likely to do so on the basis of an awareness of their own particular interest.

The origins of interest groups at work

Interest groups which are important in organisations originate from both outside and inside formal organisational boundaries. They may be composed of shareholders, suppliers, customers, or groups of craftsmen, operatives, salespeople, engineers, development scientists, managers and directors. Generally the contours of interest group formation are drawn in relation to the five dimensions of:

- relation to external groupings
- hierarchical level
- functional divisions
- geographical/national boundaries
- individual characteristics, deriving in part from wider social experience

External contacts

The extent and nature of contact between an internal group in an organisation and some wider grouping outside, such as a trade union or professional association, is often a vital ingredient of interest group formation. Groups which have a collective external identity are often easier to identify within the workplace and are more open in taking a 'group' view. Other groups (e.g. of departmental heads) may be less willing obviously to act collectively, fearing that this may undermine their individual status, but nonetheless for certain issues they may be prepared to join forces to push their particular interests.

Level and function

The second dimension of interest group formation is the distribution of the membership between different levels in the hierarchy, and the third is their location in different functional groups. Sometimes level is the overriding dimension, so that junior salespeople may form an interest group which is joined by junior production supervisors. At other times functional differences may be critical, and then the junior salespeople are more likely to ally themselves with their superiors in sales. Whether alliances are formed on either or both of these dimensions will depend on the issues which are currently at the forefront of concern. The identity of interest groups in relation to particular issues is important. For example, departmental heads may form one loose interest group in relation to the issues of job evaluation and the establishment of salary grades, whereas they may feel no common interest whatsoever when it comes to the introduction of aspects of office automation, when their ranks are more likely to be divided between the different functional interest groups of, say, administration, production and sales. The formation of interest groups in relation to hierarchy and function is obviously heavily influenced by particular organisational characteristics. For example, the technical sophistication of a fibre plant may facilitate the formation of an interest group of technical specialists. In the same plant, the fact that employees are handling some highly toxic substances may mean that the health and safety function, together with the support of government inspectors, provides the basis for a considerably stronger interest group than is often the case (Dawson, Poynter and Stevens, 1984). If most of the products are largely standardised and mass produced, a great deal of 'sales' work may be done through cartel-type arrangements with competitors. This has implications for the structure and functioning of sales and marketing and, like the other examples given above, affects the way in which interest groups are likely to develop.

Geography

In large corporations the hierarchical and functional dimensions are often overlaid by the fourth dimension of geography. This is obviously very important for multinational companies where the most senior executives are usually found in those countries where the predominant ownership resides. Different interest groups in multinationals can develop on the basis of nationality, business or product groupings, and such differences become particularly important when issues of product market strategy are involved. For example, in a declining market the crucial issues are which plants will be closed in which countries. On the other hand, in an expanding market, the issue is which plants will get the extra resources to increase production. Quarrels that arise over 'within company trading' are also good examples of different interests manifesting themselves within multinational companies. For example, a subsidiary of a multinational electrical company manufacturing light bulbs found that it could buy glass cheaper from outside the group and outside the country than from another British glass plant within the group. The interest of the works management team, conscious of the need to cut costs, appeared at first sight to be best served by switching suppliers. But the management committee decided to set this short-term gain against what it realised could be a dangerous precedent, particularly if other European manufacturers of light bulbs in the future offered cheaper products than themselves. At the same time the national headquarters were keen to keep as much production as possible in the UK and so they exerted influence on the glass factory to improve effficiency and on the bulb factory to maintain its order. Executives in multinational headquarters, considering an overproduction of glass, were anxious to find an excuse to rationalise their resources. Consequently they did not discourage the issue from developing into one of open conflict and were somewhat disappointed when it faded away.

Individual characteristics and social context

It would be naive to assume that interest groups in organisations are formed in a vacuum apart from the characteristics of the individuals involved: for example, their skills, aptitudes and experience, their perceptions of self-interest and their perceptions of appropriate strategies and tactics for the organisation. These individual characteristics are the fifth dimension of interest group formation. Chapter 1 showed how individual characteristics are strongly embedded in wider social influences, particularly social class and family background. To illustrate these influences, let us consider two caricatures. The first is of a man born to a barrister and a teacher, who achieves well at school and university where he studies chemistry. Subsequently, from among offers from all six places to which he applies, he becomes a plant chemist in an industrial chemical factory. After five years, he moves into the position of production manager in a competitor's plant. In terms of interest groups he finds himself in ones which take a senior management viewpoint and champion the cause of production and of technical sophistication on the hardware side, which is also the area in which his own career is most likely to flourish. The second caricature is of a woman born of a lorry driver and a clerk, who believes that education is wasted on a woman, who leaves school at the earliest possible opportunity and enters into erratic periods of employment as an assembly worker in various factories. She then joins the same chemical works as our earlier man, but in the packaging and labelling department. She finds herself in interest groups which defend the interests of those at the bottom of the hierarchy and are heavily unionised.

These two caricatures suggest that social class is one of the more important keys to the generation of interest groups in organisations. Those people who see contemporary society in terms of a dichotomy between two classes would argue that to give five dimensions to interest group formation is but to blur the picture unnecessarily. They would favour a radical Marxist view which emphasises a stark schism between 'them' and 'us' across the industrial relations divide between management and workers. Even people who do not hold this view so strongly would tend to think in terms of such differences when asked 'Is there much conflict in your factory?' Alternatively, other people adopt a 'unitary' view of organisations as homogeneous entities, particularly when discussing their relationship to competitors and consumers. This book tends to a middle or 'pluralistic' view on these matters, advocating that organisations can be conceptualised as a lattice of different interest groups, located in relation to the five dimensions discussed above. There are, however, some contexts where the dimension of level is so predominant in interest group formation that other dimensions are insignificant and a more radical analysis is appropriate. Table 2.1 provides a comparative summary of the characteristics of the unitary, pluralist and radical perspectives in terms of three key dimensions: namely, interests, conflict and power in organisations. These are subjects which will be raised again in Chapter 7. Further discussion on the unitary, pluralist and radical approaches may be found in Fox (1966, 1974) and Burrell and Morgan (1979, pp. 204, 388).

Given the collection of different interest groups in organisations, there are always likely to be disagreements about how scarce resources should be expended, how new resources should be created and acquired, and the nature of relationships between interest groups. Sometimes this conflict is fairly institutionalised and formally established between two or more well defined groups, as is often the case in industrial relations between management and

Table 2.1

Comparing Unitary, Pluralist and Radical Perspectives on Interests and Conflict

	Unitary perspective	*Pluralist perspective*	*Radical perspective*
Interests	Common objectives	Diverse objectives Coalition Compromise	Opposing interests
Conflict	Rare, transient from 'trouble-makers'	Inherent positive	Dynamic force for radical change
Power	Non-problematic, legitimate authority	Crucial medium for resolution of conflict	Embedded in social fabric Social domination

trade unions. In other situations, conflicts may be played out in a largely informal way, as between department heads at board level. Sometimes individuals can find themselves pulled in two or more ways at once because of their membership of different interest groups. This is often said to be the case for people who, having been thoroughly trained and grounded in a profession with a 'cosmopolitan' outlook towards work and career, are then employed by a large corporation which traditionally has developed its own executive class from home-grown talent which tends to have a 'local' outlook on life (see Chapter 1). Given the growth of professional occupations in the last twenty or so years, and their increasing importance as members of large organisations, they will now be discussed as an example of interest groups in organisations.

Professional interest groups and employing organisations

The long established professions of law, medicine, accounting, architecture and the church have been joined in this century by newer groupings of men and women with specialist training in such areas as the many branches of engineering and personnel. Table 2.2 provides a summary of characteristics which historically have been associated with professional groups who typically have developed within some form of private practice. The first three characteristics, relating to a distinct body of knowledge, specific training and restrictive entry, draw the boundaries around the subject matter and the membership of the profession. The last three, focusing on an ethical code, concern for client and peer group evaluation, are concerned with the way in which professional knowledge is developed and applied, and implies an almost unquestioning acceptance of professional authority by clients. Although their development has been justified in terms of safeguarding standards of client service, professional groups have all benefited from the exclusivity their methods of training and operation afford them, both because of the status conferred through their superior specialist knowledge and

Table 2.2
Characteristics Historically Associated with Professional Groups

- Commitment to a distinct body of knowledge
- Specific and lengthy training
- Restrictive entry
- Prescribed code of ethics and standards of behaviour
- Proclaimed concern for client groups
- Peer group evaluation, control and promotion

because of the associated restriction on entry. Professionals are now, however, frequently employed not in private practice but in large organisations, although they can still call upon the external resources of their profession when they are advancing or defending their interests. Company solicitors can refuse to act in ways which they feel would be negatively sanctioned by their peers or contrary to their codes of ethics. Professors in a university can champion a particular curriculum development with reference to the professional values of academic freedom and furtherance of scholarship, and thereby incline their colleagues to support, or at least not openly dispute, their position.

Is there a conflict between professional and organisational commitment?

The employment of professionally qualified people in a large number of different functions in contemporary work organisations has led some commentators to predict and observe clashes between organisational and professional commitment and identity and between two contrasting forms of control and regulation of work. It is argued that professionally trained people have a commitment to a subject matter, method of application and to their professional peers, not to an organisation. Certainly they are potentially highly mobile and are consequently not easily controlled by non-specialist managers or administrators. It would seem that in terms of commitment and loyalty to their employers, relative immobility and a willingness to co-operate with organisational rules, procedures and practices, one of Gouldner's 'locals' is a much better bet for employment than a professional 'cosmopolitan' (Gouldner, 1957); but therein lies a paradox. The cosmopolitan professional's training and approach to his subject matter, which are the foundation of his independence, are precisely those things which make him so desirable a commodity to the employing organisation. As an expensive resource he arguably needs to have freedom to develop and use the expertise and judgement which account for his recruitment in the first place, but he somehow also needs to be aligned to the rest of the organisation.

This issue became prominent in the 1950s and early 1960s when technological developments in industry occasioned significantly increased employment of academically trained scientists and engineers as well as accountants, lawyers and representatives of other specialisms. Would there be a clash between 'occupational' and 'organisational' interest groups? Some commentators, of whom Kornhauser (1962) was a leading protagonist, were certain that conflict between, as he put it, professional and bureaucratic value systems would occur in the employment of scientists in industry to the detriment of both the individuals and organisations involved. In particular he predicted that conflict would occur over issues of goals and control. For example, would the advancement of knowledge or commercial viability be the dominant criteria in recruitment decisions, in the evaluation of work, promotion of individuals and direction for future policy developments?

Would control, supervision and communication be geared to managerial or professional needs?

Alleviating any conflict

Although a degree of conflict between professional and organisational allegiance may be inevitable in some cases, the essential adaptiveness of people both as individuals and as members of institutionalised structures means that it is rarely as extreme as one might at first think. Furthermore, changes in the wider social economic and industrial structure create changing contexts which have important implications for the balance of consensus, adaptation and conflict between professionals and managers.

On the individual side, it has already been demonstrated how people adapt to new situations through the processes of anticipatory and secondary socialisation (Chapter 1). This is the case for professionals, not least because of the strong individual dimension to interest group formation, reflecting motivations for career, money, status, etc. For example, perceptions of personal interests may well encourage a doctor in a private hospital to toe the administrator's line as far as hours of work or the ordering of supplies are concerned, and she may also find her values changing as well as her actions. Similarly, a development engineer, professionally motivated to push back the frontiers of knowledge in his particular field, may with relative ease turn his talents to more mundane but commercially important problems and derive a great deal of satisfaction from so doing. Hastings and Hinings (1970) collected evidence to suggest that the more chartered accountants saw their personal career prospects to be dependent on non-accounting superiors, the more likely they were to give less emphasis to any professional values which conflicted with the policies and practices of management.

Occasionally, of course, conflicts do erupt. An architect employed by a property development company feels he can no longer remain with them because their overriding concern to cut costs is forcing him to design buildings which he finds aesthetically displeasing or which only have a life of twenty or so years. His decision to leave will reflect not only the conflict but his assessment of the chances that he will find suitable alternative employment. The individual career dimension of interest may be as strong as his commitment to a professional group.

Further support for individual adaptation in different organisational contexts comes from Cotgrove and Box (1970), who developed a typology of three main types of scientific role which, they argued, are typically found in different organisational settings and filled by scientists with different identities and values. First, there is the 'public scientist' fulfilling an 'academic' role in which the pursuit of knowledge is paramount. Second, there is the 'private scientist' fulfilling a 'scientific' role much concerned with the application and development of scientific knowledge and skills in order to solve practical problems. Third, there is the 'organisational scientist', who uses scientific research activities mainly as a means of earning a living and who is not concerned to develop a career in science as such.

In an empirical study of undergraduate and postgraduate chemistry students and graduate industrial chemists Cotgrove and Box found that anticipatory socialisation into different contexts and occupational choice were major moderators of potential conflict between science and industry. Where conflict remained, predominantly among 'public' and to an extent among 'organisational' scientists, it was over their lack of autonomy in making decisions about their work. Decisions about the selection and termination of projects and the planning of research were identified as particular foci for conflict.

Adaptation in the face of conflict between professional and organisational values is usually two sided. The research manager who is responsible for the development engineer will probably let him have some time to follow his own particular scientific curiosity. The hospital administrator who appreciates the distinctive way in which doctors prefer to work will try to be accommodating. In general control systems may be made more flexible: some workers may be allowed autonomy to pursue basic research, while tighter control may be introduced for those working on the development of products or the technical solution of operational problems.

Responses in terms of modifying the structure of organisations can also help to alleviate (or at least contain) some potential conflicts between professional and managerial interest groups. For example, senior managers in some organisations which are heavily dependent on maintaining a strong R & D function have instituted what have become known as 'dual career ladders' (Moore and Davies, 1977). This means that a status ladder, set apart from the managerial hierarchy, is instituted so that senior scientists can increase in status and rewards and yet remain in R & D. However, this sort of development, although a response to an acknowledged problem, has not been altogether successful as a solution, not least because by definition an 'elite' of senior scientists can only contain a few people, leaving other scientists with raised, but unsatisfied, expectations. Entry to the elite cannot be made easier without devaluing it for those it is intended to impress (Gunz, 1980, p. 117). Furthermore, Goldner and Ritti (1967) argue that since the senior scientists are not given real discretionary control over resources, the dual ladder is really no ladder at all, but has the consequence of forcing 'immobility' on the scientists who are attracted by the illusion of advancement to stay in R & D.

Another structural response to the perceived problem of accommodating valued professional experts is to develop matrix structures in which, as Chapter 5 will show, specialist functional professionals are dedicated to particular product or project groupings while still remaining partially identified with their professional colleagues.

Changes are also occurring not only within and between the professional and managerial interest groups in employing organisations, but also within the educational and training institutions which are critical agents of professional and managerial socialisation. For example, universities are encouraging a proportion of their scientists and engineers to think positively in terms of an industrial rather than an academic career by altering the curriculum to include a consideration of industrial and business problems through the study of accounting, marketing and organisational behaviour. Similarly, medical schools teach the practice of medicine within a hospital administrative system. Some social commentators argue that the institutions of higher education have not changed enough in this direction. For example, recommendation 46 of the Report of the Committee of Inquiry into the Engineering Profession chaired by Sir Monty Finniston argued that:

> every effort should be made to increase the interchange of staff between industry and teaching establishments to improve the teaching of engineering practice within engineering departments, including the intro-duction of systems of recognition (with associated additional pay) for engineering teachers who maintain close links with industry. (Finniston, 1980, p. 167)

Whether the changes in this area of professional training are sufficient and appropriate are issues of topical relevance. Suffice it to note here that the fact that debate is seen to be important is itself interesting and testimony to an acknowledgement among senior managers, professionals and academics that there are problems in offering appropriate training and employment for specialist professionals.

Thus, through the 'give and take' of human interaction, individual res-ponses to perceptions of the labour market and structural developments in employing organisations and educational institutions, many potential con-flicts between professional and managerial interest groups never openly develop. Another reason for this is that people are often more concerned to join forces with others in a similar level than they are to argue with those of a different background. The discussion about professionals in organisations has so far focused on three dimensions of interest group formation: those relating to external groupings, function and individual interest. The other dimensions of geography, and particularly hierarchical level, are also important and both of them serve to lessen the conflict between functions. Doctors in a hospital or software engineers in an electronics company may each share professional values, but the more senior among each professional group will also have interests in common with the seniors in other functions and departments. Similarly, the juniors in each group may well have interests in common which cut across professional boundaries.

The proletarian professional

Observations of this sort of fragmentation between levels in professional groups has prompted some people (e.g. Oppenheimer, 1973) to argue that conflict between professionals and managers is largely being resolved through the 'proletarianisation' of professionals who are reduced to a subservient position in their employing organisations. Their subservience is assured, the argument goes, by three developments: first, the simplification of their work tasks, so that each individual accountant or engineer, for example, undertakes fairly routine and repetitive activities in book-keeping or engineering drawing; second, the imposition of systems of accountability and tight performance measurement so that individual professionals have little discretion in their work; and third, the separation of planning and decision-making activities from the execution of work tasks, so that design decisions are made at top level and, for example, an engineer is given a tight specification from which he must produce a detailed drawing.

Such trends are not discernible for all professional work, but they are more likely to be found when at least one of the three following conditions is found: (a) if an occupational group is seeking higher status and trying to establish a foothold in the professional domain (readers should see Millerson, 1964, for a discussion of qualifying associations as a route to full professionalisation); (b) if technological developments, particularly in information technology, facilitate the simplification and fragmentation of tasks (e.g. if computer-aided design simplifies the tasks of some process design engineers); (c) if senior people consider cutting costs and 'saving' money to be of paramount importance. Such situations are just as likely to be found in the public sector under a regime of public expenditure cuts as in establishments in the private sector when they meet 'lean times'.

In response to situations in which their work has been 'proletarianised', professionals experience fear of redundancy and complain about the dwindling pay differentials between people in their position and lesser trained 'technicians'. In such situations Gunz (1978) has noted that there has been an increase in unionisation as people turn to a collective response to adversity, their individual position having been substantially eroded or difficult to establish.

The professional managerial class

In contrast to the 'proletarianisation' argument, Ehrenreich and Ehrenreich (1977) have argued that rather than an axis of dominance – subservience characterising relations between managers and professionals, the two groups have merged to become a new 'professional–managerial class' which has assimilated each other's interests and stands apart from, and in dominance over, wage labour. The Ehrenreichs do not suggest, however, that the professional–managerial class is at one with their employing capitalists, but rather it is also antagonistic to the owners of capital. Many professionals find themselves in the employment of the state rather than private enterprise, but the same separation from both 'the top' and 'the bottom' of the organisation can still be found.

Noble's (1977) historical account of engineering in the USA provides some support for this analysis by showing how the professional development of engineering was intricately linked to corporate developments. In this context corporate position was an important mark of status within the profession. Noble discusses the symbiotic relationship between engineers and their corporate employers and their relationship to academic institutions. The corporations needed technical knowledge and most engineers could only get money and equipment through corporations. Private practice was rarely a strong option for engineers and thus the individual engineer and dominant members of organisations involved in engineering and industrial development each had a great deal to gain from mutual co-operation. Indeed, members of the various groups soon became relatively indistinguishable from each other as they moved between engineering and management. The analyses by Armstrong (1971) and Cotgrove (1975) of engineers in the UK similarly suggest that they enter willingly into accommodation with managers and tend to take an instrumental view of their academic training and qualification, using it as a base for their acquisition of managerial status within their employing organisation.

The tendency for professionals to ally themselves with managers is discussed by Child (1982) who, on the basis of work by Powell (1981) and Hopper (1978), argues that it is an apt description of trends in the employment of some members of the accounting profession. Powell found accountants to be generally more interested in acting as consultants to management and participating with them in making decisions about such diverse topics as process and product development and employment than they were in keeping the accounts. In a complimentary fashion, the managers whom Powell studied welcomed accountants taking this consultancy and advisory line. Furthermore, one can note the increasing numbers of chartered accountants who find themselves in senior positions in the public, private and voluntary sectors of employment.

Three types of relationship

As well as examples of the 'professional–managerial class', accounting also affords examples of 'proletarianised' professionals engaged in the more routine aspects of book-keeping, stock control and financial control. Thus it may be more appropriate to see some professionals, particularly those trapped in more routine activities, being 'proletarianised', while others are assimilated into the 'professional–managerial class' and still others largely retain the work style that is historically associated with private practice and the characteristics identified in Table 2.2. These three types of professional–managerial relationships are summarised in Table 2.3, which identifies associated differences in predominant type of control using the typology of control discussed in Chapter 1 (Figure 1.3) and type of role in planning and decision-making about the content of professional work activities.

Table 2.3
Different Relationships between Professionals and Managers

Professional role	Professionals' relationship with managers	Predominant types of control over professional work*	Professionals' role in planning and decision-making about the nature of their work
'Proletarian' professional	Subservient	(4) Hierarchical (5) Administrative (6) Technological	Remote
Member of 'professional-managerial class'	Assimilation	(3) Output (2) Personal self (1) Unobtrusive	Participative, with varying power
Private practice	As external client As facilitator As constraint	(2) Personal self (1) Unobtrusive	Self-determined, with varying consultation

* See Figure 1.3, to which numbers relate

First, there is the proletarian professional in a subservient position to managers. The work of these people is largely controlled by standard administrative and technological systems which are supplemented by personal interventions of superiors in the hierarchy. Proletarian professionals are remote from decisions about the content of their work, both in the short term and the long term. They feel themselves vulnerable to change and fear redundancy and rationalisation. In sharp contrast, their colleagues who have become assimilated into the 'professional–managerial class' form part of the hierarchy which, among other things, defines and controls the work of the proletarians. People in this class may retain close contact with their professional skills and use them a great deal; alternatively their work may begin to bear little relationship to their initial qualifications as they move into traditional managerial and generalist roles. Their work is largely controlled by assessment of their output and performance over a financial year or some other period like a five-year plan, by their own system of personal control and by the tenets of unobtrusive control established through their prior training and experience. They are often important participants in decisions about how their work is to be undertaken, although their strength in determining the outcomes of these decisions will depend upon their power and influence with their colleagues and seniors.

Third, there are those professionals who work in ways which more closely approximate to the model of private practice. They act as consultants and advisers to clients who are likely to be corporate managers in other organisations. Their work is largely defined and controlled through the codes of practice they share with their peers, which are based on strong unobtrusive controls. Further control from market mechanisms is also important since private practices of doctors, solicitors, accountants and software specialists must all establish and retain their 'good reputations' with their clients if their services are going to be retained, assuming of course that their clients have some choice between consultants and could switch their allegiance if they so wished. Traditionally professionals working in the private practice mode have retained distance from a direct concern with a set of separate activities which they have seen as 'management'. Depending on the context and power relationships, 'management' were either 'subordinate facilitators' or 'insensitive/ignorant constraints'. In the former guise, accountants and lawyers typically hired ex-armed services officers who were charged with ensuring an adequate (and yet minimal in terms of resource consumption) infrastructure of equipment and non-professional staff. In the latter guise, hospital administrators placed limits on, or limited, medical professionals by the imposition of bureaucratic rules and other constraints. Changes are now occurring to disturb these views. Changes in the complexity and scale of professional work, in the basis of competition and the arrangements for funding mean that established approaches to management and organisation are felt to be inadequate for the challenges posed in the professional services marketplace. The master–apprenticeship mode of staff development is no longer necessarily appropriate, and neither is the loose organisational model of collections of autonomous partners sharing (minimum) overheads and professional discussions whilst individually generating and managing the flow of work in a fairly *ad hoc* but lucrative way. Management can no longer be seen as something apart from professional life.

The requirements for professionals to manage large-scale financial and human resources and make executive and strategic decisions are of necessity becoming a central part of organising the delivery of professional services. With the Citizens' Charter and prior changes in the provision of health and other public services in the UK, professionals in the public service are now being required to think about their own resource management, to be responsible for their own budgets, etc. The issues of developing professionals as managers and the organisational pre-conditions for enabling effective management of the critical 'expert/professional/skilled human resource' have now become central issues (see, e.g., Maister, 1985, 1989; Day and Klein, 1987; Lorsch and Matthias, 1987) in modern management theory.

Different occupations do not always fall neatly into one of the three categories identified above. Some professions – for example, accountancy, civil engineering and surveying – have members which fall into each category. Members of other professions – for example, solicitors and doctors – are predominantly found in approximations to the private practice mode, but it is noticeable that they employ increasing numbers of 'technical grade' associates, such as legal executives and paramedical staff, who conform more to the 'proletarian model' even within partnerships in private practice. In professions where the 'private practice' mode is rare or non-existent, the professional institution or other accreditation body is more concerned with examinations, qualifications and generally regulating entry than it is with codes of conduct once an individual has acquired membership. The practice of professional work in such cases is likely to be largely regulated by in-house administrative rules and procedures, the management hierarchy and interactions with members of other functional groups.

This section has dealt at length with the issue of the relationship between professional and managerial interest groups in order to illustrate how conflicts between interest groups can develop, how they can be accommodated and how the management of professional work has changed in response to changes in the environment.

2.2   Objectives and Goals

Personal and corporate objectives

Organisations are defined as collections of people joining in formal association to achieve objectives. The association may be through direct and full-time employment or it may be derived from stock- or bond-holding or from contracts to supply or to purchase goods and services. There is no guarantee that the objectives or goals which different people seek through their association with the organisation will be compatible. The preceding analysis of interest groups would suggest that in complex organisations where the dimensions of external relations, hierarchy, function, geography and individual differences are strongly in evidence, consensus will be rare. Nonetheless, at some minimum level there must be some compatibility, even if this is forced on the participants because of a lack of opportunity to move elsewhere for the pursuit of their goals. At a less extreme level, participants may make a positive choice to maintain their association with the organisation in view of the facilities and opportunities it offers them.

The image of organisations in which participants are feverishly and rationally pursuing their own objectives in their own particular way can not go unchallenged. Many people maintain their association with an organisation out of habit or ritual, in circumstances where it seems to afford them little opportunity to pursue any clearly identified objectives. Common ground may be found between diverse groups, and interests may quickly coalesce in the face of the threatened disintegration of the organisation. *In extremis*, interest groups may join together to try to stop a company going into liquidation or a public sector organisation being 'wound up' by the government. Alternatively, powerful interest groups may respond to the threat of liquidation or disbandment by deciding that it is in their best interests to search out other arenas for their activities. The transferability of their skills and other resources and the availability of other opportunities will vary between groups and between the task, technology and market characteristics of organisational context. Furthermore, decisions either to stay and fight and perhaps compromise one's individual or group interests, or to search out alternative arenas for the pursuit of interests are not always understandable in logical, rational terms. Strong feelings of loyalty and commitment may be very important, as may a fear of insecurity and an aversion to high-risk situations. As Hirschman has vividly put it in the title of a book, people facing problems in organisations with which they are associated make a choice, either positively or by default, between *Exit Voice and Loyalty* (Hirschman, 1972). For a variety of reasons, therefore, the ultimate 'goal' of the survival of a particular organisation may come to be the common ground on which diverse groups coalesce.

Opportunities for the exercise of choice and discretion to further personal interests are limited by a range of unobtrusive, personal, output, hierarchical, administrative and technological controls (see Chapter 1) and by constraints, created by previous activity or inactivity.

The introduction of a new process will not be feasible, however much it is pushed by a powerful group of technical specialists, if the workforce is inappropriately trained and there are insufficient resources to retain, recruit and restructure the workforce. Tariff barriers and international trade agreements and exchange rates may mean that an expansion of exports for a particular company is not feasible, however much it is pushed by the sales directorate. A move to new offices, however much the administrative section of a large accountancy practice would like it, may not be considered feasible given the money involved and the strong desire to maintain the practice within the square mile of the City of London. It need hardly be said, however, that constraints are rarely absolutely fixed, although they may for a time and for some people seem utterly non-negotiable. Certainly in the long term, constraints often become weaker and more liable to change. The preceding discussion of three modes of professional employment illustrates considerable variation in the extent to which participants can and do pursue their own interests, as opposed to the interests of other groups which are imposed upon them. Issues of power and control are taken up again in Chapter 7.

Changes in goals

The goals that are pursued within organisations change over time, as political alliances between dominant interest groups shift and external pressures and events change. Thompson and McEwen (1958) describe how different pressures lead to modifications in corporate development. For example, competition for money or people, between groups or organisations, may lead to changes in product policy. Bargaining between the interest groups and the need to 'give something in return' to a helpful supplier might lead to an adjustment in policies on stock levels. Co-option of powerful groups who are real or potential opponents might well lead to fairly dramatic changes in direction, as was illustrated in a study of the Tennessee Valley Authority in the USA (Selznick, 1949). Finally, Thompson and McEwen note that entry into coalitions with divergent interest groups might well lead to major changes in corporate plans.

A classic example of a change in direction is given in Scott's (1967) analysis of workshops for the blind in the USA. The sheltered workshops were set up initially to give employment to blind people who could not be integrated into a 'normal' working environment. However, their products became very popular and subject to increasing demand, so that a view developed among some managers that the workshops should be made more competitive. Consequently they wanted to employ more competent labour, thereby excluding the type of workers whom the workshop had been established to employ. This is an example of what is sometimes called 'goal displacement', when what have been the dominant goals are displaced even though they could still theoretically form operational objectives.

Goal displacement is particularly likely to occur where a group which holds formal authority actually has very limited discretion over the use of the resources that are crucial to the pursuit of their objectives. This was the case described by Burton Clark in his 1956 study of adult education in the USA, where the situation was compounded by the fact that the objectives pursued by the senior educational personnel were relatively ill-defined and not immediately attractive to their public sector paymasters or their political constituents. Not surprisingly, therefore, the more easily defined and quantifiable goal of 'student attendances' was imposed upon the adult education centres from 'outside', with the effect that high attendance became a more important criterion of success, and therefore objective, than educational value, however that might be defined.

Points are raised here about the seductive qualities of quantification and the importance of discretionary control of resources, which we shall return to in Chapters 7 and 8 on power and decision-making.

Goal 'succession' rather than displacement is the term used when one set of goals or objectives actually becomes redundant and is succeeded by another set. A famous example here is the National Foundation for Infantile Paralysis in the USA. Its voluntary members largely saw themselves as pacesetters in an important social movement concerned with the prevention and treatment of the disease. They encouraged and sponsored research and co-ordinated fund-raising activities. When an effective vaccination for the disease was discovered, its members shifted their concerns to encompass other crippling childhood diseases, thereby managing to 'stay in business' (Sills, 1957). More obviously the development of new products and new markets is a strong feature of commercial organisations supplying goods and services in the competitive market.

Dependency and dominance in goal-setting

Goals pursued in organisations are the creation of people, but they provide guidelines for, and constraints on, collective and individual action. The strength with which a group can further its interests varies with its power. It has been suggested that this is especially related to patterns of dependency which arise from task, market and structural considerations. Perrow (1961) was one of the first to hypothesise such a scheme in relation to his study of US hospitals. He suggested that dominance in policy-making in hospitals was shared in an unequal way at different times between trustees, doctors and administrators depending on their relative contributions towards four vital acquisitions: capital, skills, legitimation of activities within the community, and co-ordinating capacity. Perrow generalised this scheme because, he said, the four acquisitions were crucial to any organisation. In this way, Perrow proposed a scheme for identifying which groups at any one time are likely to be most influential in defining the goals which are actually pursued.

More recently, Donaldson and Lorsch (1983) have suggested that there are three important constituencies in any corporation: the capital market (sources of funds), the product market (customers) and employed members of the organisation. If a corporation is heavily dependent on external funding, the capital market interest groups are very powerful. If managers and specialists are highly mobile and yet central to operations, they will be very significant in influencing policy. If the corporation is operating in a single-product market, customers will have greatest power, but if the corporation is operating in a diversified market, and yet financially is relatively self-sufficient with largely immobile management, then the senior executives will have greater power in determining the operational objectives for the corporation.

Objectives and goals in organisations cannot then be defined absolutely; they reflect the interests of the participants and the power and influence they can muster in their support. The groups which secure dominance in the processes of determining which set of objectives is actually used as a guide for action and decision-making within the organisation are often referred to as the dominant coalition, a term first given wide currency by Cyert and March (1963). As the term coalition implies, there is no assumption that there will be consensus between dominant groups and individuals; rather that, through the process of bargaining, negotiation and influence, working agreements can be reached in which members of the dominant coalition perceive that in this way they can satisfy their objectives at least to some extent.

Personal objectives and corporate activities

The objectives that people seek through their association with others in organisations can be divided according to the extent to which they relate to the central core of activities concerned with the production and distribution of goods and services. Some are directly related to the central core; others relate to more peripheral areas of activity; and still more objectives are pursued in the organisation merely because it offers a convenient, but in no way distinctive, arena. Taking the last group first, it is easy to illustrate the way in which members use organisations as a base for pressing quite distinct, but highly individual, objectives. For example, some people may view their workplace as a meeting place for a marriage partner. Others may use it as a means to achieve long paid holidays in which they can pursue leisure or sporting activities. Others may select an organisation with flexible and relatively short hours of work, so that they can devote a lot of time during the working week to local politics. Others may choose to work where there is a lenient policy towards international telephone calls, which enables them to telephone relatives in Australia regularly without remonstration or payment.

Other people may be less specific and positive in the objectives they pursue through their association with an organisation. For example, a person may regard the simple fact of having 'a job', regardless of its content or location, as important for status in the community or for self-esteem. Others may look on their job as the lesser of other evils, in that they would rather stay with an organisation than do anything else which is likely to be available to them. The pursuit of objectives other than those related to central core activities can sometimes lead to conflict between members: for example, if two men choose the same marriage partner, or if two women want to avoid overtime which only one of them need do. But at other times these peripheral objectives are often quietly pursued without open conflict or interruption.

When it comes to objectives more directly related to the central core of activities, attention is focused on such things as levels of productivity and profitability, the distribution of profits between retained purposes, share-holders and employees, the rate and direction of technical change and the extent of market share. Most members of the organisation have a view on these matters, and there is usually disagreement on the relative values and priorities that should be assigned to achieving particular objectives. For example, shareholders may attach most weight to high profitability and growth potential, and misguidedly give little heed to patterns of technical innovation. Technical specialists may be particularly keen to influence decisions about product and process innovation. Trade union officials may push for particular payment systems or argue forcefully about the ratio of capital to labour, while the sales directorate may be most exercised over matters concerning market share. Such one-sided approaches are arguably short-sighted since the pursuit of one set of objectives often has far-reaching implications for the likelihood of achieving others, both in terms of the opportunities that may be created and the constraints (not least from competition over scarce resources) that may be strengthened. Nonetheless, most interest groups are heavily influenced by their own particular preoccu-pations.

Official and operating goals

Can this view of objectives as emergent properties of the interactions, interest and power of participating individuals and groups be reconciled with the bold statements in annual reports and charters which make the definition and pursuit of goals sound so single-minded and straightforward? At BP, for example, we are told, 'group policy recognises that BP's primary responsibil-ity to society is to create wealth by conducting its business successfully and efficiently, with group profitability being the principal measure of its success' (Annual Report and Accounts, 1980). Similarly, the Charter of Imperial College states that, 'The purposes of the Imperial College are to give the highest specialised instruction and to provide the fullest equipment for the most advanced training and research in various branches of science especially in its application to industry.' These statements give no hint of conflict between participating interest groups or between objectives for any one interest group. Such grand statements are what have been called official goals by Perrow in that they specify 'the general purpose of the organisation as put forth in the charter, annual reports, public statements by key executives and other authoritative announcements' (Perrow, 1961, p. 855). Perrow contrasts these with 'operative goals' which 'designate the ends sought through the actual operating policies of the organisation [which] tell us what the organisa-tion actually is trying to do, regardless of what the official goals say are the aims' (p. 855). In these terms the official goal of a company may be to make a substantial profit, whereas the operative goals include the quality standards for products, delivery policies and investment forecasts. Perrow, as we saw earlier, explains how he sees the operative goals as reflecting the particular interests of dominant groups as they relate to task, market and individual characteristics.

The definition of 'official goals' does not mean that they should be dismissed as mere rhetoric. They usually represent the outcome of particular debates in an organisation's history (e.g. at foundation and at significant points of change). Their significance is not that they provide a realistic description of organised activities, but that as a symbol they provide legitimacy for some actions and a rallying point for some groups. They can be used to justify or prevent proposed developments.

2.3   Defining Corporate Strategy

'Operative' or 'real' goals similarly emerge from the interactions of different interest groups, but they actually provide the basis for day-to-day and year-to-year activities and developments. Operative goals in any organisation are usually many, and again are often conflicting. The emergent package of operative goals in any one organisation provides an operational definition of corporate strategy. Following Andrews (1980) and Mintzberg (1978), Donaldson and Lorsch (1983) define corporate strategy as 'the stream of decisions over time that reveal management's goal for the corporation and the means they choose to achieve them' (Donaldson and Lorsch, 1983, p. 6).

This definition is somewhat ambiguous about the causal links which underlie the relationship between strategy and action. This ambiguity reflects a difference of view about the extent to which strategy is the originator or reflector of action and events. It used to be thought that strategy was a relatively uncontentious concept which referred to sets of decisions about long-term goals and objectives which would then guide and drive future actions and the allocation of resources (see, e.g., Chandler, 1962). Now, however, there is a great deal of discussion about the ways in which strategy can be seen as a set of *post hoc* rationalisations which seek to legitimise and make sense of actions and events which have occurred (Smircich and Stubbart, 1985). Weick (1987) talks of 'just in time' strategy which encapsulates and articulates opportunities as they arise. Through their articulation, such strategic statements are important as sources of motivation and legitimation for those involved, but they are not rational guides for action. As Mintzberg (1989) writes: 'the very notion of strategy may owe more to its persuasive power in helping us to make sense of the past than to any capacity to produce insight into the future'.

This chapter has provided evidence of the wide range of objectives pursued in organisations. Six important dimensions on which objectives vary can now be identified.

1. *Relation to central core*: the extent to which the subject matter of the objective is related to the distinctive core characteristics of the organisation (i.e. its technology, structure and specified tasks of production, distribution and sale of goods and services).
2. *Relation to interest group formation*: the degree to which the objectives an individual pursues are shared with others, and the extent of interest group formation, involvement and potential conflict.
3. *Relation to conscious cognitive processes*: the extent to which the objectives are consciously or subconsciously pursued by the individual and groups involved.
4. *Timeframe*: the specification of the short, medium or long term timeframe to be employed.
5. *Methodology*: the type of data (e.g. quantitative or qualitative, subjective or objective, single slot or time series) to be employed in assessing changes in relation to objectives.
6. *Relation to outcomes*: the extent to which specified objectives are a guide for subsequent actions or a rationalisation for previous actions.

2.4 Introducing Organisational Performance

The discussion of interest groups, objectives and strategy provides ample testimony to the difficulties of assessing 'the performance' of an organisation. As far as the achievement of goals or objectives is concerned, we know that different interest groups and individuals are likely to hold goal sets which vary both in terms of which goals are included and in the relative priority assigned to each one. Thus a set of activities and outcomes in an organisation may allow one group – for example, development engineers – to achieve their objective of developing a new product, but it may be at the cost of not achieving the financial objectives of shareholders and the finance directorate. Furthermore, operative goals themselves are the result of interaction and negotiation between different groups. As well as being in potential conflict with one another they may not be strongly related to the initial preferences of any of the groups.

Practitioners obtain little comfort from the knowledge that theoreticians are puzzled by the confusing and paradoxical nature of the concept of performance in organisations (see, e.g., Cameron, 1986). It is puzzling for several reasons. One is that there is often little attempt to distinguish between predictors (i.e. those things which may be causally related to outcome performance, such as level of R & D spending as a percentage of turnover) and indicators (i.e. those things which indicate present levels of performance, such as trends in market share or profitability).

Another source of confusion is that even for indicators *or* predictors a variety of indices are suggested and used, and yet they often give conflicting messages. Practitioners should, however, take heed of this confusion since it reflects reality. They need to note that when they are trying to assess the performance of an organisation they need to adopt a variety of approaches. Performance is multifaceted and thus a variety of assessment methods are required in order to construct a profile of an organisation's performance. Only in this way can its members gauge those things which are being done well and those things which are being done badly.

Table 2.4 suggests three general areas in which assessment needs to be conducted. The first is that of effectiveness in terms of goal attainment. In this area questions need to be asked as indicated earlier about which goals are important and the timescale for their assessment. Quinn and Cameron (1988)

Table 2.4
Assessing Performance in Organisations

A. *Effectiveness* = Extent of Goal Attainment
    Questions:
        What goals?
        Why are these important?
        To whom are these important?
        What is an appropriate timescale for their assessment?
    Some suggested goals
        Level and rate of change in profits
        Level and rate of change in market share
        Level and rate of change in turnover

B. *Efficiency* = Ratio of Value of Inputs to Value of Outputs
    Questions: criteria for determination of values
    Some suggested indices:
        Unit cost
        Unit quality
        Price
        Delivery time

C. *'System' or Process Characteristics*
    Ability to 'manage' environment
        • to secure scarce resources
        • to detect/create new opportunities
        • to detect/avoid threats
    Ability to 'manage' within the organisation
        • financial resources
        • human resources
        • capital assets

---

demonstrate that it is appropriate to adopt different effectiveness criteria at different stages in the life-cycle of an organisation. For example, growth is all important for a new venture, whereas productivity is more important for an established venture. It is also important to pay attention to long term as well as short term concerns when seeking to assess effectiveness.

The second area identified in Table 2.4 is that of efficiency. How efficient is the organisation in generating output of a certain value from input of a certain value? The values must be assumed to be those 'paid' or 'received' by the corporate organisation. However, as Francis (1990) has shown, what is 'good value' for the corporation in terms of unpaid overtime may be very 'poor value' for employees. From the corporation's point of view, however, it is important for assessments to be made of cost, price, quality, etc.

Finally, there are characteristics of the system which are considered to reflect upon performance. How 'good' is the organisation in managing or creating its environment to secure scarce resources and to detect or create new opportunities? How good is it in managing and developing its human resources? Is it, for example, paying enough attention to its invisible assets located within the brains of its experts? And is it making the best use of its capital assets? These 'system' or 'process' characteristics are difficult to assess but, as Pettigrew and Whipp (1991) show, their critical importance should not be underestimated. Subsequent discussions in this book about managing the environment (Chapter 4) and managing the organisation will enable the ideas introduced in this section to be developed into an agenda of both outcome and process performance measures, which will become the main subject for the concluding chapter.

The literature on organisational effectiveness and performance reveals many problems and few solutions (see, e.g., Goodman and Pennings, 1977; Steers, 1977; Mohr, 1982; and Legge, 1984). This should not surprise readers who have been introduced to the concept of organisations as arenas in which a variety of interest groups associate in order to achieve certain often disparate and sometimes conflicting objectives. In this scheme it would be naive to assume that one could generate a simple linear measure of performance for the organisation, or indeed that one can adequately conceptualise an organisation as a unitary system.

Practitioners need to pay attention to information concerning their performance in all three areas identified in Figure 2.4. This will help them form and reform their views about areas of good performance and areas where they need to do better. Even then they will have to grapple with the need to achieve a *balance* between apparently conflicting forces. These are Cameron's (1986) paradoxes and they again serve as a reminder of one of the themes of this book. Acting upon analysis, the practitioner has to juggle: she has to secure consensus and disagreement, change and continuity, and so on. To increase our understanding of performance we need to know more about organising and organisation; we need to read on before we can conclude in the final chapter with a further discussion of performance.

Technology: A Social Product **3**

One of the most immediately obvious signs of variety between organisations is their production of a wide range of different artefacts, extending to all forms of manufactured finished goods, components, refined natural products, communication hardware and software, management consultancy and medical, welfare, educational, leisure and other services. Yet this variety can be interpreted in terms of a common model which focuses not on the products but on their production. All organisations have a core, illustrated in Table 3.1, which comprises the acquisition of inputs of natural, human, financial and fabricated resources and their transformation through a variety of ways

Table 3.1

Organisations as Arenas for the Transformation of Inputs into Outputs

Inputs into products and processes	Transformation processes	Outputs of goods and services
Raw materials	Labour	Finished products
Energy		
Manufactured components		Components
Data/information	Skills	Information
Cash	Data	Services
Services	Plant	Skills
Skills	Energy	Knowledge
Knowledge	Machinery	Experience

into the production and distribution of outputs of goods and services. For example, people in an electronics factory use mechanical and computer-controlled equipment, skills, labour and knowledge to transform raw materials, energy and components into finished consumer products. Doctors in a hospital admit patients and try to transform them through medication, surgery and advice into healthier people. A construction company assembles supplies and skilled people on a new site and they use tools, plant and energy, labour and skill to transform the derelict land into a new office building.

The overall 'transformation process' in any organisation involves a variety of integrated smaller workflow sequences which cover the identification and acquisition of appropriate raw materials through to the distribution of the outputs. Figure 3.1 takes the example of a man-made-fibre plant and illustrates three very different transformation processes which characterise the development, production and sales functions. This variety means that technology, as Mohr (1971) describes it, is essentially a multidimensional concept. For example, British Rail has an apparently fairly homogeneous

---

FIGURE 3.1
Functional Workflows in a Man-made Fibre Plant

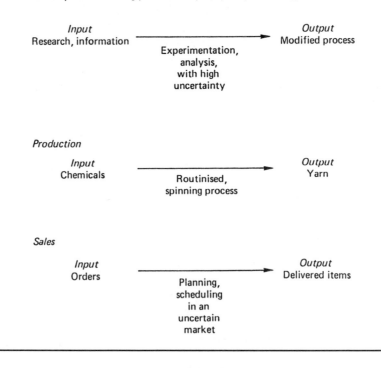

Development: tackling problems of yarn quality and energy reduction

Input		*Output*
Research, information	Experimentation, analysis, with high uncertainty	Modified process

Production

Input		*Output*
Chemicals	Routinised, spinning process	Yarn

Sales

Input		*Output*
Orders	Planning, scheduling in an uncertain market	Delivered items

---

product range, yet displays great variety in the technologies it employs. There is unit production for the overhaul of preserved steam locomotives, small batch production for prototype power cars being built for a new type of train, and large batch production for the construction of mainline coaches, not to mention the variety of technologies used in maintenance and development.

3.1   Technology: The Concept

The term technology is used in this book to encompass the materials and processes used in transforming inputs into outputs, as well as the skills, knowledge and labour that are part of their present operations and which enabled the technologies to be developed in the first place. Technology thus has both hardware (materials and operations) and human (knowledge) components. It is the product of human endeavour, and its operation is dependent on a degree of human co-operation and involvement. This definition emphasises that technology cannot be seen as either a 'neutral' or a single 'given' force in organisations (see, e.g., Dennis, Gillespie and Mornsey, 1978). For a start it appears to affect some people adversely in the sense of giving them boring, repetitive jobs, or grimy, greasy working conditions, or carcinogenic materials with which to work, while bestowing on others beneficial effects in the form of interesting, exciting work, a clean environment, good share dividends and a flexible working day. But more fundamental than the manifest inequalities of its effects, and indeed underlying these inequalities, is the fact that technology is created by and used by people who, as we have seen in previous chapters, have particular interests which they are pursuing through their association with organisations.

In the preface to his book, *America by Design*, which traces the history of engineering in the interrelated contexts of academia and industry, David Noble eloquently summarises this definition of technology:

> Although it may aptly be described as a composite of the accumulated scientific knowledge, technical skills, implements, logical habits and material products of people, technology is always more than this, more than information, logic, things. It is people themselves, undertaking their various activities in particular social and historical contexts, with particular interests and aims. (Noble, 1977, p. xxii)

Noble documents how engineers designed the technical systems which formed the basis of manufacturing industry in the nineteenth and twentieth centuries and how as managers, educators and social reformers they also designed the work organisation and, in a sense, a whole new social order.

The production processes used depend on the outcome of debates about what is available in terms of knowledge, expertise, ability to pay, materials and energy, and what is seen to be desirable, appropriate and advantageous.

For example, imagine a situation in which process and product innovations are being considered. R & D has a vested interest in pushing for technical sophistication; production an interest in a system which facilitates easy retooling; sales an interest in producing a high-quality, up-market product; and the operators' trade union an interest in preserving jobs and securing the extensive retraining of people who are redundant. Decisions about the purchase of new hardware, changes in the way work is done and relationships structured, as well as the practical implementation of such decisions, must be understood in the organisational context that has been described in the previous chapters. Just as structure is a tool for the achievement of interests, so too is technology. But a problem arises, both for practitioners and analysts of organisations, because many participants do not share this view. This is particularly the case for many people who have had a fairly narrow education in science and engineering and who feel that scientific values and discoveries and their application merely reflect the inexorable and somehow neutral or independent march of progress. Engineers may consider that they merely advise on what is technically the best within the financial limits prescribed. Financial advisers may say they are merely ensuring that costs are kept within budget. In this way each group may say that the selection, creation and operation of technology results from 'rational' judgement which is somehow universally the 'best' in the circumstances. For such an analysis to be valid, organisations would need to be unitary, consensual systems with fairly comprehensive knowledge about alternative, as well as the chosen, technologies. Furthermore, simple linear relationships between a few variables would be the predominant type of interaction between parts of the organisation.

A contrary view is presented in this book. Organisations are shown as encompassing several different interest groups and being characterised by many variables which are linked in an interactive and uncertain way (see Introduction).

In an effort to defuse the myth of technology as neutral and to summarise some of the important findings of the many studies of technology in organisations, the remainder of this chapter will deal with the relationship of technology to developments in work organisation and management structure. This involves an examination of the work of those who have tended to see technology as 'given' or 'neutral', requiring human adjustments to its demand. The limitations of this form of analysis will be discussed with the object of generating a more realistic picture of the opportunities and constraints that are created (by people) when decisions about technology are made and implemented.

3.2   Technology and Work Organisation

The concept of technical controls on job requirements and job performance was introduced in Chapter 1, when it was shown how the design and operation of technical hardware affected levels of discretion, type of supervision, and degree and type of specialisation. For example, on a mechanical assembly line, job-holders undertake repetitive activities in a carefully controlled and monitored working environment in which there is a great deal of task fragmentation. An extreme statement of the meaning of this type of technology for operators is given in Beynon's *Working for Ford* (1974). In contrast, a technician in a biochemistry development laboratory may have a great deal of discretion, be subject only to loose supervision, and be responsible for carrying out a whole range of tasks which she considers necessary for the accomplishment of overall work objectives. The three elements of discretion, supervision and division of labour are often collectively referred to as 'work organisation', and this is the general term that will be used here. A selection of classic but now somewhat outdated studies will be discussed as a prelude to considering contemporary approaches which, among other things, focus on developments in new microelectronic technology.

The Tavistock Institute and socio-technical systems

A group of researchers working at the Tavistock Institute of Human Relations pioneered modern studies of the implications of technology for work organisations (see Trist, 1981, for a summary). Taking the analogy of biological organisms, they developed the concept of organisations as socio-technical systems in which inputs and outputs to and from the environment were exchanged. Rice (1963) argued that any enterprise has a multiplicity of tasks which are performed simultaneously, but one of these is *primary* in that its primary task is generating sufficient money to stay in existence. The more precisely the primary tasks are defined, the greater the constraints on task performance. In achieving the primary task, organisations utilise both a technical system and a social system, each of which sets requirements for the other. The extent to which the requirements are met to the mutual satisfaction of both systems was reflected, the Tavistock researchers argued, in production effectiveness.

Some of the most important Tavistock work was conducted in the Durham coal mines and weaving sheds in India, where managers were advised that they could and should choose a form of social structure that was appropriate to the technical system. Furthermore, when technical changes were being made, the designers of technical systems should pay attention to their social implications. Readers should see Trist *et al.* (1963) for a full description of the work undertaken in the Durham coalfields. Table 3.2 provides a brief account of the changes made in the technology and the social system, and shows that an incompatible mixture of technology II and social system II was associated with a loss of productivity and poor morale. When the social system was changed to one which was more compatible with technology II, the coal mines were more successful in terms of indices of both production and morale. Thus

---

Table 3.2
Summary of the Research and Consultancy Programme Undertaken by Members of the Tavistock Institute in the Durham Coal Mines

---

Phase 1: Traditional system
Technology I: traditional handgetting of coal
Social System I:
- work groups of six assigned to particular locations, with two members of the group attached to each of three shifts;
- work group shared an equal payment bonus
- self-regulating and largely self-selected, cohesive work groups
- 'deputy' (supervisor) acted more as a provider of services to the group than as a direct controller

Phase 2: Technical change was introduced
Technology II: mechanical conveyor belt introduced so that coal face worked as a long wall. This change created, by default, a 'new' Social System II:
- established social system destroyed
- tasks divided up between workers
- great problems of supervision and control
- deputy 'forced' to take much more control of the workforce which was resisted

Results of interaction between Technology II and Social System II: loss of productivity; poor morale (which incidentally was exacerbated by the poor economic conditions of 1930s).

Phase 3: Development of Social System III: composite method (as a result of Tavistock consultancy). In place of formal division of labour, a team of forty miners was established with greater 'structured interdependence' between the sub-groups. Workers carried on with the next sequence of work when their own was completed. Development of common pay not based on fixed rate and production bonus. Greater self-regulation in working group; management no longer had to provide all control and co-ordination.

Steady state: Interaction of Technology II and Social System III: more successful in terms of production output, costs, absenteeism, flexibility in division of labour and generation of mutually supportive, semi-autonomous work groups which Tavistock championed here and elsewhere.

---

the Tavistock analysis showed that both the technical and the social system of an organisation can be seen as the subject of choice, and that decisions made in one area should be compatible with those made in the other. They felt that, unlike mechanical systems, socio-technical systems could achieve a steady state from differing initial conditions and in different ways. No longer, they argued, could it be the technologist's job simply to design the technical system, the personnel department's job simply to organise it, and the finance department's job simply to identify the financial constraints and opportunities. The technical system comprising the equipment and production layout, the work organisation comprising the structure of relationships between people, and the economic organisation comprising the financial constraints and opportunities were, the Tavistock group argued, all interdependent – and subject to choice.

The social implications of different production systems: Blauner, Goldthorpe, Gallie

In spite of the work at the Tavistock Institute, which appeared to throw a large question mark over the idea that technology as such could have universal deterministic effects on work organisation, findings from several significant studies nonetheless suggested strong links between technology, work organisation and workers' attitudes.

Blauner (1964) concluded from a study of four USA enterprises using craft technology (print), machine-minding technology (textile mill), assembly lines (car plant), and continuous process technologies (chemical) that the type of technology had a profound effect on work organisation and workers' attitudes. He found that discretion and satisfaction were higher in enterprises employing unit or process as opposed to large batch or mass production systems. Conversely he found that management control and worker alienation (which he defined in terms of feelings of meaninglessness, powerlessness, self-estrangement and isolation) were higher in mass production. Blauner did note, however, that the effects of strong local communities could counterbalance the negative effects of machine-minding to some extent and could lead to higher than expected levels of satisfaction if workers belonged to strong social groupings which transcended the boundaries of the firm. In short, he felt that the development of continuous process technology, particularly in contrast to mass production systems, would increase workers' control over their work, reduce structural divisions between workers and management, decrease the likelihood of a minute specialisation of tasks, and increase the likelihood of team work. Labour would become a fixed rather than a variable input, and since, he argued, managers would want to keep their experienced workforce, they would be generous in their terms and conditions of employment. In this way Blauner argued that many of the sources of resentment and alienation felt by workers would be removed.

Accordingly, workers would become more committed to their employing organisation, less interested in militant trade unionism, and more compliant towards management.

Woodward (1965) also found in her study of 100 enterprises in Southern England that process technology appeared to be associated with higher levels of social integration. With developments in technical control systems, she argued that the need for close supervision was eliminated and therefore better relations were facilitated.

Goldthorpe *et al.* (1968) were critical of conclusions which drew a direct causal connection about the relation between technology and workers' attitudes. In Chapter 1 their concept of 'prior orientations to work' was discussed, and it is this which they regarded as the crucial link between technology and attitudes. Their studies of workers in a car plant, ball-bearing factory and chemicals plant did not lead them to dispute that technology was a major factor in affecting the level of intrinsic satisfaction derived from jobs, the facility to form cohesive work groups and different forms of supervision. What Goldthorpe *et al.* did dispute, however, was that one could immediately draw conclusions from these relationships about individual employees' attitudes and values. This relationship, they argued, depended much more on the workers' 'prior orientations' to work and thus their present expectations:

> For instance, technological constraints on collaboration in work tasks or on work group formation generally will be far less likely to lead to frustration and pervasive discontent among workers for whom work is an essentially instrumental activity than among men who are in fact seeking for 'social' satisfactions in their employment in addition to economic returns. And, similarly, technologically necessitated methods of control of a bureaucratic and impersonal kind will tend to have far more disturbing and dysfunctional consequences for the latter type of worker than they will for the former. (Goldthorpe *et al.*, 1968, p. 183)

Wedderburn and Crompton (1972) took a somewhat middle view in this debate. In a single case study of Seagrass chemical works they concluded that production tasks and the control systems associated with them did create situations where the actual experience of work and supervisory relationships differed markedly, but that the importance attached to these different experiences did bear a relationship to the workers' expectations and prior orientations.

In contrast to Blauner and Woodward, Gallie (1978) tells us that Mallet (1969) developed a thesis that new forms of process production and the use of electronic control systems, far from easing relations between workers and managers, would stimulate workers to see the indispensability of their skills to management and to recognise that the controls upon them were less irrevocably tied to features of the production technology. Thus Mallet argued that technological development, far from leading to more harmonious industrial relations, would prompt a resurgence of working-class solidarity, class conflict and struggles for control within the enterprise.

The empirical evidence to support these divergent views was thin, and consideration of this issue led Gallie to conduct a study of two similar pairs of BP oil refineries, one pair in France and the other in England. Within each country one refinery was relatively backward and the other relatively advanced in terms of technology. His main concern was to explore whether technological developments had major and direct implications for managerial control and industrial relations in the plant, or whether wider social, cultural, institutional and historical patterns were equally or more important in effecting these things. Gallie's study showed that modern process technologies were not devoid of sources of grievance, although these were focused less on boring, repetitive work, and more on the structures of shift work and manning levels. In general he concluded that:

> the nature of the technology *per se* has, at most, very little importance for these specific areas of enquiry. Advanced automation proved perfectly compatible with radically dissimilar levels of social integration and fundamentally different institutions of power and patterns of trade unionism. Instead our evidence indicates the critical importance of the wider cultural and social structural patterns of specific societies for determining the nature of social interaction within the advanced sector. (Gallie, 1978, p. 295)

The implications of the microelectronics revolution for work organisation

Just as developments in process technology in the 1950s and 1960s stimulated interest in the implications of technological change for work organisation, so more recent developments in what is generally called 'new technology' have sparked renewed interest in this subject. The generic term of 'new technology' is used to describe processes which depend on miniaturised electronic circuitry to process information. It is found in commercial organisations such as banks and building societies, where it can have a large impact on counter service, credit control and investment policy; in retail enterprises, where it facilitates the integration of cash desk data and stock controls; and in manufacturing industry, where its ultimate manifestation is in the development of flexible manufacturing systems in which activities of design, tooling, assembly, sales and quality control can all be streamlined into one system.

Microelectronic technology can process information in systems which handle an immense amount of data speedily and produce analyses which derive from considering far more variables simultaneously than any other system ever invented. The advantages of the new technology in all sectors are said to be its cheapness, its reliability, its compactness, its speed of operation, its accuracy and its low energy consumption. For example, it can facilitate faster and more precise knowledge of operating conditions and results (e.g. in an oil refinery or a nuclear power plant, where a single screen can show all relevant information and facilitate easy forecasting of production data on the basis of altering any number of variables). Similarly in retail, EPOS (electronic point-of-sale) systems facilitate presentation and analysis of disparate sets of data on price, sale rate, stock levels, and so on. In this way the new technology unifies previously segmented control systems and provides the opportunity for a more comprehensive assessment of present and forecast performance. But offsetting these advantages which largely accrue, at least initially, to management, there are many who would argue that the new technology will also herald increasing unemployment, increasing degradation and deskilliing of work for many of the workers who can find employment, and an ever tightening grip of a small, select group of managers and specialists on other employees. Is this a reasonable, if depressing, scenario for the future?

In answering such a pessimistic question one must reiterate that we are not considering some immanent law of technological determinism. Technology is not an independent force, but one which can be differently developed and utilised according to the objectives and beliefs of those in positions of power. In this analysis it therefore seems appropriate to start with the objectives of managers in so far as they can be determined, before looking at the evidence on the effects of the policies and practices they have adopted in relation to new technology.

Why new technology is introduced

In a summary on 'New Technology and Developments in Management Organization', Child (1984b) identifies four management objectives which available evidence from case studies and surveys suggest are prominent in decisions to introduce new technology. The first two of these objectives are reducing operating costs and increasing efficiency. Reductions in the size of the workforce, relocating and retraining employees, and a growth in sub-contracting work to 'home workers' are all ways in which the new technology facilitates these two objectives. Sub-contracting arrangements with workers sitting at home with their own microcomputer or terminal, connected into the enterprise by electronic processes, not only ensures that the 'outworkers' bear their own overheads for space, furniture and facilities, but it can facilitate easy and quick performance monitoring and possibly a payment system which relates only to the actual hours worked as identified by the information system. Increasing efficiency can also come through improved technical services, such as stock-keeping or production scheduling, and from self-diagnostic systems which provide an early identification of process problems in need of maintenance before a breakdown occurs. Easier and earlier fault diagnosis can be complemented by the use of modular components which are easily replaced, often by the operator who looks after the machines. In this way excessive dependence on maintenance personnel is avoided. In manufacturing there is also the possibility of improved flexibility, so that a variety of products can be produced from the same computer-controlled facility with a minimum of cost and delay at change-over times.

The third objective is to secure improvements in quality. The checks and measurements previously undertaken by people can now often be built into the production facility. Finally, the fourth managerial objective often cited as important in decisions to introduce new technology is that it will facilitate improvements in managerial control. This arises from the improved processes for generating and transmitting performance information and the increasing opportunities for decreasing the amount of skill in jobs and the indispensability of workers. This is the area in which there has probably been most debate about the relationship between new technology and work organisation.

The effect on skills and control

Braverman (1974), somewhat echoing Mallet's earlier analysis, was particularly important in the 1970s and 1980s in prompting a resurgence of interest in a Marxist analysis of the labour process. A general theme of his work is that automated production systems are inextricably linked with deskilling, increasing technical and administrative control over the deskilled labour force, and an increasing polarisation of social divisions under 'monopoly capital'. This is a theme largely shared by Noble (1984) in his historical account of the US machine tool industry. He argues that rather than developing numerically controlled machines, engineers could just as easily, and with equal technical flexibility, have developed a 'record/play back' (R/P) technique which would have depended not on specialist computer programmers as CNC (computer numerically controlled) systems largely do, but on skilled machinists 'teaching' new jobs to the machines. He argues that the choice of CNC over R/P was not based on 'technical efficiency' but on increasing managerial control and deskilling.

Littler and Salaman (1982), although generally supportive of Braverman's part in a revival of interest in labour process analysis, point out that there is no single or simple means of controlling labour: technological control is important, but so too is bureaucratic or administrative control, together with other aspects of the employment relationship which ensure compliance. Furthermore, for senior managers of some multinational companies, issues of control of the production process become less important if they have the option of geographical relocation of plant and equipment to areas where the workforce will conform to 'indigenous modes of regulation and motivation'. Littler and Salaman comment: 'The first priority of capitalism is accumulation, not control. Control only becomes a concern when profitability is threatened' (p. 265). This echoes to some extent Marglin's (1974) analysis, that senior managers and entrepreneurs are interested both in productivity (to make money) and control (to keep the money they made).

The available evidence suggests considerable variation in relations between the introduction of new technology and the way control is exercised, the degree of discretion afforded workers, the basis and extent of the division of labour, and the type of supervision. The variations reflect in part management's view, but they also reflect the processes of local negotiations which often result in considerable modification of the views originally held by management (e.g. Wilkinson, 1983; Rose and Jones, 1984). Moreover, the requirements for flexibility and frequent job changes often mean that, in the case of CNC machines, for example, the operators are given considerable discretion (Sorge *et al.*, 1983). In an international context, data from 1340 organisations in twelve countries with over 8000 respondents found that advanced technologies were not necessarily associated with an increase in the proportion of lower skilled jobs in enterprises (IDE, 1981). This IDE project also gave more support to Gallie's view that culture or country is often more important than sector or technology in influencing the attitudes and behaviour of workers.

Much of the new technology itself can be used either to facilitate or curtail discretion and skill among workers. For example, Wilkinson (1983) shows that there is a choice with CNC machines about whether shop-floor workers or specialist programmers do overriding editing or programme development. He found that although generally specialists were employed to undertake more skilled work, in a few cases management had deliberately instructed its operatives in the skills. Even where workers were formally denied access to the skills of machine programming, Wilkinson found that they often attempted to develop the skills by studying programming in their 'spare time' and making keys so that they could get access to the control boxes and so practise their skills.

Similar variation is reported by Child (1984a) from contemporary studies on the role of supervisors in the new technology. He identified three distinct roles: (a) they may become glorified 'provisioners', merely ensuring that the necessary equipment is available; (b) they may develop programming ability; (c) they may develop strong interests in the technical performance of the equipment and thus play an active part in operating the new technology. The supervisor's job in relation to stock control, progress-chasing and crisis management may also change if improved information systems lead to a more streamlined stocking system and self-diagnostic features of new equipment lead to fewer emergency breakdowns.

There is evidence that some managers will use new technology as an opportunity to enhance the skills of their workforce: to develop, for example, a workforce of 'allrounders', capable of operating, programming and routinely maintaining the new equipment. In response to these developments, particularly in times of high unemploymeent, the managerial hope is not only for an efficient workforce, but for one which responds to greater security and job interest with increasing commitment to the enterprise. In this way new technology is being used to augment, rather than replace or degrade, human skills. The success of such a strategy will, of course, be dependent in part on the expectations and orientations of the workforce.

At the other extreme, some managers are involved in using the new technology specifically to degrade skills and to reduce workforces. This might happen, for example, after the introduction of flexible manufacturing systems in which the production, transport, quality control and packaging of goods can all be performed routinely by programmed machines. Similarly, banks may largely use the new technology to handle all routine matters while retaining a group of specialists to handle special tasks. It is suggested that where work can be standardised and handled routinely without detriment to the finished product or service, then managers are inclined to follow a 'replacing people' rather than an 'augmenting people' long-term strategy. If, on the other hand, the work is unpredictable and dependent on personal service or poses considerable risks (of danger to life, theft, or some other disaster) if the electronic system were to break down, then an 'augmenting' strategy is more likely (Child, 1984a, p. 251).

3.3 Technology, Organisation and Management Structure

The arguments and theories relating technology to the shape of the organisation structure and role of management show a similar progression to those concerning the relationship between technology and work organisation. Captivated by the discovery that one could talk in terms of an appropriate fit between technology and organisation structure and that not all organisation structures were equally appropriate to all technologies, some commentators developed fairly mechanistic and deterministic theories about the place of technology in explanations of organisation structure. But these were then overtaken by a fuller appreciation of the role of choice, both of technologies and organisation structures and the political processes involved in their selection. This section will be concerned with reviewing some of the relevant studies and commentaries.

Joan Woodward: a pioneer of links between technology and structure

Woodward (1958, 1965) is one of the well-known scholars who first focused on the implications of different forms of production processes for management behaviour and structure in organisations. She conducted an empirical survey of 100 firms in one small area of south-east England. One of the objectives of this research was to investigate how and why industrial organisations varied in structure and whether, as some management theorists of the 1940s and 1950s would have people believe, there were particular forms of structure that were associated with commercial success. In her survey she did indeed find variations in structure and success, but she could only begin to make sense of them when she grouped her surveyed organisations into the three technological groups of (a) unit and small batch, (b) large batch and mass and (c) process, which were derived from the eleven-point scale of production systems shown in Table 3.3. This classification was an elaboration of a division normally used by production engineers and was taken to reflect the complexity of the technology – that is, its inherent controllability and predictability – although Starbuck (1965) has argued that it is more a scale of smoothness or continuity than of complexity of production. The scale ranged from the production of custom-made unit articles, through the batch and mass production of standardised goods, to what Woodward saw as the technically most complex stage, namely the continuous flow production of dimensional products. She also included two residual categories for combined systems which did not fit into any of the other categories.

Table 3.3
The Classification of Production Systems Used by Woodward

A. *Integral products*

	1.	Production of simple units to customers' orders (e.g. 'made-to-measure suits')
Unit and	2.	Production of technically complex units (e.g. prototypes for small units)
small batch		
production	3.	Fabrication of large equipment in stages (e.g. radio transmitting stations)
	4.	Production of small batches to customers' orders
Large batch	5.	Production of components in large batches
and mass	6.	Production of large batches, assembly-line type
production	7.	Mass production

B. *Dimensional products*

	8.	Intermittent production of chemicals in multi-purpose plant
Process		
production	9.	Continuous production of liquids, gases and crystalline substances

C. *Combined systems*

	10.	Production of standardised components in large batches subsequently assembled diversely
	11.	Process production of crystalline substances subsequently prepared for sale by standardised production methods

---

SOURCE: Woodward (1965), p. 39.

Grouping her organisations into the three main categories of unit and small batch, large batch and mass and process production allowed her to identify three trends of direct relevance to the relationship between technology and organisation structure. First, she found a linear relationship between a firm's technical complexity and such features of its formal organisation chart as the length of line of command, the span of control of the chief executive, and the ratio of managers to total personnel. Second, there was a curvilinear relationship between a firm's technical complexity and the extent to which it had, in Burns and Stalker's (1961) terms, an organic informal, or a more mechanistic formal, system of management (see Chapter 4). Third, Woodward found that firms were more successful financially when they conformed to the median organisational characteristics for their 'technology' group than when they diverged from it. Thus Woodward concluded that there was 'no one best way to manage', but that it was important to consider the nature of the technical context before deciding on appropriate forms of organisation. The classical principles of management, with their clear definitions of responsibility, seemed to be appropriate to firms with large batch or mass production systems but, perhaps not surprisingly, to be detrimental to success in both unit and process production.

Management control systems

The initial findings relating technology to organisation structures were particularly well supported at either ends of the technology scale, but the relationships were less clear-cut in the middle areas of large batch and mass production, where it appeared to Woodward that there was more scope for managerial choice between options. With these types of production,

> physical work flow did not impose rigid restrictions with the result that technology did not so much determine organization as define the limits within which it could be determined. The separation of production administration from production operations, rationalisation of production processes, and attempts to push back the physical limitations of production resulted in the emergence of a control system that depended in part on the physical work and in part on top management policy. (Woodward, 1965, p. 185)

This observation led Woodward and her team, now established at Imperial College, to conduct further investigations into the way in which management control systems were developed. They adopted Eilon's definition of a management control system as encompassing the activities of planning, co-ordinating, monitoring and providing feedback about progress in achieving the task of the organisation (Eilon, 1962). A four-fold typology of control systems was developed in terms of variations on two dimensions (Reeves and Woodward, 1970). The first dimension was the degree to which control was exercised personally or indirectly. At one end of this scale one would have personal, hierarchical control of the owner–manager who decides what should be done and monitors progress. At the other end are the sort of bureaucratic and technical systems of control found in complex programmes for production planning and cost control or built into the production processes and operated through mechanical or electronic devices. The second dimension was the degree to which the control systems were integrated or fragmented. At the integrated end were firms where all the standards set for the product (e.g. cost, delivery, quality) and the adjustment mechanisms when one or other standard was being underachieved, were built into a single, integrated system of managerial control. This is clearly more feasible with automated and programmable production systems or those under the control of a very few people. In contrast, at the fragmented end were firms where such standards were set and controlled relatively independently by different departments. Some fragmentation of control was also noted in establishments where many different products were made for different markets.

Putting these two scales together, Reeves and Woodward identified four categories of control and suggested that the normal processes of industrial and technical development were such that firms started in the first cell with a single, integrated system of personal control, developed and monitored by an entrepreneur who personally resolved conflicts between time, quality and cost. As the business grows with increased specialisation, delegation and fragmentation, the second cell becomes the norm in which controls are still essentially personal through direct supervision but are now more fragmented, with different departments being responsible for different aspects of production. With the post-war growth of production engineering and operational research techniques, process control and mainframe computerisation, administrative controls proliferate and control systems become more mechanised and automated – but still fragmented. This characterised the third cell. Only with integrated data processing and computer-aided programming and design – in short, 'the new technology' – can a masterplan be developed into the single, integrated, impersonal control systems of the fourth cell.

When Woodward's original 100 firms were classified into one of the four categories, it was found that 75 per cent of unit and small batch firms fell into the first cell, and 95 per cent of process firms into the fourth. But the large batch and mass production firms were not so neatly accounted for, with 35 per cent falling into the second and 40 per cent falling into the third. It seemed that the similarities of social structure which Woodward had noted between unit and process production firms could be attributed to some extent to the fact that both could operate integrated control systems, the one through personal administration, the other through automation, whereas people in the middle ranges felt constantly harassed by different sectors of a fragmented system. This harassment was graphically illustrated in a study by Reeves and Turner in which they compared the nature of control systems in three firms, as summarised in Table 3.4. Similar degrees of chaos were found in the

Table 3.4
Relationship between Production System, Information Handling and
Behaviour in Three Factories Studied by Reeves and Turner

Hollington	*Rose Engineering*	*Mass Bespoke*
Manufacturing	Manufacturing	Manufacturing
Large, complex electronic equipment	Precise hydraulic equipment	Men's bespoke suits
500 employees	700 employees	1000+ employees
Batch production	Batch production	Batch/mass production

1. Hollington and Rose Engineering had similar systems for planning and control of production which were much more complex than Mass Bespoke. In the first two factories there were continual crises caused by shortages; much energy devoted to progress-chasing; and a lack of complete knowledge about the state of play in the different versions of progress held by different functions. There was more certainty and less chaotic revisions in the suit factory.

2. The complexity of their production systems was a function of (a) their market position and how it was interpreted by management, and (b) the nature of their products. In the first two factories there was a much larger number of products, production operations, components and production sequences than in the third. There was also greater uncertainty about the market.

3. Underlying procedures could be detected as a basic strategy for controlling manufacture in the first two factories, including

- checking overall load on the factory by crude aggregate means
- preparing a notional production programme to allow preparatory work to be scheduled
- revising a notional programme as new information becomes available
- creating a list of priority work and updating it as new information becomes available
- coping with shortages, bottlenecks and late deliveries on an *ad hoc* basis

4. The problem of collecting and collating information in complex batch production systems is great. The existence of different sets of information is not just a manifestation of poor communications; the complexity of the situation *makes complete communication impossible* (given limited resources of time, money, etc.). The inability to gather all the necessary information in each of the two batch production factories is a good example of *limited knowledge/ bounded rationality*. Complete consensus on what information is required, let alone on its content, is unlikely to occur. This situation may be aggravated by the ability of some people to use power to get their own set of information accepted.

SOURCE: from Reeves and Turner (1972).

planning and control systems of two of the firms: Hollington electronics, making discrete batches of heavy electronic equipment from a large number of components, and Rose engineering, also engaged in component manufacture of enginering products. The planning and control information in these plants was subject to constant review and amendment. Much energy was devoted to progress-chasing the 'current most important order', in the absence of hard information on either production capacity or the 'relative importance' of other orders. Reeves and Turner compared this apparently chaotic system to the much calmer situation they found in the third factory, which was engaged in supplying weekly batches of mass produced suits from a factory where both the capacity and the number required each week were known. Scheduling and control were therefore comparatively easy. They explained the relative chaos of the batch engineering plants in terms of their diverse and fluctuating markets and the nature of their products. They pointed out, for example, that in scheduling nine jobs on to three machines, with three operators per job, there were millions of ways of completing this task. Thus complete agreement on what to do was almost impossible. There was, in their terms, a 'variable disjunction of information'. It is precisely these sorts of production situation which are greatly improved by the new micro-electronic technology which facilitates easy updating and realignment of different parameters. The form of planning and control system that was found to be characteristic of the Hollington and Rose batch production situations is likely to become less common with the adoption of new techniques.

Technology and relations between functions

Woodward also gave some thought to the implications of different technical systems for relations between departments; that is, to the horizontal as well as the vertical dimensions of structure (Chapter 5). Thinking overall about the flow of work in different contexts, she suggested that in unit production the key central function was development, in the sense that it was here that most money would be made or lost, because it is often the idea of a product and a conviction that the firm could make it, rather than the product itself, which is sold to the customer. Consequently marketing people have to be technically competent, but it is the development engineers who are the elite. In large batch and mass production the functions can be much more independent, with no clear elite and with considerable tensions between departments, not least because of the fragmented control system. Nonetheless, in Woodward's view the key activity is efficient production. In process production sales usually assume greater importance since once the system is in production it is vital to ensure a smoothly expanding market. There are usually fewer tensions between departments, not least because co-ordination of production is largely achieved automatically. Woodward relates an anecdote about Standard Oil of New Jersey, who at the beginning of the twentieth century distributed kerosene lamps free of charge to Chinese peasants in order to obtain a market for kerosene which was a by-product of a new refining process.

Woodward and her team at Imperial College were thus significant in popularising the idea that organisation structures should be designed to fit the constraints posed by the technology. Although her concerns with control as an intervening variable showed that she did not adhere to a strictly deterministic view of the relationship, there is little doubt that she was more excited by the discovery of the link than she was in discussing the limitations of her analysis or why particular technologies were chosen.

Support for a direct link between technology and organisation structure was not confined to Woodward's work. Burns and Stalker (1961) highlighted the importance of characteristics of technology and markets as sources of uncertainty and complexity which, they argued, could be best accommodated through developments in organic (for high uncertainty) or mechanistic (for low uncertainty) forms of organisation (see Chapter 4). Coincidentally with Woodward and Burns, others (notably James Thompson and Charles Perrow) were studying organisations in the USA and coming to similar conclusions.

James Thompson: technology, interdependence and co-ordination

Thompson's classification of production systems is based on the nature of the linkages between various parts of the organisation. It is summarised in Figure 3.2. At the simplest level, there is what he calls 'mediating' technology, wherein the units are linked together by virtue of sharing a common resource from, or being subject to common constraints which are controlled by, a single headquarters. Thus the manufacturers of different components which will be assembled into an aeroplane are all subject to the common constraint of overall weight. Similarly, the branches of a supermarket chain are subject to the common constraint of the availability of their own brand name of baked beans and the administrative procedures of headquarters. Such technologies, Thompson suggests, are operated by units with pooled interdependence, each working separately but giving a discrete contribution to the whole. Transfers between the units can be handled in a co-ordinated and standardised way which lends itself to bureaucratisation and the impersonal application of rules.

At a more complex level of interdependence, long-linked technologies require operating units to be linked to one another in serial interdependence in which the outputs of one unit become the inputs of another. This is typical of many mass production assembly plants where, Thompson argued, co-ordination is best achieved through planning systems as well as rules and procedures. This point is reminiscent of Woodward's work on control systems for large batch and mass production firms.

The third form of production process Thompson calls intensive technology. This involves using a variety of techniques to achieve a change in a specific

FIGURE 3.2

The Classification of Technology, Interdependence and Co-ordination Used by Thompson

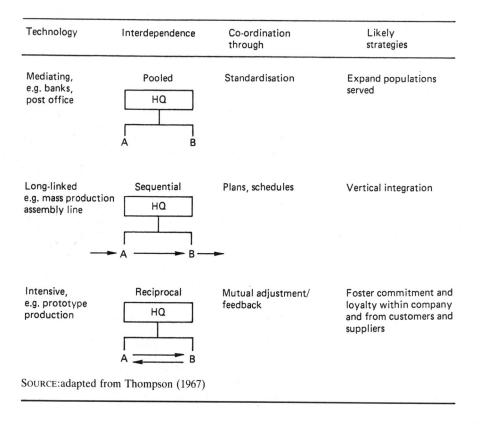

Technology	Interdependence	Co-ordination through	Likely strategies
Mediating, e.g. banks, post office	Pooled	Standardisation	Expand populations served
Long-linked e.g. mass production assembly line	Sequential	Plans, schedules	Vertical integration
Intensive, e.g. prototype production	Reciprocal	Mutual adjustment/ feedback	Foster commitment and loyalty within company and from customers and suppliers

SOURCE: adapted from Thompson (1967)

object. The selection, combination and order of application of these techniques are determined by feedback from the object itself and between the people involved. The best way to co-ordinate such activities, Thompson argues, is to place heavy reliance on feedback and mutual adjustment between the parts and the object. This is a characteristic of organisations involved in providing health services, in renovating old buildings and in the development of military strategy.

Thompson was concerned with the way firms attempt to gain as much control as possible over those things that are necessary for the generation of their products but which, if uncontrolled, represent significant sources of uncertainty. He documented the ways in which firms tried to organise the acquisition of their inputs and the disposal of their outputs, so as to minimise the control that others have over them. He discussed ways of buffering inputs (e.g. through stockpiling or the constant recruitment and training of personnel). He was also concerned with ways of smoothing the production process itself through progressive planned maintenance, systems for the allocation of priorities, as with the distinction in the UK postal service between first or second class mail or, in other contexts, the maintenance of significant inventories of finished product.

Technology and corporate strategy

Thompson's concern with the way people in organisations seek to control significant sources of uncertainty leads him to suggest how the particular characteristics of an organisation's technical system are important when making decisions about expansion and development. Thus, he argued, long-linked technologies lend themselves to vertical integration, whereby a firm incorporates control over input and output units. Mediating technologies, on the other hand, can benefit greatly from an expansion of the populations they serve, while organisations with intensive technologies should give consideration to incorporating the objects of their work. Thompson also focused attention on the nature of product (especially their concreteness or versatility and abstraction) and the adaptability of the technology as being important sources of constraints and opportunities when it comes to decisions about corporate strategies. Thompson and Bates (1957) used these two dimensions as a basis for suggesting how senior executives could diagnose where they should concentrate their policy attention. For example, a highly concrete product and a low adaptability technology, as in organisations like TB hospitals or coal mines, meant, they suggested, that attention must be paid to possible avenues of diversification should product markets disappear. On the other hand, manufacturing organisations with concrete products but adaptable technologies need to be especially concerned with the decision about when to shift products.

Charles Perrow: the characteristics of raw materials

Whereas Woodward and Thompson were important in focusing attention on the implications of different forms of production or transformation process, Perrow concentrated on the inputs to the transformation processes (Perrow, 1967, 1970). He became particularly interested in the implications for people and structure of differences in two basic dimensions of inputs; (a) the degree to which raw materials used in an organisation were standardised, and (b) the nature of the response when non-standard raw materials were encountered.

The degree of standardisation of the raw materials

The purity and testability of inputs and the frequency with which production workers have to cope with exceptions to the norm in their raw materials are questions that can be asked equally of the feedstock entering an industrial chemicals plant, the microchips entering an electronic assembly factory, the components entering a mechanical engineering jobbing shop, and the clients entering a counselling service. The replies one gets are important considerations in the planning and operation of the organisation. They have a bearing on the following sorts of question. Would more emphasis on the search for alternative materials or alternative testing procedures be worth while? What sort of people, in terms of qualifications and experience, should be selected and recruited for the preparation and handling of the raw materials? How should clauses of the contract between supplier and user be phrased with regard to specifying quality and delivery? How should stores and inventory control be structured to relate to production, and where, if anywhere, should input quality testing be located?

The nature of the responses when non-standard raw materials are encountered

Perrow's second dimension concerns how exceptions are dealt with, if and when they are encountered. Are the problems that account for their sub-standardness sufficiently well understood to be handled by standardised procedures; in other words, can highly programmed responses follow the discovery of an inadequacy in the raw materials? For example, if a batch of chemical feedstock was not of the required strength, it is likely that standard operating instructions exist which specify the circumstances for rejection and the circumstances for specific changes to be made in the content or strength of mix. Similarly, standard operating procedures specify reactions to the identification of sub-standard components in mass production. Alternatively, the reasons for inadequacy may be neither so well understood nor so amenable to immediate action. A great deal of 'searching' may then be required to find a solution to the problems posed by non-standard raw materials. Such is often the case in prototype or unit production of a high specification product like an aeroplane engine. Here particular metal pieces may be specified and yet their properties under different points of stress be difficult to determine. If they are found to be inadequate, then the process and product engineers have to decide what to do. Should they refashion the components themselves, treat them with some chemical, request that they be made of an alternative material, rethink the whole design of that particular sub-assembly, or any combination of these strategies?

The extreme end of non-standard search procedures is found in organisations where the raw materials do not respond in a uniform fashion to screening tests, or indeed for which there are no known screening tests. A patient facing a doctor may not be easily categorised as needing a particular sort of treatment, and there may have to be a great deal of investigation to establish the nature of his condition. Where materials or processes are just being developed, as in the case of contemporary bioengineering, there is often a lot of searching required into the nature of the raw material's uncharted variability. In the early days of the commercial manufacture of microchips, 'yield' was a big problem largely because it was often not clear to production that chips were sub-specification until they had been incorporated into the assembly of the final product.

The more general implications of differences in the types of response to non-standard raw materials can be seen from the following questions. What sort of investment should a company make in gathering and processing information on raw materials and the reasons for their deviation from a specified norm? To what extent are comprehensive standard operating instructions appropriate in the stocking and production areas of the plant? What sort of people, in terms of qualifications and experience, should be employed to detect and to rectify deviations in raw materials? What in-house training is required to facilitate the development of discretionary judgement? How can changes in scientific and engineering know-how be monitored so that people in a company will know when, if at all, it is appropriate to increase standardisation in production procedures?

If the two dimensions of variability and search are put together, a four-cell model can be constructed. Perrow provides a convincing argument that organisations falling into each of these four cells are most appropriately structured in different ways. Whereas, he argues, a formal mechanistic hierarchy is appropriate for routine production where there is little variability and minimal search, a greater degree of informality is needed to cope with non-routine prototype development with high variability and extensive search requirements. These ideas are taken up again in Chapter 5.

Technology, structure and size

Further support for links between technology and organisation structure came from studies by others such as Hall (1962), Hage and Aiken (1967, 1969) and Khandwalla (1974). Hage and Aiken conducted a study of sixteen health and welfare agencies in the USA. They found significant relationships between the routineness of the technology and the degree of centralisation, formalisation and specialisation. By the time of the publication of their work, a debate had developed as to the relative priority between technology, as advocated by Woodward, Thompson and Perrow, and size, as advocated by Pugh and Blau and their colleagues (see Chapter 5). However, as Hickson, Pugh and Pheysey (1969) pointed out, it is likely that the relationship between production technology and structure will be strongest in those areas most in contact with the operations technology. Thus variations in the number of personnel and their form of organisation on inspection and maintenance was found to be highly related to type of technology, whereas this relationship was not found for indirect specialist functions. Arguably, therefore, the smaller the organisation, the more its structure will be pervaded by technological effects, whereas the larger the organisation, the less pervading will be the effects of technology. In larger organisations specialists and administrators will be 'buffered' from the effects of the technical core by the sorts of standard procedure and formalised paperwork which, all other things being equal, are associated with increases in size.

Management structure and new technology

Before leaving this discussion of the role of technology it is worth noting that the three main studies discussed in this section, namely Woodward, Thompson and Perrow, all pre-dated the operational introduction of new technology. To date most of the work in this area has focused on its implications for work organisation, but some comments in relation to management structure can be made. Underlying the relationships between technology and organisation structure suggested by Woodward, Thompson and Perrow is a concern for uncertainty and complexity. A common strand of argument is that characteristics of the technology pose uncertainties or create complexities which can somehow be coped with through the development of appropriate management structures: for example, by fostering flexible working relationships between specialists, maintaining buffer stocks of raw materials, and placing more or less emphasis on the different forms of administrative, technological, hierarchical and output systems of control. The fascinating importance of developments in new technology is that they may lead to a reduction in uncertainty and complexity precisely because they can facilitate the collection, interpretation and analysis of a mass of hitherto disparate information. Thus these developments in microelectronic technology may lead to a reduction in the emphasis on organisational forms as tools for coping with complexity and uncertainty, and an increase in the significance of personal networks of highly committed groups. This is the scenario presented by Drucker (1989), in a book entitled *The New Realities*. But this line of argument must be temporarily suspended until Chapter 5 in order to conduct an analysis of the 'environment' in a similar way to that made of 'technology'. In this way a fuller picture will be created from which to continue the discussion.

The Environment: Opportunity and Constraint 4

Maud and George Budd own the only shop-cum-post office in a medium-sized village in the English west country. They operate their sub-post office under licence, and they sell basic groceries, sweets, tobacco, soft drinks and inexpensive children's toys, stationery and novelties. Their customers are of two main sorts. Most importantly there are the residents of this relatively thriving village, where at least one or two members of many of the households are locally employed in farming and agriculturally related occupations, in light industrial work in three nearby towns, and as building and other crafts people. Other residents, but by no means as many as in some other villages, are retired or weekend owners of holiday cottages. There is also a degree of passing casual custom which is mainly derived from visitors to the local stately home or celebrated village pub. When George and Maud bought the shop, its annual accounts revealed that it was just about breaking even, but that its turnover had declined substantially in the previous three years when their predecessors had deliberately cut down on their range of goods and had all but stopped selling groceries because of difficulties they encountered with efficient stock-keeping. The post office business had shown a steady increase over the past ten years but now looked to be levelling off. George and Maud decided they could manage all the work associated with the shop themselves, except for employing one part-time assistant who would serve in the shop three mornings a week. They came into the shop determined to develop good relationships with customers and suppliers in order to increase demand for their goods and services and to avoid unexpected and large price rises or shortages. They began to look for ways to attract new customers and encourage existing ones to buy more. They began meeting other shop-keepers with a view to negotiating bulk discounts on their supplies, and they also paid a great deal of attention to following the Post Office rules and procedures so that the District Postmaster would be pleased to maintain their licence. Apart from these present concerns they began to think about future developments. On the positive side they considered whether a fairly cheap personal computer would make stock-keeping more efficient and economical. They also wondered whether the proposed cuts in bus services would mean that some people would buy more from them and, if so, how they should alter their service to meet this change. They also anticipated some difficulties. Would economic recession and rising unemployment make it impossible to sell luxury items? Would Post Office policy change to allow the postal delivery of some benefits from a regional centre? In this way, George and Maud were concentrating their attention on the opportunities and constraints presented by their business environment.

4.1   'Environment': The Concept

Inverted commas are used in this sub-heading because the environment is inevitably an arbitrary concept in that it embraces everything 'outside' any particular organisation that is being focused upon. It is composed of a large variety of individuals, groups and organisations who are regarded 'collectively' simply because they share a linkage with whatever 'focal' organisation is the object of interest, whether for a practitioner, researcher or observer. To identify a focal organisation is not to assume that it is necessarily significant in its environment other than for the reasons that have led to its identification. Similarly, the designation of people, groups, other organisations and institutions as part of the 'environment' is idiosyncratic. As Starbuck (1976) has commented, 'Assuming organisations can be sharply distinguished from their environments distorts reality by compressing into one dichotomy a melange of continuously varying phenomena' (p. 1069). This is an extremely interesting point for our general understanding of activities within organisations and relations between people and groups in different organisational and institutional contexts. It leads directly to the subject of the final section of this chapter which concerns 'networks and inter-organisational relations'. However, notwithstanding the value of a general analytical perspective for any practitioner, it is also the case that members of a particular organisation are naturally interested in the opportunities and constraints that are presented by the people, groups, events and history which can be said pragmatically to constitute 'the environment' of their organisation. Accordingly, the first part of this chapter suspends the analytical issue of distinctions between 'organisations' and 'their environments', and discusses critical features of the links between people in particular organisations and those in the political, social and economic context of their operations.

4.2 Interactions across the Boundaries of Organisations: A Practical Guide

William Evan (1966) pioneered a pragmatic approach to the environment of organisations when he coined the term 'organisation set' to characterise all the 'organisations in interaction with a focal organisation'. He described how the interactions varied in terms of their frequency (regular, occasional, infrequent), formality (high, medium and low formalisation) and the extent to which they were co-operative, neutral or conflicting. The applicability of these sources of variation can be illustrated in terms of the Budds' village shop. They have regular interactions with particular suppliers of groceries and with the District Postmaster, infrequent contact with 'chance' customers, and occasional contact with the VAT inspector. Their relations with the Post Office are highly formal, their relationship with regular village customers much less so. They have a general inclination to co-operate with other village stores in order to secure good deals with regional suppliers, but there is potential conflict with anyone who threatens their own village market.

There is also a fourth variation in the extent to which the linkages are specific to an establishment, an industrial sector, a region, a nation state or an international grouping such as the EC or the Commonwealth. For example, some of Budds' customers give them all their cigarette trade and thus provide a unique organisation–environment link. Other customers use many sources for their sweets and notepaper but are geographically limited to a particular area for supply. Post Office rules apply to all sub-post offices in Britain, and national economic conditions affect the whole range of establishments. Taking an industrial example, a batch engineering workshop has one or two unique suppliers; it deals, together with others, with a national trade union organisation; its geographical location affects its ability to get skilled workers; and its national location in Britain makes it subject to the British government's approach to international trade.

Looking at these interactions, it may be said that they fall into three broad categories of content. There are interactions to secure the supply of inputs, there are interactions to secure the disbursement of outputs, and there are interactions which have the effect of regulating the operations and transactions of the focal organisation.

Inputs and outputs

Inputs and outputs are fairly self-explanatory. They are the goods (raw materials, components, finished articles) and services (skills, labour, knowledge, creativity) that are taken into the organisation and disbursed from it. Both inputs and outputs vary in the extent to which they are standardised and predictable and thus in the ease with which they can be subject to routine planning and control systems. Similarly, they can both present uncertainties and special requirements which need to be 'coped' with in a more direct fashion. The discussion of Perrow's work in the previous chapter dealt with sources of input uncertainty, which is also relevant to current debates about whether to 'make or buy' components for manufacturing (see, e.g., Butler and Carney, 1983).

When it comes to outputs, senior executives often face a dilemma about the extent to which they feel they should standardise their products for a mass market or diversify for specialised markets. Essentially this involves judgements about the growth potential of different market sectors and whether they can recoup the additional costs incurred in terms of investment in the personnel, administration and technology required for specialist luxury items, or whether a cost-cutting mass production strategy is likely to offer the 'best' returns.

External regulation

Sources of regulation are often less tangible and obvious than sources of inputs and depositories for outputs. Regulation can be thought of in two forms: first, there are formally established laws, rules and procedures which affect operations and transactions within and between organisations. These may be embodied in government decisions and national laws, in national agreements between employers' associations and trade unions or in the corporate or divisional policy of 'parent' organisations. The other major source of regulation is located in the informal cultural, attitudinal and value characteristics of the members of both the focal organisation and constituents of its environment. Attitudes and values, as seen in Chapter 1, are largely influenced by associations with significant individuals and groups, both within and outside the organisations. Friends, family, work groups, trade unions, professional associations and leisure groups are particularly important in this context. Members' views on what is desirable and feasible are thus formed in relation to significant parts of the environment, while members' views of the environment are often clearly important regulatory influences. For example, members of a government's views on the advantages of the free market or a more planned approach to industrial development will affect commercial and industrial operations and transactions, and important customers' views on the desirability of trade with South Africa may well regulate a focal organisation in terms of where it purchases its raw materials. The strength of either formal or informal regulation on a focal organisation will reflect not only the content and formality of relationship but, most importantly, also the relative power and influence of the parties involved, a point which will be further considered in Chapter 7.

Mapping the environment

To speak of organisation is thus to speak of environment as well. The inevitability of needing to secure inputs, to disburse outputs and of attempts to regulate, inextricably links the members of any focal organisation with the members of its environment in a form of 'love–hate' relationship: 'love' because of the opportunities the environment provides and 'hate' because of the constraints and losses it can impose; 'inextricably linked' because of an inability for anyone to have the opportunities without the possibility of constraints. Figure 4.1 provides an illustration of the conceptualisation of the links between an organisation and its environment in terms of constraints and opportunities. The people, groups and organisations which are variously responsible for inputs, outputs and regulation for any focal organisation can be charted in these terms. Maps for different enterprises will have similarities and differences depending on the extent to which organisations share individual, industrial, regional and national characteristics.

FIGURE 4.1
Conceptualising the Environment

Sources of change

So far a static cross-sectional view of an organisation's environment has been constructed, but three further complexities require a longitudinal perspective. To begin with, the constituent parts themselves are not static. As they change, grow and decline, the interests and the intentions of their dominant coalitions may alter. A policy of acquisition and diversification may make one supplier less dependent on a particular customer. A change of government may lead to a reversal of policies on regional employment subsidies. The bankruptcy of a competitor may open the way for the significant growth of another. Second, there is change in the patterns of interaction between the parts as communication, co-operation and conflict ebb and flow. Competitors may band together and may include or exclude a focal organisation. A government edict may be much influenced by the lobbying of employers' associations or trade unions and dramatically change the market position of a group of organisations. Third, the extent to which the constituent parts of its environment are subject to power and influence from the focal organisation, and vice versa, also changes over time.

These three dynamic factors, which will be the subject of further discussion in the next section of this chapter, mean that the environment is to some extent always a source of uncertainty for a focal organisation. This explains why many of the activities and decisions which link a focal organisation to parts of its environment are concerned with two things: (a) generating and collecting information about relevant environmental segments; (b) attempts to influence and control aspects of the environment.

4.3 Generating and Collecting Information about the Environment

People in organisations need to 'know' their environment in order to recognise and take advantage of the opportunities it offers, to recognise the constraints it imposes and to seek to turn the constraints into opportunities. Given the structure of different interest groups discussed in Chapter 2, it must be remembered that the definition of opportunities and constraints will not necessarily be a matter for consensus even within one organisation.

Information about inputs: In pursuit of objectives, dominant groups in organisations look on the environment as a source of skills, labour, knowledge and creativity, raw materials, components, finished articles and energy. In order to secure what they consider to be the most favourable transactions in terms of whatever criteria they consider appropriate, they need as much information as possible about potential inputs. For example, it is likely they will need to know the following information:

1. What is available in terms of quantity (i.e. are the inputs readily available or scarce?)
2. Are there any alternatives (i.e. are there any alternative inputs which would ultimately serve the same purpose? For example, is there a shortage of compliant labour? Is there justification for more automation?)
3. What is available in terms of quality and efficacy (i.e. how appropriate are the various alternatives in terms of the tasks they are expected to fulfil?)
4. What is available in terms of price (i.e. what resources – especially money and space – already controlled within the organisation will be needed to secure the identified input?)
5. What is available in terms of opportunity cost (i.e. if the transaction is made and a particular input secured, what other things will have to be forgone?)

Information about recipients of outputs: In pursuit of objectives, dominant groups in organisations look on the environment as a recipient of the goods and services they produce. Accordingly they need to have information about the motivation and resources of potential recipients.

1. What expectations or needs are the outputs likely to satisfy?
2. What is the likely rate and direction of change of these expectations or needs?
3. What costs are they willing to incur for acquisition?
4. Most importantly, what is the availability of alternative sources of satisfaction by other means through competitors?

Information about sources of regulation: Some regulative pressure will come from people in other organisations for whom there is a happy coincidence between the preservation of their comparative advantage and the protection of some public good. For example, professional groups in the process of seeking regulation to protect lay clients can also secure a comparative advantage by restricting or barring entry into their activities by unqualified people. Indeed, much regulation is couched in terms of offering protection to specific groups: for example, the deliberations of the Monopolies Commission and the activities of the British Standards Institute are formally concerned with protection of the consumer; aspects of employment legislation are concerned with protecting the rights of either trade unions or employers; and regulations relating to environmental issues like pollution formally offer protection to the general public.

Regulation, while it constrains the activities of some organisations, offers opportunities to others. A small company trying to survive and grow but threatened with takeover by a near monopolist may benefit from the activities of the Monopolies Commission. Alternatively, a large company may be thwarted in its takeover bid for a small but growing competitor. Some governments in Britain have placed emphasis upon positive intervention in industrial and employment matters as a 'good' thing and thus have used regional and industrial policies to promote particular kinds of activities: for example, locating new offices or plants in selected regions, youth training or export credit guarantee schemes. But such promotions are often inextricably linked to regulating, discouraging or even prohibiting other activities. Even governments, such as those under Margaret Thatcher which protested a non-interventionist policy, nonetheless indirectly exercise considerable regulation and intervention in the activities of organisations through their financial policies of controlling public sector borrowing or their disbursement of grants, allocations and subsidies. Whatever the interpretation put upon particular forms of regulation, members of organisations need to collect information about them so that they can determine on a policy of acceptance, compliance or evasion, otherwise ignorance emerges as the 'default' option.

Other forms of regulation are more informal and are based on people either consciously or subconsciously adopting the taken-for-granted assumptions, attitudes and values which prevail in dominant parts of their environment. If a small group of software engineers working together as consultants know that their large corporate clients always expect a smart city-suited appearance before they will take anyone seriously, then they will probably comply with this form of regulation. Similarly, and with more penetrating effect, if these same clients always like to see a merchant banker on the board of a consultancy, the engineers may also comply unless they are certain of sufficient business without this custom.

Gathering information on inputs, outputs and regulation is a costly business. A point is reached where decisions have to be made about the extent of benefits from more and better information as against the costs of ignorance. But such decisions in a sense only affect the tip of the iceberg of potential information. More often people are not aware that they are missing knowledge or information, as its omission from their information store is by default and not by design. Perfect knowledge and information is rarely to hand, particularly when its generation and collection will itself consume scarce resources, a feature of organisational life which is further discussed in Chapter 8.

4.4   Controlling and Reacting to the Environment

Gathering information is linked to the second group of activities concerned with attempting to achieve greater control over the supply of inputs, disbursement of outputs and regulatory activities. The environment is rich in both opportunities and constraints, their definition depending upon position and interest. Efforts to achieve greater control are broadly related to attempts:

- to take advantage of opportunities
- to work within constraints
- to turn constraints into opportunities
- to reduce uncertainty and make operations more predictable, plannable and amenable to the pursuit of particular interests

Of the many ways to attempt to achieve the general objective of greater control, power and strength in the environment, four major ways are selected for discussion here. They are summarised in Table 4.1.

Direct influence on particular people

Six main approaches to direct personal influence are identified in Table 4.1. At an informal level there is the whole range of business hospitality (e.g. taking potential clients out to lunch, for a day at the races or an evening at the opera). More formally, significant people like MPs or merchant bankers may be 'co-opted' on to the board of a company with a view to creating a special interest for the company within Westminster or the financial world. Co-option or incorporation on a large scale occurs when people in a focal organisation make a successful bid to acquire complete additional enterprises, rather than the hearts and minds of individuals. Acquisition to effect vertical integration involves the purchase of suppliers or customers, thereby giving the focal organisation greater and possibly total control over its immediate inputs or outputs. Horizontal integration involves acquiring competitors or diversifying product ranges and so is also concerned with achieving greater control over the market place, spreading liabilities and reducing degrees of dependence on a smaller market segment.

Third, greater direct influence may be secured through bargaining and exchange. It is now commonplace, for example, for property developers to give some socially useful development such as a gallery or a swimming pool as a planning gain in return for planning permission for commercial developments. Similarly, large users of energy, using the threat of switching supplies, bargain with the national utilities about price. Randall (1973) discusses how senior executives seek to gain control over sectors of their environment by establishing their legitimacy, status and influence and securing a 'policy' space for their organisation apart from competitors.

Fourth, coalitions may be formed between groups of different and possibly competitive interests. For example, a cartel agreement among the manufacturers of washing powder may maintain prices at a high level and facilitate greater control over the market. Joint ventures between a building company and a property developer may secure planning permission from a local council for housing. Fifth and more formally, parties may enter into contracts with one another.

Table 4.1
Ways to Achieve Greater Dominance and Control of the Environment

---

A. *Secure greater influence in a particular set of relationships*

1. *Personal informal interactions*
    (e.g. hospitality: lunch, visits to races or opera)

2. *Co-option/incorporation of individuals, groups, organisations*
    (e.g. appointing MPs and merchant bankers to the board; appointing
    ex-factory inspectors as corporate safety advisers; buying up suppliers
    or customers (vertical integration); buying up competitors (horizontal
    integration))

3. *Bargaining (exchange of valued scarce resources)*
    (e.g. property company gives local authority 'planning gain' of a new
    swimming pool in return for planning permission for new office
    block)

4. *Coalition*
    (e.g. cartel of competitors to achieve high price stability)

5. *Contractual arrangement*
    (e.g. with suppliers to ensure delivery dates or with employees over
    'ownership' of ideas developed within the company)

6. *Technological advance*
    (e.g. product or process innovation)

B. *Achieve greater influence generally within particular environmental
    sectors*
    (e.g. secure competitive advantage in obtaining supplies, in offering
    products, in influencing regulators)

C. *Alter internal operations to 'buffer' against unpredictabilities of
    environment*
    (e.g. large inventories of finished goods, preventive maintenance,
    systematic training and recruitment programme)

D. *Adjust internal structure to make it more sensitive to the environment
    and geared towards*
    • information gathering
    • control and influence

Lastly, technological developments which facilitate process or product innovation can have a direct impact on particular sets of relationships with competitors, suppliers and customers.

These six different ways of influencing relationships directly are not mutually exclusive but are often interlinked. An informal lunch may lead to a seat on the board or a components contract. An MP co-opted on to the board can sometimes attract sufficient prestige to the company's notepaper for other notables to offer their services. Bargaining between competitors can lead to the establishment of a coalition, and so on. All the strategies listed under Section A in Table 4.1 are concerned with attempting to influence particular relationships, but success with one sector may be at the expense of difficulties in another. For example, a contract with a developer of the latest technology may give a development director potentially greater control over the supplier and over his competitors, but it may create difficulties with the unions over the introduction of new technology.

General promotional activity

The focus for Section B in Table 4.1 is on how focal organisations can secure a basis for their competitive advantage, so that they can make 'the best deals' in obtaining supplies, selling products and influencing regulators. This is a central area of study for courses in business policy. For example, as far as customers are concerned, we need to note the possibility of competing on the basis of cost, quality and differentiation: that is, the production of goods and services which are cheapest, best or of the most appropriate quality or somehow distinctly different from those offered by others. Texts such as Johnson (1987) from the UK and Porter (1985) from the USA deal comprehensively with these issues.

There is also the issue of general promotions, in which organisations attempt to bring the activities and the image of an organisation to the forefront of the minds of people in different environmental sectors such as domestic consumers, the government, or the trade union movement. Lager advertisements, for example, are directed at drinkers, at publicans and even at leisure wear manufacturers who may be interested in a joint venture for promotional tee-shirts, etc. Public relations consultants, advertising agencies and point-of-sale advisers are all concerned to offer a wide range of promotional activities that will serve to distinguish a company's products from those of their competitors. The decade of 1980s has seen the growth of consultancies which specialise in helping organisations to create and maintain a new corporate image and identity. Olins (1989), a leading consultant who has worked with BT, the Prudential and the Natural History Museum, discusses the place of such general promotional work in securing greater control of an organisation's environment.

Creating 'buffers' against the environment

The concern of interested parties to achieve greater control and dominance in their environment is also likely to lead them to modify their internal operations, as suggested in Section C of Table 4.1. In particular they may be concerned to 'buffer' their activities against the unpredictabilities of the environment by maintaining large inventories of finished goods or storing significant quantities of components. In this way managers are seeking to reduce their dependence on suppliers and yet be capable of responding quickly to increases in market demand. Another way in which buffers against environmental influences are created is to undertake programmes of preventive maintenance and systematic training and recruitment so that plant, equipment and the workforce can more easily respond to unexpected change. Thompson (1967) gives one of the first comprehensive accounts of the way in which organisations seek to control and, if that is not possible, to buffer and protect themselves from unexpected or adverse effects. He describes attempts to gain power and defend domains against environmental influences, but he acknowledges that whatever success was forthcoming in this direction, there would always be residual uncertainty because of a lack of perfect knowledge and information.

Appropriate structures

Finally, a fourth way to increase control and dominance in environments is to structure internal operations so that roles and relationships are appropriate for maintaining the critical activities of gathering information and attempting control in different segments of the environment.

Burns and Stalker: mechanistic and organic forms of structure

As early as 1961 Burns and Stalker had suggested that, through a judicious design of organisation structure, firms could greatly increase their ability to secure their position within their environments. Their ideas about organisation structure arose out of an empirical study of electronics firms in Scotland. They identified two extreme forms of organisation, mechanistic and organic, although they freely admitted that many organisations would fall in interim positions. The summaries of each type in Table 4.2 show that, at one extreme, a mechanistic organisation displays strong specialisation, formalisation, standardisation and hierarchy. At the other extreme, an organic structure displays flexibility in task definition, a weaker hierarchy and greater importance is given to co-ordination and communication within networks of lateral relationships as well as within the hierarchy.

The importance of Burns and Stalker's study was that it suggested that mechanistic structures were more appropriate where employees do not have high expectations of discretion and autonomy and where there is a high

Table 4.2
Mechanistic and Organic Forms of Organisation

Mechanistic forms	Organic forms
Tasks	
Highly differentiated tasks, precise formal role definitions	Specialist tasks contribute to overall tasks in ways which are largely not predetermined
Predominant types of control (See Figure 1.3)	
Hierarchical Administrative Technological	Output Personal Unobtrusive
Predominant forms of communication	
Instructions and decisions passed down through hierarchy	Advice and instructions passed through network of lateral as well as vertical relationships
Knowledge relevant to task definition	
Concentrated at top of hierarchy	Distributed through network of levels and functions
Types of personnel (see Chapter 1)	
More 'locals'	More 'cosmopolitans'
Importance of industrial, technical and commercial contacts outside organisation	
Less important	Great importance

SOURCE: adapted from Burns and Stalker (1961), *The Management of Innovation*, pp. 120–1.

degree of stability and certainty in the technology and environment. This is likely to be the case, for example, in monopolies or oligopolies with long product life-cycles, as in the insurance business. In such situations flexibility, far from being an asset, was a liability. However, with changes in the organisation of the financial services sector in the UK it is interesting to note that many large companies have now found it important to develop more flexible decentralised structures as the market for new products has become much more competitive. In general the more highly trained and qualified the personnel, the more complex and uncertain the technology and environment, then the more appropriate an organic form of structure becomes.

The conclusion which Burns and Stalker reached was that there was nothing absolutely right about an organic or a mechanistic structure, and neither did they represent immutably fixed characteristics. Structures, they showed, were the subject of choice and decision-making, albeit within constraints. What was appropriate to one environment might be wholly inappropriate in another. In other words, as Chapter 5 will demonstrate, structures are tools which can be created, selected and used by groups to attempt to achieve co-ordination and control in relation to their objectives. They will, like all tools, incur costs as well as benefits. The art of organisation design thus becomes one of selecting the most appropriate tool, given the nature of the environment. This theme runs through much of the literature concerned with the relation between organisations and their environment as the following selected references demonstrate.

Dill (1962) and Thompson (1967) noted that, when faced with heterogeneous and changing environments, people in high-performing organisations sought to identify homogeneous segments and to establish internal structural units to deal with them. Internal specialisation was thus related to the diversity of the information and its ease of collection, and the assessed importance of particular environmental segments. Where there was a lot of stability and predictability, focal organisations established rules and bureaucratic procedures for categorising events and selecting appropriate responses. If, however, the range of responses was vast, unwieldy and unpredictable, then great importance needed to be attached to localised units to monitor segments of the environment and plan the responses. However, specialist groups are expensive to maintain; thus where possible it was noted that managers preferred to categorise, routinise and standardise their dealings with environmental segments. The development of appropriate structures to facilitate environmental scanning and control has maintained its place as a major theme in organisational analysis for more than twenty years. It is a major subject for discussion in Chapter 5. However, such is its significance to our understanding of the environment as well as that of structure, the broader discussion will be foreshadowed here by a summary of the work of Lawrence and Lorsch who, with their fellow-American Galbraith, were pioneers in developing the theory and practice of structural responses to environmental conditions.

Lawrence and Lorsch: diversity and uncertainty

In a comparative study of ten establishments, six developing and manufacturing plastics, two manufacturing consumer foods and two manufacturing containers, Lawrence and Lorsch (1967) focused on the way people in different industries and departments interacted with different environmental sectors. In particular they observed that the environments of some, but not all, firms were highly diverse and that different sectors embodied different amounts and types of uncertainty, as measured by the subjective assessments of chief executives. Not surprisingly, Lawrence and Lorsch found overall differences in the amounts of uncertainty faced by firms in different industrial sectors. The plastics firms, operating in a diverse and dynamic environment in which there were frequent changes in technologies and a fair degree of volatility in the markets, faced more uncertainty and diversity in their environments overall than the food firms, which were characterised by a fairly stable technology but a slightly higher degree of uncertainty in the market sector than for plastics. Both the plastics and food firms faced significantly more uncertainty and diversity in their environments than the firms in the container industry, where there was at that time little change in technology, materials or markets. More interesting than these overall differences between firms in different industrial sectors, however, was the finding that there were often substantial differences between the degree of uncertainty faced by different departments within a single firm in their interactions with sectors of the environment. In the plastics firms research departments faced most volatility and uncertainty, followed by development and then sales, with production facing least uncertainty and diversity in its environment. In each industry those departments which faced the highest level of uncertainty also tended to be the most influential departments in the firm.

A main thesis of Lawrence and Lorsch is that managers in different departments, dealing with different amounts and types of uncertainty arising from their environments, should adopt different managerial styles and strategies. They summarised such differences in their concept of 'differentiation', which they defined as 'the difference in cognitive and emotional orientation among managers in different functional departments'. They operationalised this concept through interview and questionnaire techniques, collecting responses from 30–50 managers in each industry about their goals, the normal timespan for feedback from the results of activities, and the extent to which interactions with others are biased to task or social elements. They also found that departments were differently structured on a Burns and Stalker type of mechanistic-organic scale (see Table 4.2). Differentiation between management styles, together with differences in structure, create a variable need, they argued, for what they call 'integration'; that is, 'the quality of the state of collaboration which exists among departments which are required to achieve unity of effort by the demands of the environment'.

Given the paradoxical nature of life in organisations, it will come as no surprise that they found differentiation and integration to be complementary rather than alternatives: the greater the differentiation, the greater the need for integration. Thus differences of strategy and structure could flourish between departments, while at the same time special mechanisms for integration ensured that centrifugal forces did not pull the organisation apart. They found that links between differentiation and integration were related to a firm's financial performance as measured over a five-year period by changes in profits, sales volume and new products developed as a percentage of current sales. They had selected both high and poor performing firms in each industrial sector. Within each sector they found that the successful firms were those that matched the extent of differentiation with appropriate integration strategies. The most successful differentiated firm was manufacturing plastics; it also topped the league as far as the range and extent of integrative devices was concerned. It had specialist integrative departments to link highly diverse specialist departments and permanent teams providing integration in other areas. It also had three basic integrative mechanisms which were found in firms in all sectors: namely, the use of paper systems and rules, a formal hierarchy with associated systems for planning and goal-setting, and direct personal contact between managers of different departments. The high-performing food firm, facing medium environmental uncertainty and diversity, requiring moderate differentiation and hence integration, used individual integrators and temporary teams as well as the three basic mechanisms. The high-performing container firm merely relied on three basic mechanisms of procedures, hierarchy and direct contact. Poor performers in each sector were those that did not match environmental demands with appropriate inter-departmental diversity and did not match such diversity with appropriate integration. Lawrence and Lorsch concluded, in a similar vein to Woodward, Perrow and Thompson, that there was nothing inherently good or bad about any level of differentiation and integration. Rather, the key to business financial success, they argued, lay in matching levels and types of both to environmental demands. It was equally inappropriate for container firms to have high differentiation and high integration as it was for plastics firms to have low differentiation and low integration. Similarly, a combination of high differentiation and low integration or vice versa would not be appropriate to any firm. In this way people were warned not to assume that they necessarily needed a complex, highly differentiated and integrated 'modern' approach to organisation, since it could be that low levels of uncertainty and diversity in their environment made this a costly and an inappropriate response. Equally dangerous would be to assume low uncertainty and diversity when in fact the situation called for high levels of differentiation and integration. They cited the example of a low-performing food company which maintained research as a single structural entity, whereas they felt that applied and basic research had to deal with sufficiently different environmental segments for them to be structurally separated. In contrast, a low-performing plastics firm had two research departments with essentially the same task and should therefore, they argued, have been amalgamated.

In an extension to this work, Lorsch and Morse (1974) included the members of the focal organisation as a significant feature for analysis and demonstrated the importance of securing a three-way fit between (a) the critical demands and conditions of the central tasks and the environment of an organisation; (b) the management structures and strategies; and (c) the personal predispositions of its individual members. Such a fit, they argued, will normally result in better financial performance as well as rewards to individual members through a heightened sense of competence.

Subsequent commentators – for example, Duncan (1972), Tosi, Aldag and Storey (1973) and Downey, Hellreige and Slocum (1975) – have taken issue with Lawrence and Lorsch's methodology and findings. For instance, there has been considerable criticism of simply using a subjective measure of uncertainty and of their rather mechanistic model of adaptation. Whatever the criticisms, however (and we shall return to them in the next chapter), Lawrence and Lorsch's work, particularly when put with other 'foundation' studies of a 'contingency' type (notably, Woodward, 1965; Perrow, 1967; Thompson, 1967), was extremely important in shifting the views of managers and analysts alike about the structure and dynamics of organisations. Indeed, it was in their book that a chapter tentatively entitled 'Towards a contingency theory of organisations' first brought together this collection of work, with its emphasis on the need to design appropriate structures to fit the environment.

Jay Galbraith: strategies for coping with uncertainty

Just as one of the themes of contingency theory is that 'there is no one universally best way to organise', so another, albeit often implicit, theme is that whatever structure is adopted, or emerges by default, its establishment will incur costs as well as benefits. This theme is brought to the forefront of analysis in the writings of Jay Galbraith (1973, 1977). Following Thompson (1967) and Lawrence and Lorsch (1967), Galbraith's starting point for his analysis of the design and operation of organisations is the complexity of technology and environment. He suggests that the complexity faced by any establishment is a function of its division of labour, required level of goal performance and goal diversity, which in turn reflects capital, labour and product markets and technologies in its environment. People in an organisation in which there is a complex pattern of specialisation, with a strong emphasis on high performance and with a wide range of products and associated goal diversity, are in Galbraith's terms having to cope with a large degree of complexity. This complexity, in turn, is reflected in the amount of information that has to be acquired and processed for effective task performance. The greater the complexity, he argues, the greater the amount of information that has to be acquired and, I would add, transmitted to the right place at the right time. Unfortunately there is normally some information which cannot be acquired or processed, possibly because it has not yet been 'discovered' either by people in the organisation or by anyone else, or because, as Chapter 8 will show, its acquisition or transmission is thought to involve too many economic or social costs.

The difference between the amount of information acquired and processed to the right place at the right time in any organisation and the amount of information required for task performance can be taken as a measure of the uncertainty an organisation faces: that is, the information that would be needed if a given level of task performance were to be achieved. Galbraith proceeds in his analysis by saying that faced with a degree of uncertainty, people in organisations can adopt a variety of strategies to seek its reduction. These strategies are summarised in Figure 4.2. Three of them are found generally, although in different degrees of importance and intensity, in all organisations. They are, following Thompson (1967), the operation of the hierarchy, the development of rules and procedures, and activities concerned

FIGURE 4.2
Alternative Strategies for Coping with Complexity and Uncertainty in Organisations

1. Rules and programmes
2. Hierarchy
3. Planning

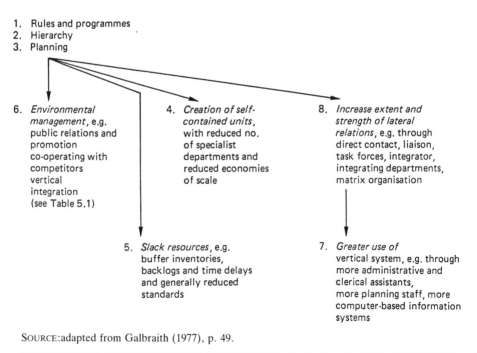

6. *Environmental management*, e.g. public relations and promotion co-operating with competitors vertical integration (see Table 5.1)

4. *Creation of self-contained units,* with reduced no. of specialist departments and reduced economies of scale

8. *Increase extent and strength of lateral relations,* e.g. through direct contact, liaison, task forces, integrator, integrating departments, matrix organisation

5. *Slack resources,* e.g. buffer inventories, backlogs and time delays and generally reduced standards

7. *Greater use of* vertical system, e.g. through more administrative and clerical assistants, more planning staff, more computer-based information systems

SOURCE:adapted from Galbraith (1977), p. 49.

to plan and schedule work. As we have seen in earlier chapters, these activities are associated with desires to standardise and control internal operations so as to facilitate interaction over inputs, outputs and regulation with the environment. Beyond these basic responses, however, Galbraith suggests that if the degree of complexity and uncertainty demands it, people make choices about adopting other strategies which broadly fall into two groups: first, they can attempt to reduce the amount of information required; second, they can endeavour to increase the coverage and efficiency of information acquisition and transmission.

Reducing information required

Attempts to reduce the amount of information required involve reducing the complexity or strength of factors identified as the major influence on information requirements. Thus a choice may be made to reduce the division of labour by the creation of self-contained units. This involves moving from an organisation based on functional or discipline groups in which 'specialists' are then 'loaned' to product groups, to an organisation based on product groupings which are then 'self-contained' as far as access to specialist help is concerned (see Chapter 5 for further discussion of function-based and product-based structures).

Alternatively, the level of goal performance may be reduced by operating with slack resources (e.g. by maintaining larger inventories of finished goods or stocks of components). Third, remembering Table 4.1, programmes of 'environmental management' may be initiated to gain greater control within their environment. The strategies described in Table 4.1 were direct influence, participating in price fixing, cartels, joint ventures, bargaining with suppliers, general promotion, and vertical or horizontal integration.

Increasing information available

Attempts to increase the amount of information that is processed within the organisation can be approached in vertical terms, between levels, or in horizontal terms, between functions. In terms of level, attempts can be made to improve vertical information systems through supporting the hierarchy with electronic data processing systems and/or more clerical, administrative or planning personnel. Such a strategy was found by Khandwalla (1977) in his study of Canadian enterprises, where experience of complex diverse environments was associated with greater investment in information, planning and control systems.

Lateral relations across boundaries between functions can be improved in a number of ways, as the preceding discussion of integration in the work of Lawrence and Lorsch illustrated. Direct contact or other liaison mechanisms between specialists can be a great help, as can the establishment of integrative positions or departments. Another alternative is a full-blown matrix structure, which will be the subject of detailed discussion in Chapter 5.

None of the strategies which Galbraith summarises are mutually exclusive, and neither are they necessarily the result of conscious choice. Galbraith's argument is that if they are not 'chosen', some of them may emerge by default as a result of people's attempts, albeit possibly unco-ordinated or subconscious, to respond to complexity and uncertainty. On the 'bad' side, performance may be lowered as production finds itself under increasing pressure and no one takes up opportunities to influence suppliers, customers or regulators. Alternatively a great deal of effort may be put into managing one sector of the environment whilst neglecting others, or neglecting to see that internal structures and operations facilitate an appropriate response. On the 'good side' of events happening 'by default', specialists may begin talking to each other informally, thereby developing lateral relations as a way of solving complex problems.

Choosing the right strategy

Although expected benefits may accrue from whichever course of action is chosen or emerges by default, costs will also be incurred. The costs may be in terms of such things as financial investment in new data processing or opportunities missed by reducing scanning or advertising, or higher turnover among valued staff. The critical question for practitioners is, are the costs justified by the benefits or should alternative strategies be chosen? The 'right' balance of tactics and strategies is one which ekes out the scarce resources to just those areas that will facilitate the seizing and creating of opportunities and the working within constraints which cannot, at least in the short term, be altered. Identifying such a 'right' balance and trying to solve it for both the short and the long term is often very difficult, particularly as solutions for one time-scale may spell disaster for another.

Concluding the practical guide

Figure 4.3 summarises the main approach that has been developed in the preceding pages. Of course, one must beware of making simple generalisations or seizing too early on an apparently neat solution. This section of the chapter has suggested that environmental analysis is an important activity for practitioners. The determination of strategies and tactics in the light of analysis, or their emergence by default, will, it is argued, have far-reaching consequences which can be represented as both costs and benefits for different interest groups.

The work of the 'contingency theorists', of whom Thompson, Burns and Stalker, Lawrence and Lorsch and Galbraith are in some ways representative, leads to two general practical conclusions. The first is that the greater the degree of variability and change in the environment, the more adaptive and

FIGURE 4.3
Practical Guide to Managing Interactions across the Boundaries of a Focal Organisation

Given objectives of interest group

↓

Make (or consult) environmental analysis of

↓

    suppliers of inputs

↓

    repositories of outputs

↓

    sources of regulation

↓

What further information is needed?

↓

How can environmental scanning be maintained or improved?

↓

What are the critical sectors over which attempts will be made to increase control?

↓

What tactics are appropriate?

↓

- Focus on greater control in particular set of relationships
- Focus on greater influence and general promotion
- Adjust internal operations
- Adjust internal structure

↓

Given tactical package which is determined or emerges by default:

1. What are likely to be its consequences in the environment in short and long run?

2. What are likely to be its costs in terms of groups within the focal organisation, for example in terms of finance, manpower, morale?

3. Do these costs outweigh likely benefits given objectives of interest groups?

4. Should the tactics or strategy be modified? And so on.

open the structure should be. The second is that the greater the heterogeneity and diversity of environmental sectors, the more specialised the internal structure should be, and consequently the more elaborate the means of integration and co-ordination. On the basis of this guide practitioners can make their own analysis to suggest tactics for a given environmental sector to achieve greater dominance, control and predictability. In doing so they should not forget to look beyond the immediate and intended effects to pick up any second or subsequent order effects in relation to other segments. And, of course, the costs, in terms of time, finance, morale, and so on, must be carefully weighed against any expected benefits. A discussion of the advantages and disadvantages of contingency theory will be contained in the next chapter.

4.5   Analysing the Environment: Turbulence, Dominance, Interorganisational Relations and Networks

Contingency theorists share a concern to help executives cope with or, better still, control the uncertainties, problems or other difficulties that arise in their relationship with parts of their environment, in which they are trying to secure inputs, disburse outputs, and respond to regulation. This approach inclines to a view of organisations as relatively mature dynamic systems which adapt themselves to changes in their environment. The resulting assumption is that powerful people in organisations can and do make and implement plans to cope with disturbances from the environment, even if they are unable to eradicate the source of the disturbance entirely. Those who are unable to emulate their more successful brethren may, by default, preside over their organisation as its slides to decline and ruin. Such a perspective is easily justifiable in practical terms, particularly for larger companies. However, since it is essentially based on a particular position and methodology, it does not facilitate a critical analysis of a number of important issues relating to the social, political and economic context of activities in and between organisations. This will now become the focus of the chapter.

Creating the environment

Selznick's pioneering study of the Tennessee Valley Authority (1949) and C. Wright Mills's (1965) classic analysis of *The Power Elite*, both of which owed obvious debts to the founding fathers of modern sociology, Marx and Weber, opened the way for contemporary students of organisations to develop their work in this direction. However, few people rushed to follow them until the late 1960s and early 1970s, when interest in networks of organisations grew significantly among economists and sociologists as well as investigative journalists – particularly in the USA, but also, for example, with the Insight Team of the *Sunday Times* in the UK and its 'exposures' of the operations of large multinational corporations.

J. K. Galbraith's publication of *The New Industrial State* (1967) was a significant contribution to this resurgence of interest. His commentary on the activities of large corporations in the USA argued that long lead times, heavy capitalisation, specialisation and inflexibility of modern technology meant that market mechanisms were distorted. Consequently, large corporations sought to eliminate markets by vertical integration, control markets by horizontal integration and suspend markets by agreements with 'competitors' on price and output. Rather than 'adapting' to their environments, such corporations were apparently creating them.

Barker (1968) and Weick (1969) were also important in stressing the complexity and political processes embodied in inter-organisational relations. In sympathy with the theme of this section, they argued that people in organisations can take control of other organisations (sectors of their environment), particularly if they have sufficient knowledge about them to appreciate the depth, type and timescale of the constraints they represent. Weick coined the phrase of the 'enacted environment' in the following terms: 'The human creates the environment to which the system then adapts. The human actor does not react to an environment, he enacts it' (1969, p. 64). Similarly, Starbuck (1976) later commented on the way organisation--environment relations became the subject of 'self-fulfilling prophecies': 'the organisation selects the environment it will inhabit, and then it subjectively defines the environment it has selected' (p. 1078). The theme of enactment is now very important in discussions on strategy (see Chapter 2 and, e.g., Smircich and Stubbart, 1985; Mintzberg, 1989).

Crozier's analysis of contemporary France as the 'blocked' or 'stalled' society (1973) fostered further interest which was then taken up by Karpik and Benson in their calls in 1974 to the 8th World Congress of Sociology (subsequently both published in Karpik, 1978a) for more analysis of networks of organisations as political economies. Resonance with these statements was found in Hirsch (1975), who argued that there was a need for studies of organisations in different industrial sectors in order to understand their market conditions and strategies for control. More recent work in this area is found in Morgan (1989).

Far, therefore, from either adapting to changes in their environment or facing extinction, organisations, or at least the people in them, were shown to be managing and creating their own operating condition. Brief mention has already been made to this in the discussion of Jay Galbraith's (1973) strategy of 'environmental management', showing that, even within contingency theory, organisations were not always considered the objects rather than the originators of 'environmental conditions'.

Williamson and institutional economics

Within economics a small school of 'institutional economists' who treated the economic system as part of a complex social system was also gathering force. The publication in 1975 of Oliver E. Williamson's *Markets and Hierarchies:*

Analysis and Antitrust Implications was a landmark for this movement, and it once more focused attention on the structure and dynamics of interorganisational relations. Williamson compares two alternative means of co-ordinating activities between groups and organisations, either through market mechanisms of voluntary exchange and contracts or through degrees of hierarchical structure and legally and procedurally based authority. He maintained that the choice of mechanism is governed by the relative transaction costs involved in each, and that ultimately criteria of efficiency are reflected in the choices made. He argued that the costs of writing and executing complex contracts across a market vary with the characteristics of the human decision-makers involved and the characteristics of the market environment. In an efficient market there are many participants and the price gives all the information required. But transactions via the market become 'inefficient' when there is a condition of 'information impactedness' (i.e. incomplete, biased, inconsistent information) often because the parties possess idiosyncratic knowledge or bounded rationality and there are a small number of participants. These sets of conditions are reflected in, and encourage, some strategic advantages for one and more parties; prices fail accurately to convey all the necessary information and transactions become increasingly costly to execute. Small numbers invite opportunistic behaviour in which those involved make false or empty threats or promises for personal advantage and thus the uncertainties and complexities of the market are aggravated. Hierarchies, Williamson argued, can alleviate market failures by monitoring membership behaviour, establishing procedures for resolving conflict and for providing information and control. Thus the contracting parties have greater control over and knowledge of the uncertainties associated with the transaction and over personal opportunism of the parties involved.

Williamson explored the conditions under which hierarchy will reduce transaction costs in the following three cases: employment relationships, in which he noted movement between sub-contracting and corporate employment, and vertical and horizontal integration between corporations. In his examination of vertical integration in the context of a debate on monopolies policies he argued that vertical integration is a defensible approach for specialised firms that are technologically separable but transactionally interdependent.

Subsequent comment on Williamson's model has criticised it for an over-emphasis on efficiency, which ignores issues of power and domination as criteria which also underlay decisions about the organisation of transactions both within and between organisations (see, e.g., the collection of essays edited by Francis, Turk and Willman, 1983; also Perrow, 1981). Others have argued that markets and hierarchies are not distinctively separate phenomena but that it is possible to find elements of each in the other and indeed to identify a third form of organisation wherein transactions based on trust and co-operation between the parties are the dominant form (see, e.g., Ouchi, 1978, 1981). Whatever the debates and criticisms, however, Williamson is very important for his part in establishing an institutional school of economists committed to analysing the economics of networks of interorganisational relations within a wider social context.

Interorganisational relations

The growth of academic interest in interorganisational relations was also influenced by a popular realisation that large multinational and multidivisional organisations were huge repositories of power and influence in national and international affairs. Vernon (1971) and Mandel (1975) describe how some multinational companies manipulate their financial affairs so that, with mechanisms such as transfer pricing, they can declare profits in those countries where they are liable for least tax. Sampson (1973) graphically described the role of the American-based ITT Corporation in the downfall of the left-wing Allende government in Chile. In less dramatic fashion, large corporations are often wooed by national and local governments who want them to establish their next 'new plant' in South Wales, or the London docklands, or some other area in which they are hoping to generate significant increases in employment. Not surprisingly, therefore, senior executives of these corporations get the 'best deal' they can and often end up receiving considerable grants and subsidies, as well as benefiting from having the ear and sympathies of important politicians.

The growth of complex interorganisational relations is not limited to the industrial and manufacturing sectors. Hall *et al.* (1977) point out that complex social programmes often require increasing interdependence between a variety of agencies. For example, the courts, custodial institutions, statutory and voluntary social work agencies, schools, colleges, employment bureaux and many other agencies might be interlinked in attempting to generate solutions to the problem of youth. They comment that some linkages will be mandatory, like that between the courts and custodial institutions, whereas others will be voluntary and will reflect felt needs collectively to acquire clients and resources, share services and 'carve up' policy spaces.

One of the first contemporary attempts to approach the subject of the environment from a broader perspective rather than from one focal organisation was an article by Emery and Trist (1965b) entitled 'The Causal Texture of Organisational Environments'. They introduced the idea of variation according to the amount of change and structure in the relationships between different parts of environments. An environment of perfect competition with a random distribution of suppliers and customers exhibited little patterned change or structure. Structures of imperfect competition and oligopoly were at an intermediate point, and at the extreme were what they called 'turbulent' environments, where there was a great deal of change which was largely beyond the control of any focal organisation. Thus, although concerned with 'the environment', they had not fully emancipated themselves from the focal organisation; indeed, they suggested that the more turbulent the field, the more decentralised a structure is needed to cope appropriately and the more senior executives need to rely on unobtrusive and personal control through values and norms, rather than on hierarchical or administrative control. Terreberry (1968) developed their suggestion that with rapid changes in technologies, markets, commodity prices, and so on, the late twentieth century was going to be a period in which organisation had to deal with increasingly turbulent, and by implication largely uncontrollable, environments.

The population ecology model

Recent developments of a population ecology model of organisation environments, with its analysis of the 'survival of the fittest' organisational form in a jungle of competitors, lends credence to this view of turbulence. This approach, developed by Aldrich (1979a), among others, for organisational analysis, offers a three-stage model. First, there are variations of organisational forms which are 'specific configurations of goals, boundaries and activities' (Aldrich, 1979a, p. 28). The model is said to be 'indifferent to the ultimate source of variation' (p. 35), which may be planned or unplanned, random or predictable.

The second stage is the selection of those forms that fit their environment best and find a 'niche' within it. A niche is 'created by the intersection of resource constraints – an abstract resource space consisting of a unique combination of resources (information, access to materials, customers, and so on) that could permit a form to survive there' (p. 40). Aldrich stresses the importance of external pressures – for example in product or process innovation – on selection, but also acknowledges that internally members can influence choices. He suggests that people have a tendency to prefer compatibility of forms and congruence with past history. In this way there is a degree of inertia in that criteria used in the past have a currency which may actually outlive their relevance. Anticipating some of his critics and pointing to other directions for the analysis of interorganisational relations, Aldrich notes two features of industrial society which further limit the applicability of a pure form of selection. First, wealth is concentrated into relatively few large organisations which are apparently less vulnerable to failure and rarely disappear into extinction except by merger or acquisition. Second, the growth of the public sector, with contemporary Western governments being concerned to some extent with the disbursement of between two-fifths and three-fifths of national income, is a major factor in giving some institutions and organisations an 'artificial' advantage in the selection process. Thus Aldrich admits that environmental selection of entire organisations is largely limited to small businesses, voluntary associations and those firms which are not liable for receipt of public funds. Nonetheless, he maintains that particular structures and activities within large organisations are subject to selection processes.

The final stage of Aldrich's model involves the retention of positively selected variations in accordance with such factors as 'competitive pressures on business firms, members' pressures on voluntary associations, and political pressures on public agencies' (p. 48).

Elsewhere the author has described how this approach leads Aldrich to underplay issues of power, interest and political processes which are of crucial importance in interorganisational analysis, even in the private sector of small and medium-sized enterprises which is his main arena (Dawson, 1980). It is not that Aldrich never mentions the conscious pursuit of particular interests and the associated politics within and between organisations: it is that they are mentioned almost in passing as a residual form of explanation to be employed when a full explanation of change cannot be based simply on the dynamics of natural selection. In fact, in the later chapters of his book, which deal more with relations between large enterprises institutions and the state, Aldrich himself warms to this theme of politics and domination, but he does not allow it to encourage him to modify his model.

The politics of interorganisational activities

In contrast, Benson's accounts of 'the interorganizational network as a political economy' is centred on the idea of a network of organisations engaged in a significant amount of interaction with each other. The network, an emergent phenomenon, is inextricably linked to struggles to secure the scarce resources of money, authority and legitimacy (Benson, 1975, 1978).

Similarly, Pfeffer and Salancik stress the importance of political activity by members of different organisations as a central part in their analysis of *The External Control of Organizations* (Pfeffer and Salancik, 1978), not that they paint a lurid picture of perpetual seething politics. They acknowledge that at some points political activity is captured into set outcomes (e.g. statements, events, purchases of plant and equipment, or measured aspects of performance), and that these set outcomes present a degree of constraint at least in the short to medium term. They would not dispute Aldrich's two reservations about the limitations of developing any model of conscious strategic choice: first, that the environment is not an ever open purse and there are significant legal, financial and cultural barriers which limit choice, even if these limitations were at some point the result of organised activities; and second, that there are cognitive limits to change such that new opportunities may be unnoticed (Aldrich, 1979a, Chapter 6). Pfeffer and Salancik discuss the social control of organisational change and identify conditions arising from patterns of dependence on and control over resources which predispose interorganisational relations towards degrees of compliance and dominance. They argue that people try to secure favourable patterns of interdependence through securing discretionary control of important resources. If, however, they fail to secure single control of resources, they will try to mitigate the effects of dependence by negotiating favourable collective structures of interorganisational action, possibly through cartels, acquisitions, joint ventures, interlocking directorates and coalitions. Attempts will also be made to lobby governments and their agencies to secure legal and social sanction for their activities and to curtail the activities of those with whom they are in conflict. For example, in Britain the oil companies have been engaged in a long series of discussions with various governments about taxation on North Sea oil. Their pressures for more favourable terms have been rewarded by lower rates of taxation, particularly in relation to new fields, since 1981. The companies argue that lower rates are essential to encourage the development of North Sea oil; but, of course, they also facilitate higher rates of profitability.

Crenson (1971) provides another example of the way networks of powerful organisations can preserve their interests. He compares two steel manufacturing cities in Indiana, USA. Each had similar populations and at one time similar levels of air pollution. One, East Chicago, with a number of steel firms and no strong party organisation, passed an effective clean air ordinance act in 1949. The other, Gary, dominated by US Steel and having a strong party organisation, did not have an anti-pollution ordinance act until 1961, and even then it was not as effective as its counterpart in East Chicago, passed twelve years previously. Crenson argues that US Steel, which dominated Gary as an employer, for a long time prevented the issue from being articulated as a grievance because people 'knew' they would not succeed. Once it became an open issue, US Steel thwarted attempts to do anything about it until at last some action was taken, and even this was strongly influenced by the corporation. All this was accomplished without US Steel formally entering the political arena. This account raises issues of the covert exercise of power which is dealt with in more detail in Chapter 7. In another area, Evan (1972) and Fellmeth (1970) describe how the Interstate Commerce Commission, created in the USA with the formal purpose of regulating interstate commerce in the area of transportation, was 'captured' by the interests of the transport operators to the detriment of consumer interests.

Further evidence in support of the importance of studying interorganisational relations is given by Hirsch (1975), who made a comparative study of industrial performance in pharmaceuticals and musical records. He selected these two industries because he maintained that firms in both sectors shared similar environmental and technological characteristics. They were each dependent on a relatively simple, highly mechanised production process. They shared a strong dependence on 'external gatekeepers' who, as general practitioners or disc jockeys, could effectively control access to their customers. Each industry had experienced strong growth in the 1950s and 1960s and had demonstrated the importance of maintaining high rates of product innovation, as the 'life' of any one drug or any one record was soon put into shadow by new rivals. Yet in spite of these similarities in their environments, the 'best' of the pharmaceuticals firms showed far greater levels of financial performance than the 'best' of the record firms, and this pattern was maintained with those firms which were relatively medium or poor performers in each sector. Hirsch explained this industrial variation in terms of the pharmaceutical firms being much more successful during the 1950s in controlling aspects of their environment. They negotiated pricing and distribution agreements with their competitors, whereas this was not done between the many record companies. They secured support from the federal government and were able to use patent law to stop piracy, whereas copyright law in relation to records was largely ineffective. They also secured a position of strong influence with important opinion, namely leaders in the American Medical Association, whereas those involved in radio and television were not so easy to identify and influence. The role of the state in facilitating organisations in their attempts to gain control over their environments – for example, by passing legislation to prohibit the substitution of chemically equivalent drugs (at reduced rates) to brand names – is clearly extremely important. It should be noted, however, that the state can also sometimes block attempts by organisations to control their environment; for instance, in the UK a reference of a proposed merger to the Monopolies Commissions, or some other regulation against 'unfair trading' (e.g. deceptive advertising) may have this effect.

Hirsch (1975) concludes that firms, and indeed whole industrial sectors of firms, vary in the extent to which they are subject to environmental 'constraints' and the extent to which they can 'create' those 'constraints' for others. In his comparison of pharmaceuticals and records over a decade or so Hirsch describes strategies which both succeeded and failed to secure 'control'. Variation in the success of control attempts is found not only between sectors, but also over time in any sector. In their extended studies of pop music, Hirsch (1972, 1975) and Peterson and Berger (1971) showed how the giant recording studios in the 1920s and 1930s did in fact have strong control over their environment until changes in recording technology, the advent of television and changes in public taste – such as the growth of rock and roll and other changes in the ownership and structure of the indus- try – broke their monopoly power. Furthermore they show that after the 'turbulence' of the 1950s, which was the period in which Hirsch makes his comparison with pharmaceuticals, large corporations in the record industry emerged once more as a source of dominance, both in relation to smaller or 'would be' entrants and to consumers.

Consideration of the findings of Hirsch and his colleagues leads Perrow (1979, p. 213) to a number of conclusions which are important for this analysis. First, while organisations 'adjust' to environmental changes (e.g. technological developments), the 'drive is to control and manipulate the environment'. Second, turbulence can be the result of their own efforts to rationalise and introduce new innovations: 'As Pogo might say: "we have met the environment and he is us".' Third, 'the most salient environment for the majors is other majors; despite competition between them, they collectively evolve strategies to eliminate or absorb threatening minors'. Related to this view is Perrow's argument that the costs of turbulence and change, when it occurs, are 'externalised' to dependent parts of the industry. Thus, in the case of the popular music industry, the costs were borne by the creative artists or producers or support firms and not by the recording companies themselves. Perrow therefore argues the need for practitioners and analysts to be aware of what networks exist, to judge how tightly or loosely the parts are connected, how strong is the dependence and other links between the parts, and also to understand the rationalisations and the logic which provide a 'gloss' to cover the real dynamics of power, domination, resistance and submission.

4.6   Concluding Remarks

Developments in the study of networks of interorganisational relations provide a very important context for understanding relationships between a focal organisation and parts of its environment, which must be seen to include national and international agencies and loose networks, as well as more easily identifiable formal organisations. As always, there is no absolutely right model. Some organisations appear at particular times to be comparatively helpless in the face of events which are not within the control of their members. Many of them consequently decline and disappear. But an injection of new blood and different perspectives and strategies, or other changes in technologies or markets, may create conditions in which adaptation is possible. At the other extreme are the large and powerful organisations which are the creators of turbulence for others. Examples of each type of organisation tend typically to come from different methodologies. Detailed studies of individual, usually large, firms provide evidence for adaptation and dominance, whereas population studies of whole sectors, and indeed a cursory glance at bankruptcy rates, tend to support the maxims of the 'survival of the fittest' and the 'failure of the unfittest'.

Undoubtedly people in organisations do face a lot of change and uncertainty. The evidence is available for all to see: the effects of world recession, sharp changes in commodity prices and interest rates, political upheavals in many parts of the world, startling rates and directions of technological change, the growth of multinational and multidivisional organisations, joint ventures, cartels and dramatic changes in political and social values. But here is the paradox. These are changes that are largely created by the activities of political, economic and business organisations. Only when thus 'created', often in response to an opportunity or constraint located in the 'environment', do they become 'turbulence out there' for other organisations (which, incidentally, are usually those of less power and strength than those creating the apparent chaos).

Although many people employed in enterprises of every shape and size do feel that the world in the late twentieth century presents an appallingly complex and changeable jungle, only some of them would see the jungle as totally impenetrable. The view of environments and organisations that must be carried forward from this chapter is that the distinction between the two is arbitrary and idiosyncratically related to particular positions and points of view. But for the practitioner, who has a particular position and point of view, this chapter has attempted to draw as accurate a map of the jungle as possible to help the individual plan the route forward and understand how she entered the jungle in the first place!

Co-ordination and Control: Structure and Organisation Design **5**

5.1 Addressing the Imperative for Co-ordination and Control

Organisations have been discussed as collections of interest groups backed up by varying degrees of power and influence. Neither strategy nor tactics can be thought of as objects of consensus, so how is an operational consensus imposed or developed? How are the centrifugal forces inherent in collections of diverse interest groups contained? In other words, how is co-ordination across different activities and control across different levels achieved?

Co-ordination becomes a challenge to people in any organisation as soon as there is any form of division of labour. It is required to some extent in all situations in which goods and services are produced, except in those cases where one person alone begins and completes a job, whether it be making shoes, cultivating land or entertaining. As soon as other people are involved and the tasks and responsibilities are divided in some way, the issue arises of choosing an appropriate means of co-ordinating the different activities. How else, for example, can one ensure that parts that are to be manufactured separately will fit together and be compatible, that they are made in appropriate numbers, that work is not duplicated, and so on? Even if different individuals and groups do different jobs and yet co-exist within totally consensual groups, some means of co-ordination must still be found.

However, in most collectivities consensus is never fully attained (see Chapter 2). There are often differences over major issues such as future strategies, how current work should be done, and how proceeds should be disbursed. Sometimes such differences are explicit, sometimes they are implicit and sometimes they are resolved before their potential has been developed. Nonetheless, even if just at a potential stage, the possibility of differences arising creates another imperative: that is, to develop some means of control, by which individuals and groups are influenced, guided or forced to act in ways determined by others.

In addressing the question of how co-ordination and control are achieved, one needs to consider the development of structures and cultures within organisations. The structure of an organisation refers to the socially created pattern of rules, roles and relationships that exist within it. The culture of an organisation refers to the collection of values and beliefs which are found within it.

Structures and cultures are important reference points when thinking about organisations. Customers notice whether or not they are seeking a service from a very hierarchical organisation with everyone conscious of their place on a formal ladder; new recruits wonder how and where they they will fit in; clients question whether the organisation is 'geared up' to provide the sort of service they require and managers consider whether their workforce has too little or too much discretion to do their job. The responses to these questions will depend on the appropriateness of the fit between the organisation's structure and culture on the one hand and its strategy on the other.

The next two chapters are concerned with the definition and place of structure and culture in organisational analysis, the relationship between these two constructs and their place in acting as the 'glue' which facilitates co-ordination and control. The metaphor of glue can be developed. The imperative is not for some 'super strong glue' which sticks fragments together 'for ever' but rather for a 'post-it' type glue which is just strong enough to hold the present constellation of fragments together but which will allow the parts to be refixed if regrouped or reformulated. The imperative for structures and cultures is that they should be strong enough to secure stability to facilitate the achievement of objectives, and yet encourage flexibility for growth and such responsiveness to and creation in environments as environmental scanning suggests is appropriate (see Chapter 4). The remainder of this chapter deals with structure; Chapter 6 deals with culture.

5.2 Defining Structure

Structure is a social creation of rules, roles and relationships which at best facilitates effective coordination and control, as far as corporate governors are concerned. Other groups may, however, find that the created structure effectively frustrates the pursuit of their objectives and interests. At other times structures seem to serve no one's interests but to represent remnants of history and misjudgement. The corollary of structure as a means for securing coordination and control for dominant interest groups is that it can also be the means by which people resist control and fragment attempts at coordination. In short, depending upon one's interests, structure can be seen to be appropriate or inappropriate and to facilitate control *or* resistance and coordination *or* fragmentation. The practical task is to design structures which create appropriate levels of control and coordination. Figure 5.1 provides a summary of the elements of structure. This shows it is the shorthand label attached to the collection of things which defines how jobs are to be done, how job-holders will relate to one another, and the rules and procedures which formally govern work activities. Issues associated with the definition and control of individual job-holders have already been discussed in Chapter 1, including the six main ways in which control can be achieved (i.e. through unobtrusive, personal, output, hierarchical, administrative and technological means; see Figure 1.3). The processes of communication and decision-making are discussed in Chapter 8. Thus, of the elements in Figure 5.1, the middle element concerning relationships in organisations will be the major focus of the first part of this chapter. It will be analysed in terms of two dimensions: boundaries and formality.

5.3 Relationship Boundaries: Where to Draw the Lines

There are two important boundaries between different parts of organisations: those between levels in the vertical plane and those between groups in the

---

FIGURE 5.1
Elements of Structure in Organisations

SPECIFYING INDIVIDUAL ROLES

Allocation of tasks

Job definitions

SPECIFYING RELATIONSHIPS

Reporting relationships

Delegating relationships

Grouping individuals into teams/
departments

SPECIFYING RULES AND SYSTEMS

Control systems and procedures

Communication systems

Rules governing terms and conditions of
employment

Rules governing processes of planning and
decision-making

---

horizontal plane. Grossly simplifying, one can say that relationships across levels are broadly concerned with the control/resistance axis of structure, and those across functions with the co-ordination/fragmentation axis, although elements of each are found in both. There is great variation in the extent and form of boundary crossing between levels and functions.

Vertical relationships between levels

Organisations where the vertical boundaries between levels are clearly marked and assume great significance for participants are said to have a strong hierarchy. Ones with a flatter structure, with fewer levels and possibly less significance attached to the boundaries, have a weak hierarchy. Commentators and consultants on organisation structure have been much concerned with the balance between the height or number of levels in the hierarchy and the span of control or the number of subordinates answerable to each superior. Simplifying, one can see that there is a trade-off to be made between the number of levels and the average span of control. The advantages of tall structures, apart from the relative reduction in spans of control which arguably lessens the load on superiors and increases control, are sometimes said to be in terms of personnel policies. Taller structures contain more steps for promotion, which some would argue helps to maintain the commitment and loyalty of valued specialists and highly regarded generalists. However, personnel policies can also be supported by grading and evaluating schemes, whereby individuals can move between grades without having to move between levels on an organisation chart. The disadvantages of a tall hierarchy are that it can exacerbate problems of communication and implementation of policies if they are decided by people at the top. There are now many advocates for 'flatter' organisations, for less emphasis on hierarchy and formal authority and for more emphasis on creating shared feelings of belonging and commitment to one organisation (Kanter, 1983). These approaches will be further discussed in the section on culture.

Where there is great dependence on hierarchical controls or a high frequency of unexpected problems, there are strong arguments for limiting spans of control. If, however, output, administrative and technological controls are important, the arguments for limiting spans of control are much weaker. The degree of similarity and geographical distance between activities is also a relevant consideration in decisions about spans of control and numbers of levels.

Horizontal relationships between groups

Moving to consider horizontal boundaries between functions or departments, three basic forms of established relationships can be easily identified. First, organisations where the horizontal divisions are predominantly in terms of different functions are said to have a functional structure, as illustrated in

Figure 5.2. This contrasts with a second form of organisation where the predominant horizontal boundaries are between product groups in which case, as in Figure 5.3, one has a product organisation.

In accounting for the development of different organisational forms, Stewart (1983) suggests that functional structures are usually the first to develop in response to the tensions which arise when a group of people first get together as an embryonic organisation to produce goods and services. The functional structure emerges from a pioneering phase in response to crises which are articulated in terms of 'We're getting too big', 'We want guidelines', 'There's too much firefighting round here', 'We need a way of deciding on priorities.' Thus Stewart argues that a functional structure, with its clear

FIGURE 5.1
Typical Example of Functional Organisation

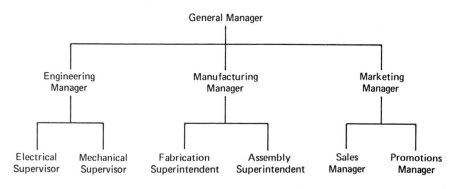

FIGURE 5.3
Typical Example of Product Organisation

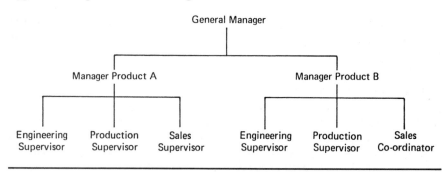

systems, clear lines of responsibility and the facility for people to belong to specialist groups, answers the needs of the pioneers who find it too chaotic and ineffective to continue with a lack of organisation. However, the problems of a functional structure are that it can lead to a lack of integration between the specialists, a growth of bureaucratic paperwork, an 'unhealthy' attempt to build and defend specialist empires and, above all, the construction of barricades against the customer.

A switch to an organisation based on products rather than functions appears, then, to provide a solution to these problems. Even then, however, growth presents other problems as product groupings demand more autonomy so that they can develop in ways which are independent of other product groupings, and yet more appropriate to their environmental context.

In this way, Stewart argues, we can understand the development of a divisionalised or 'M' form of structure, in which operational decision-making and profit responsibility are assigned to general managers of divisions. In this structure corporate headquarters is mainly concerned with strategic planning and decision-making, project and policy appraisal, the allocation of resources between divisions, overall financial control and corporate performance. This allows for the development of synergy in terms of financial management and strategic policy, and yet preserves operational autonomy: in other words, an attempt to secure the best of both a 'centralised' and a 'decentralised' approach.

Matrix structures

A similar impetus to combine the advantages of contrasting forms of organisation can be found in the development of matrix organisations as a third form. Figure 5.4 shows that in a matrix neither a product nor a functional organisation predominates but there is a product organisation overlying a functional organisation. In such cases individual specialists are dedicated to a clearly identified product group in which they have a product or project manager, while at the same time maintaining a formal relationship with their functional manager.

The development of matrix structures is usually accounted for in terms of offering solutions to the difficulties of ensuring the quality and extent of lateral relationships required from people working with high technology or in rapidly changing markets.

Experience in the late 1950s and early 1960s suggested that the advantages associated with functionally-based structures made them appropriate in contexts other than those which were best suited by the development of a product-based structure. Where technically high standards of work were at a premium, particularly in small organisations in a relatively narrow field of activity and where long-term growth was important, the functional structure appeared to be the most appropriate. Co-ordination could be made at the top of the hierarchy, specialist overheads could be shared out economically, and

FIGURE 5.4
Typical Example of Matrix Organisation

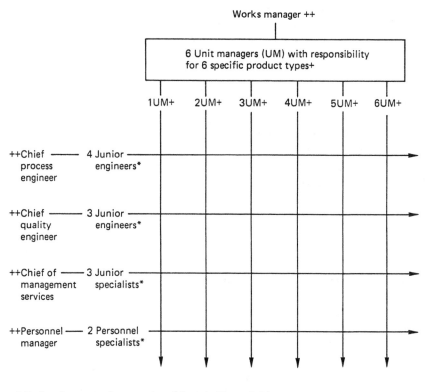

+ Each unit manager has a product 'hierarchy' beneath him.
* Each specialist is dedicated to one or more product types.
++ Members of management committee of factory.

an excellent career path was available for the specialists who had such important roles to play. Where, however, short-term financial considerations or a focus for customer contact were important, and where the enterprise had several diversified product markets or geographical areas to serve, or utilised a wide range of different technologies, then product groupings had a lot to recommend them. But what, the question arose, were people to do if they were involved in senior positions in an organisation where they felt it was important to try to foster technical excellence and yet produce articles which satisfied the customer in terms of quality, were produced to budgeted cost and were delivered to agreed delivery dates?

In a fascinating account of the development of matrix structures in the US aerospace industry, Kingdon (1973) chronicles how people had been content with functionally-based technical excellence until the newly elected President Kennedy publicly promised to have a man on the moon by 1970, and hence time became an important variable. At the same time American taxpayers and members of Senate and Congress wanted to see evidence of 'value for money'. In response to the felt need to try to get the best out of both the product and functional worlds, matrix structures like that illustrated in Figure 5.4 were developed within NASA. Furthermore, those responsible for procuring components or services for the space programme looked for evidence among their suppliers and sub-contractors that they were similarly organised.

In matrix structures, specialists retain membership of a functional group and some allegiance to their specialist manager, but at the same time they are dedicated to particular product or project teams. Placed in the somewhat unenviable position of answering to two bosses, members of these structures often find them somewhat uncomfortable workplaces. They also find that they have to spend a great deal of time in meetings, sorting out priorities and relationships. Thus matrix structures emerged as fairly costly to maintain. Nonetheless, their protagonists feel that such local and personal difficulties are easily offset by the improvements in communication, decision-making and implementation that were said to result (Knight, 1977). Matrix structures are the fullest expression of investment in lateral links which Jay Galbraith advocated in his analysis of strategies to cope with uncertainty and complexity (Figure 4.2). However, regardless of the theory, in practice they sometimes become highly formalised and bureaucratised, and the free flow of information that was envisaged by their creators is not always a dominant feature.

5.4 Formality of Relationships

Just as roles may be more or less formally defined in job descriptions, so the relationships that exist vary in the extent to which they are formally defined in organisation charts, written rules and procedures and other manuals. But beyond the formal prescriptions of roles and relationship (which in a sense are the bare bones of structure) there are also informal prescriptions which provide the flesh for the bones and so make significant contributions to the form that is perceived. The informal side reflects custom, practice and tradition, and is displayed in actual rather than formally described behaviour. At an intermediate level, the effects of such things as payment systems and appraisal schemes will profoundly affect the way work is undertaken. If payment is on a piecework rate, then it is likely that the job-holders will place more emphasis on the number of completed items than on minimising materials wastage, whereas if there is a bonus paid at the end of the day for efficient use of materials and minimising wastage one would expect a different work pattern to emerge. The patterned regularities of formal and informal roles, rules and relationships are influenced by, but do not simply reflect, individual personalities. This is one of the reasons why organisations are always more than a collection of people, but yet are collective entities definable in terms of their own structures and processes.

Bureaucracy

One of the most celebrated and widespread forms of structure is a bureaucracy, in which there are clear formal prescriptions of roles and relationships, an extensive rule book and set of procedures. Characteristic of early forms of government and industrial organisation, bureaucracy received much consideration from and after the analysis by Max Weber.

Albrow (1970), in an excellent critical commentary on bureaucracy, notes that there is a problem with the original sources of Weber. He comments:

> In terms of the influence it has exerted and the argument it has stimulated Weber's writing on bureaucracy is more important than the sum total of [other] contributions. Yet there is a dearth of detailed exposition of his work, as opposed to straightforward borrowing of particular ideas on the one hand, or critical discussions of some fragment of his writing on the other. (p. 37)

Much of the commentary on Weber has, in fact, derived from the Parsons and Henderson translation of his *Theory of Social and Economic Organisation* (1947), rather than from original sources, and some of the problems discussed subsequently seem to arise more from the translation than from the original.

Weber developed his ideas of bureaucracy on the basis of an analysis of three different forms of authority which at different times and in different places in world history had, he argued, provided the basis for willing compliance to a ruler's command. His first base of authority is charisma, where the position of the powerful is maintained through the strength of individual personality or sacred characteristics. Second, there is tradition, where positions of authority are assigned according to custom, practice and birthright. Third, there is what Weber called legal rational authority, whereby the positions of the powerful are enshrined in laws that are accepted by those involved as being rational for the pursuit of objectives. In this context the laws and rules provide the basis for legitimate authority, with obedience and compliance being due to the office, not to the person holding it.

Weber's definition of bureaucracy follows directly from this analysis. His specific characteristics of bureaucracy follow directly from the principle of legal rational authority. In addition to rules, these characteristics include: official tasks organised on a continuous, regulated basis; tasks divided into functionally distinct spheres; offices arranged hierarchically; full-time officers engaged on contract; training of officers, recruited for expertise; and separate resources for individual officers and collective organisation.

Weber felt that bureaucracy represented a technically efficient form of organisation, but that in government it might lead to a concentration of power which would be a threat to democracy and freedom. He was far more concerned with these wider social and historical analyses and with broader issues of legitimacy, control and compliance, than he was with the practical results – whether good or bad – of bureaucratic functioning for the achievement of goals of dominant groups or individuals. Subsequent analysts of behaviour and organisation have, however, taken Weber's typology of bureaucracy and commented on its implications for people and organisation. With developments in scientific management and the search for 'rationalisation' to secure the elimination of waste associated with names such as F. W. Taylor (1911), L. Urwick (1929) and Henri Fayol (1916), there was much support in the early twentieth century for bureaucratic systems of organisation for their efficiency and stability. They were also praised for their apparent emphasis on fairness and justice for employees, clients and customers.

Human responses to bureaucracy

With changing managerial philosophies, a greater emphasis on 'human relations' and a concern about the effects of impersonal bureaucratic systems on motivation and co-ordination, some commentators became less enthusiastic about formal bureaucracy. During the 1950s and 1960s a number of important studies emphasised the 'unanticipated' consequences of bureaucratic forms of organisation. Merton's commentary on the bureaucratic personality suggested that the bureaucratic requirements for reliability could well lead to an overrigidity in the behaviour of bureaucrats. At its most extreme this meant that the means of administration (form filling, following rules and procedures, etc.) became ends in themselves, and the 'real goals' of the organisation were forgotten: for example, accountants might be more concerned with neat and tidy ledgers and less with interpreting accounts. Merton described this response as 'trained incapacity' – quite the reverse of the efficient model suggested by Weber and yet nonetheless the result of graded career structures which emphasised impersonality (Merton, 1957, Chapter 6). In another area, Selznick's (1949) study of the Tennessee Valley Authority highlighted how the delegation of authority to specialised groups of officers could lead to the formation of strong sub-groups who could effectively pursue their own sectional interests, often to the detriment or neglect of others in the organisation. Furthermore, Gouldner's (1954) study of a gypsum mine and processing plant showed how the imposition of rules which were resented established basic minimum requirements for behaviour which were never exceeded. This led to an increase in direct control and supervision which increased tension between levels and so increased the emphasis on rules and on close supervision. In a sense Gouldner was documenting a crisis of 'legitimacy' in a situation where rules were no longer seen as legitimate and control was restricted.

In commenting on these three cases of 'unanticipated consequences', March and Simon interpreted them as the inappropriate imposition of a mechanistic control model which disregarded people and generated a vicious circle of negative human responses, which was 'answered' by increasing emphasis on the 'offending bureaucratic principle', whether that was reliability, delegation or impersonal rules (March and Simon, 1958, pp. 41–5).

Discussion of the unanticipated consequences of bureaucracy was associated with a growth of interest in 'informal' aspects of organisation which apparently flourished outside the stipulations of hierarchy and rules. These could, as in the three cases given above, act against the achievement of objectives of those at the top of the hierarchy, but the reverse was equally possible.

An awareness that everything could not always be preordained and subject to hierarchy and rules led some commentators to question the viability of bureaucracy as an appropriate form of organisation in uncertain circumstances. For example, it seemed inappropriate if its members were dealing with high rates of technical, market or political change involving the employment of technically excellent professional specialists who may not easily fit into a bureaucratic context. Bennis, for example, concluded that 'Bureaucracy was a monumental discovery for harnessing the muscle power of the industrial revolution. In today's world it is a lifeless crutch that is no longer useful' (Bennis, 1966, p. 263). He suggested a basic shift in managerial philosophy based on a different, more complex conception of people as not so easily manipulable and a new concept of power with emphasis on collaboration, consultation and democracy.

In spite of misgivings about the efficiency and flexibility of bureaucracies for those at the top of the hierarchy and the concern about their effects on those at the bottom, bureaucratic features are still the hallmark of many contemporary organisations. Even if all Weber's characteristics are not always found together, sufficient of them are found often enough to make bureaucracy the most common form of organisation in the middle and late twentieth century.

Size and structure

It has been suggested that the spread of bureaucratic systems is associated with trends towards an increase in the average size of organisations. The Aston studies in the UK by Pugh and his colleagues (1969a, 1969b, 1976a, 1976b) of forty-six work organisations, and studies by Blau and Schoenherr (1971) of fifty-three US employment security agencies, including 1201 local offices and 387 major functional divisions, suggested a strong relationship between bureaucratic structure and size: the larger the organisation, the greater the degree of bureaucratisation, with more formal means for control and co-ordination. This suggested relationship accords with experience to some extent, but the studies relating size and bureaucracy have been subject to some criticism. To begin with there has been criticism of their measures of bureaucracy, such as standardisation, formalisation, specialisation and centralisation. Second, it is argued that causal relationships have been improperly deduced from cross-sectional data. For example, Aldrich (1972), re-examining the Aston findings, suggested that rather than increases in size 'causing' increases in bureaucracy, a number of environmental and technological factors created conditions conducive to bureaucratic forms which then facilitated increases in size. There is insufficient space in this introductory text to dwell on these criticisms, but students should consult Mindlin and Aldrich (1975), Pennings (1973) and Donaldson (1976) for further discussion.

Leaving aside issues of causality, one can conclude that size and bureaucratisation are correlated, although this is more likely to be due not to 'size *per se*' but to its implications for problems of control and co-ordination and the alternative solutions that are offered for solving these problems (Weick, 1969, p. 25). This was rather the conclusion of the national study of eighty-two organisations by Child and colleagues which was the follow-up to the Aston study. Child and Mansfield (1972) found that size, technology and degree of contact with the environment were all positively associated with complexity, by which they meant specialisation and expertise; complexity in turn was associated with formalisation and standardisation. Size was also found to be independently associated with decentralisation, which in turn had a positive relationship with formalisation and standardisation (Child, 1972). Thus Child concludes that organisational complexity, rather than size with which it is correlated, is a major predictor of standardisation and formalisation.

Variations in bureaucratic forms

The Aston studies were also important in demonstrating that bureaucracy was not a unitary concept. Using three dimensions, Pugh and his colleagues identified the seven different types of 'bureaucracy' shown in Figure 5.5. The first of the three dimensions concerned whether control over work activities was exercised in a personal fashion through the line, or whether work was impersonally controlled by administrative procedures or technological controls. The second referred to the extent to which activities were highly structured in terms of standardisation, formalisation, specialisation and the number of levels in the hierarchy. The third covered the extent to which authority to take decisions was highly concentrated and centralised or dispersed and fragmented. Organisations which were impersonally controlled, with highly structured activities and concentrated authority, were given the name 'full bureaucracies' and these largely conformed to the Weberian type. Varying degrees of 'workflow bureaucracies' were identified as being impersonally controlled, but with dispersed authority and variation in the extent to which work was structured. Personal line control and

FIGURE 5.5
An Empirical Taxonomy of Bureaucratic Structures

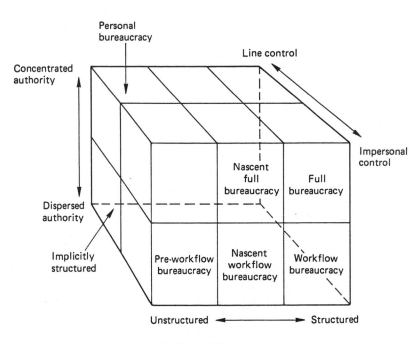

SOURCE:from Hickson and Hinings (1969), p. 123.

unstructured activities were represented as 'personal bureaucracies' (with concentrated authority) or 'implicitly structured' (with dispersed authority: Pugh, 1969b).

Thus it was suggested that elements of bureaucracy were not necessarily always found together but could vary independently of one another. In particular, one could have highly structured activities and impersonal control and yet dispersed authority. Indeed, it has been argued that the structuring of activities actually facilitates decentralisation because many of the parameters and premises that will form the basis of decision-making are established through bureaucratic and unobtrusive controls, and thus dominant groups can encourage delegation within these well-defined, or well-internalised, limits.

5.5   Contingency Theory

As scholars and practitioners became aware of the co-existence of different forms of structure in organisations, as they noted that firms, apparently equally successful or unsuccessful, could be structured in different ways, interest became focused on the question of what makes some structures appropriate and desirable in some circumstances and inappropriate and undesirable in others. The work of Burns and Stalker (1961), Lawrence and Lorsch (1967) and Galbraith (1973) discussed in Chapter 4 displays how scholars discovered the importance of fitting the structure to characteristics of the environment. Similarly the work of Woodward (1965, 1970), Thompson (1967) and Perrow (1970), discussed in Chapter 3, displays the importance of fitting the structure to characteristics of the technology in order to secure strong corporate performance. The common key characteristics of the environment and technology which were seen to underpin these relationships were the extent to which they created complexity and uncertainty which had to be handled within the organisation.

It was through such research and discussion about the applicability, efficiency and effects of different organisational forms in different contexts that a 'contingency theory' of organisation structure was developed. Grossly simplifying, a central theme of this analysis was that the more uncertain and complex the context (as determined by age, size, technologies, product, capital and labour markets) the more organic and flexible the structure needs to be, and the more need there is for information to flow vertically between levels and horizontally between functions. In contrast, the more certain and less complex the context, the more, it is argued, structures can be mechanistic, with greater emphasis on hierarchy and standard rules and procedures. Age and size were also often considered as contingent factors, with longer histories and larger sizes being associated with more mechanistic structures.

Subsequent developments in contingency theory have led to more complex models, as is shown, for example, in the papers by Lawrence on 'The Harvard Organization and Environment Research Programe', and by Van de Ven on 'The Organization Assessment Programe', which were both published in 1981 following a conference in 1980 at the University of Pennsylvania on recent developments in organisation design and behaviour. But, whatever the complex embellishments, the more systematic measurements and the more precise definitions of variables, the main thrust of the contingency arguments remains largely unchanged. Rather than summarising a variety of recent developments, one example of the more complex, more reflective contingency analyses from Mintzberg (1979) will be discussed. This is not to imply that this is necessarily more convincing than that of Lawrence, with his nine-cell analysis of structural forms in terms of variations in resource tensions and strategic uncertainties, or that of Van de Ven, with his nine-cell grid of different types of horizontal and vertical differentiations, or indeed the schemes of other people. The text concentrates on Mintzberg as an example of these more complex contingency developments since space does not allow for a detailed description of other, similar endeavours.

Mintzberg: five structural configurations

Mintzberg's synthesis of contingency theory is based on his conception of organisations in terms of five basic parts. At the bottom is the *operating core*, 'wherein the operators carry out the basic work of the organisation – the input, processing, output and direct support tasks associated with producing the products or services' (p. 19). This includes purchasing agents, machine operators, assemblers, and people in sales and distribution. They are supervised by people in superior levels who are in the *middle line*, which includes production, marketing and distribution, supervisors and managers. Above this group are people in the *strategic apex*, who are 'charged with ensuring that the organization serve its mission in an effective way, and also that it serves the needs of those who control or otherwise have power over the organization' (p. 25). Members of the board of directors and their immediate associates usually constitute the strategic apex. As well as differentiation between levels, there are significant differences, within the operating core and middle line, between different departments of production, sales and distribution. In addition, two significant groups of specialists are identified. First, members of the *technostructure* establish and maintain the administrative and technological controls which standardise and specify activities, outputs and skills relevant to the operating core and middle lines. This group includes industrial engineers, budget analysts, planners and personnel specialists. Second, *support staff* are concerned to make the organisation more self-contained and less dependent on outside services (e.g. legal counsel, industrial relations, mailroom and cafeteria). Mintzberg argues that each part represents a 'pull' on the organisation as it attempts to increase its power and importance. The strategic apex represents a 'pull to centralise', the technostructure a 'pull to standardise', the operating core a 'pull to professionalize', the middle line a 'pull to Balkanize', and the support staff a 'pull to collaborate'. In a way reminiscent of Woodward, Lawrence and earlier contingency theorists, Mintzberg argues that the degree of complexity and certainty generated by specific configurations of contingency factors supports different patterns of relative dominance between the five parts.

Using this basic model Mintzberg suggests five configurations of internal structure and function as most appropriate to deal with different sets of contingency factors, reflecting variation in the organisation's age, size, technical system and environment (Mintzberg, 1979, pp. 466–7). Mintzberg's discussion will be briefly summarised and related to the six different types of control already identified in Chapter 1 (see Figure 1.3). The *simple structure* has little or no technostructure, few support staff, a loose division of labour, low specialisation and a small managerial hierarchy operating in an organic fashion. Direct supervision is the key co-ordinating mechanism, with a hierarchical form of control being typical. Important decisions are handled centrally, and the strategic apex – often one or two people – is the dominant part of the structure. Mintzberg suggests that many organisations conform to this model in their early years of formation. However, some mature organisations, particularly those operating in simple but dynamic and sometimes hostile environments, with simple technologies which do not in themselves control the work of operators, remain in this form.

The *machine bureaucracy* thrives in typically old and large organisations, with technologies which regulate and control work in a non-automated way, in stable and simple environments. Standardisation of work is the key co-ordinating mechanism and administrative and technological forms of control predominate. The technostructure, which provides the analysts who standardise the operators' work within the parameters of the regulating technology, emerges as dominant. Rules and regulations, formal communication and hierarchical chains of authority and decision-making are the hallmarks of this mechanistic system.

In contrast, the third form, *professional bureaucracy*, flourishes with technologies which are relatively simple but dependent on a complex knowledge base, and in environments which are complex but stable. In this context the professionals in the operating core control their own work of diagnosis and problem-solving, and there is a high degree of both vertical and horizontal decentralisation. The professional operating core predominates in a situation characterized by unobtrusive controls and co-ordination through the standardisation of skills. Nonetheless, there is a fair degree of bureaucratisation which particularly affects the categorising of clients and the application of collective means for peer control work. Both of these characteristics can give rise to conflicts: the former with clients or their representatives, and the latter with administrators (see Chapter 2).

The fourth, *divisionalised* form flourishes where a very large organisation has reached a mature point in several product markets. Its technical systems are often similar to those of machine bureaucracies but they are more easily divisible and provide products for relatively simple and stable but diversified markets. The middle line reigns comparatively supreme, and control is largely exercised through the standardisation of outputs and the careful measurement of performance. This is often done in terms of direct profit and loss accounting in private enterprises. Communication between headquarters and the divisions is highly formalised and often restricted to the exchange of targets from headquarters with results from the divisions.

Mintzberg calls his final typical configuration *adhocracy*, and argues that it flourishes in complex, dynamic, sometimes disparate environments. Co-ordination is largely achieved through mutual adjustment and control exercised in a personal or unobtrusive way. Adhocracy is said to have two forms. First, there is the operating adhocracy in which the support staff and operating core predominate and spend their time innovating and solving problems directly on behalf of their clients. This form displays a complete blend of administrative and operating work and is often found in the early stages of organisational formation. In contrast, the administrative adhocracy makes a sharp distinction between the dominant administrative support component and the operating core, with the latter severely truncated. The administrative adhocracy is thus concerned, in Mintzberg's words, not to serve clients but to serve itself. It is found particularly in organisations that are characterised either by sophisticated automated technologies, which in themselves standardise and control operations, or else make extensive use of sub-contracting in their operations. In both forms of adhocracy, people in the administrative adhocracy are 'free' to develop and innovate for the future. The support staff are the dominant group and the structure is characterised by everything that is organic rather than mechanistic. Other characteristics include highly trained specialists deployed in market-based project teams which override traditional line-staff distinctions and place a strong emphasis on liaison devices to encourage mutual adjustment within and between teams. Innovation and change rather than stability are the gods of this form of organisation.

As in most contingency approaches, Mintzberg acknowledges that while each of these forms of organisation is appropriate to different contexts, they each nonetheless create problems. For example, the simple structure risks alienating its members who may resent their lack of involvement in decision-making. The machine bureaucracy may be resented for an overrestrictive approach to job design and decision-making. Moreover, the centralisation of information and decisions may overburden top management and quickly create problems if and when change is required. As regards the third form, Mintzberg comments that the professional bureaucracy does in many ways succeed in

> answering two of the paramount needs of contemporary men and women. It is democratic, disseminating its power directly to its workers (at least those who are professional) and it provides them with extensive autonomy, freeing them even of the need to coordinate closely with their peers, and all of the pressures and politics that entails. (p. 371)

However, he notes that for outsiders, particularly clients, there is virtually no check or control on the professional's work apart from the oversight of other professionals. Another problem is that there is often no home for the slightly 'off-centre' professional, even though she may be developing valid responses to client needs which eventually will become highly recognised and respected. There are also all the problems which Chapter 2 discussed concerning the relationship between professionals and their administrators.

The fourth form, divisionalisation, is similarly beset with problems that are inextricably linked to its positive features. For example,

> it trains general managers, but then gives them less autonomy than does the independent business . . . it protects vulnerable operations during economic slumps, including some that later prove to have not been worth protecting; its control systems encourage the steady improvement of financial performance yet discourage true entrepreneurial innovations

. . . overall the pure Divisionalised form (i.e. the conglomerate form) may offer some advantages over a weak system of boards of directors and inefficient capital market; but most of those advantages would probably disappear if certain problems in capital markets and boards were rectified. (p. 423)

Lastly, the adhocracy, with all its advantageous encouragement of innovation, is nonetheless seen as the least stable form of structure. Many forces encourage greater degrees of bureaucratisation within adhocracies, not least individual intolerance of ambiguity and the high costs of communication. Yet Mintzberg comments on the fashionable element of adhocracy: 'if simple structure and machine bureaucracy were yesterday's structures, and professional bureauracy and the divisionalised form are today's, then adhocracy is clearly tomorrow's' (p. 459).

It is said to be especially suited, it will be recalled, for complex and dynamic environments, for sophisticated and automated technologies, and for educated and highly trained specialists. One of the most usual manifestations of an adhocracy is in some form of matrix structure. In a sense the development of matrix structures marks a pinnacle of development in contingency theory. Indeed, Paul Lawrence said of the book he wrote with Davis on matrix structures (Davis and Lawrence, 1977) that it was a practical application of contingency theory (Lawrence, 1981, p. 313). The spread of matrix structures marks the choice of a form of organisation which is advertised to those in positions of power as the best way to meet the demands of particular technological, political and economic environments.

Variants of the matrix theme are now found in many different industrial sectors and in the realms of educational and social service agencies. The extent and speed with which this 'new' organisational form has been adopted is testimony to the persuasiveness (and possibly the inherent validity) of a contingency approach.

However, in considering why organisational forms emerge in the way they do, it is difficult to unravel cause and effect and to know to what extent there is a 'bandwagon' with a trendy new form of organisation being seen as the solution to a range of problems. Just how valid is contingency theory as a form of analysis? And can this question be separated from the issue of whether it provides a satisfactory pragmatic prescriptive guide for reorganisation? It is to questions such as these that we now turn.

5.6 The Analytical Validity and Practical Applicability of Contingency Theory

Material already presented in this and previous chapters on technology and environment suggests that contingency theory has some face validity and appears supported by common sense at a general level. Yet the fruits of its application in specific cases appear to be limited, and it has been subject to considerable methodological and analytical criticism (see, e.g., Donaldson, 1976; Wood, 1979). Contingency theory is a good but limited prescriptive guide for the practitioner when it comes to making decisions about structures. Furthermore, structures have a real, but limited, contribution to make to organisational performance. On the other hand, contingency theory leaves quite a lot to be desired as an analytical basis for understanding the dynamics, activities and outcomes associated with organisations. The reasons for its genuine but limited practical applicability and its limitations as a form of analysis are interrelated and will be discussed together. They are summarised in Figure 5.6 and Table 5.1. Figure 5.6 schematically illustrates the main thrust of contingency theory and identifies three problem areas that limit its practical and analytical strength. Table 5.1 summarises the main problems in each of these three areas, and it is to these that we now turn.

Problem area A: linkages between contingencies and structures

Variety and diversity between contingencies

There has been considerable scholarly debate, even within contingency theory, about the relative strength and importance of technology, environ-

---

FIGURE 5.6
Contingency Theory: The Problem Areas

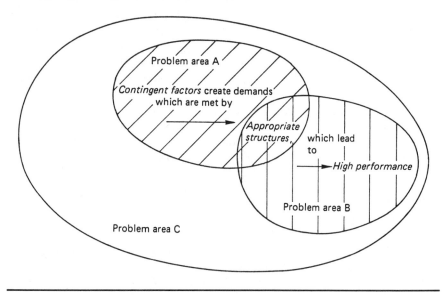

Table 5.1
Summary of Practical and Analytical Problems with Contingency Theory

A. *Linkages between contingencies and structures*

1. Which of the contingencies is the most important in determining structure?
   At any one time different contingencies require different responses.

2. Contingencies change over time at different rates and in different directions.

3. Any 'fit' between contingencies and structure is the result, to some extent, of *choices* made with constraints. Alternatively, structures emerge by default but are still tied to actions and decisions of people.

B. *Linkages between structure and performance*

1. Which of the multiple measures of performance is one using?

2. What is the direction of causality of any links that are found?

3. What other factors affect performance (e.g. interest rates, commodity prices, social and political change, values and attitudes)?

C. *The overall concept: linkages between contingencies, structure and performance*

In so far as the links are created through the perceptions, meanings and interpretations associated with different contingent, structural and performance factors, then attitudes, values, interests, power and action are concepts which are undervalued in a contingency approach. 'Appropriate structures' are sometimes important intervening variables between contingencies and performance; at other times they are irrelevant to performance, and at yet other times it can be counter-productive in concentrating attention on structures to the neglect of people and values.

---

ment and size. Readers should refer to Aldrich (1972), Pugh *et al.* (1976a and b), Child (1972) and Hickson, Pugh and Pheysey (1969) for this material. The debate is in fact not easily resolved because of the methodological and epistemological problems of unravelling relative cause and effect within limited cross-sectional case studies or relatively small-scale surveys.

Related to the debates about which factor is the stronger are the problems that arise when one tries to use contingency theory as a practical or analytical tool, simply because the various contextual factors for any one organisation may be giving different signals. For example, there may be a fairly certain technology but a highly uncertain and dynamic environment. Lawrence and Lorsch (1967) have attempted to answer this by arguing that such variable contingencies can be met by developing different strategies and styles for different departments. But different signals may be received by the same function: for example, part of the production facility may employ the latest in computer-controlled machinery, while other parts may still be largely characterised by labour-intensive batch production. In such circumstances the contingency argument would be to divisionalise, as Chandler (1962, 1977) and more recently Mintzberg (1979) have suggested. But divisionalisation can itself be a difficult structure to maintain, as our discussion of Mintzberg's analysis suggested. For example, people in one division may resent being treated differently to their counterparts in others. Not surprisingly, then, there is some evidence from Khandwalla (1973, p. 493) and Child (1984a, p. 234) that even though diverse signals may be received from the environment, internal consistency in structural design is very important. This means that some elements of structure may be inappropriate to some signals, but nonetheless overall consistency creates a working environment which on balance leads to improved performance. Child (1984, p. 236), citing Marks & Spencer in Britain, argues that the history, tradition and culture of an enterprise can provide a strong base for consistency and for encouraging employee commitment, which can be more important than adapting to every change in technology or organisation which a strict adherence to contingency theory might suggest. Not only do contingencies vary between product groupings but also at different stages of the life-cycle for one product (Kimberley *et al.*, 1980; Quinn and Cameron, 1988).

Nash (1983) proposes a systematic device for strategic business planning which identifies different forms of decision-making, planning, control, vertical and horizontal structures, leadership and motivation in order to meet the contingencies created at different times according to whether the product market is emerging, developing, maturing or declining. His scheme is summarised in Table 5.2. Nash argues, for example, that an emerging product market typically has a small but rapidly increasing number of competitors, low price elasticity and limited profits. In such conditions he advocates limited delegation, with strong leadership, informal and output-oriented control systems, highly differentiated structures beneath strong entrepreneurial leadership, and high discretionary rewards to attract the 'right people' to come and stay. This contrasts with a mature product market largely taken over by a stable number of fairly large competitors dealing in products with high elasticity and displaying moderate to high profitability and excellent short-run cash generation. In such circumstances there can be some delegation and flexibility in meeting goals providing there is strict application of profit and loss principles, sophisticated risk-averse managers, established reward systems, and well understood technologies. However, when the product market moves into decline, delegation needs to be limited, cost controls made stricter, and so on (Kimberley *et al.*, 1980).

A problem becomes apparent with this approach because people move within and between product life-cycles and hence need a nimbleness which managers and specialists do not always possess – often because of a highly parochial approach and maybe, as we shall see later, because of an overemphasis on structures as the solution to organisational problems.

Coping with change

Although a contingency approach should alert organisation designers to the problems of change, there is still a problem of holding on to both short- and long-term perspectives. This can be particularly problematic if present circumstances suggest a high degree of certainty such that one would opt, all other things being equal, for a formal bureaucratic structure. However, will this mean that people in the organisation become insensitive to the need for change in the future? For example, Direct Labour Organisations (DLOs) for building works in labour-controlled local councils in the UK used to be in a dominant position for obtaining any council building work. However, with the requirement of the 1981 Land Act that all work be the subject of competitive tendering, their near-monopoly position was broken and they needed to become more active in terms of both marketing their services and in providing operational management to ensure competitive performance. A mechanistic structure was no longer appropriate. Nonetheless, some DLOs struggled on in a mechanistic fashion apparently ignorant of their change in circumstances.

An opposite example is given by a 'hi-tech' establishment that has grown from very small organic beginnings with a high density of research scientists and engineers into a large manufacturing concern which now employs fairly well understood plant and machinery in order to mass produce items for a large consumer market. The organic flexible and informal ethos of the enterprise's origins is unlikely to continue to be an appropriate basis on which to structure the growth of large-scale manufacturing operations. Yet the directors are loath to become associated with an apparently inflexible formal enterprise, even though they accepted the 'logic' of it as a solution to their management problems.

Action and choice

Both the above examples illustrate the importance of the attitudes and values of the people involved as an important facet of analysis. The 'objective' facts of the context do not have an automatic effect on internal operations. They may be noticed and interpreted by individuals, all of whom have their own particular interests to safeguard and their own perceptions of the appropriate

Table 5.2
Meeting Contingencies at Different Stages in Product Life-cycles

Product cycle	Emerging	Developing	Mature	Liquidating
Industrial structure	Rapid increase from small number of small firms	Medium-sized firms jostling for position (mergers & casualties)	Moderate, stable number of relatively large firms	Moderate but declining number of large firms
Product-market characteristics				
Price structure Demand structure	Low price elasticity Small, homogeneous	Some price elasticity Expanding buyer segments	High price elasticity Highly segmented demand	Very high price elasticity Saturated demand
Product characteristics	High differentiation	Moderate differentiation	Limited differentiation	Commodity
Financial characteristics				
Typical profitability	Negative to low	Low to moderate	Moderate to high	Declining
Technological availability	Limited possession of proprietary know-how	Expanding base	Public knowledge	Practical know-how
Delegation Autonomy Risk Innovation	Limited delegation by strong leadership; variety of schemes are possible	Highest degree of delegation & freedom supported	Delegative to controlled: flexibility in meeting fixed goals	Very limited delegation and freedom
Decision-making	Formalised goals virtually non-existent Information limited	More information for decisions General goals exist	Information-based decisions	Information for control Rigid goals Clear goals

Planning & control systems	Information, highly qualitative (milestone-oriented)	Capable of setting broad goals and measuring results (programme-oriented)	Supportive of careful goal setting and control (Profit and Loss-oriented)	De-emphasise long-term planning: quantitative controls (balance-sheet-oriented)
Responsiveness to external conditions	Limited responsiveness at first: focus on establishing a position	Highly responsive; adapt to market opportunities	Less responsiveness required because of decreasing rate of change in markets	Responsive but under very limited conditions
Integration and differentiation	High degree of differentiation Integration at top	Decreasing differentiation Integrative function becoming more 'local' to markets, products	Continuing decrease in differentiation Integration 'local'	Low differentiation Integration at the top (corporate)
Leadership	Entrepreneur, strong, leader	Entrepreneur/business manager	Sophisticated manager	Administrator
Motivations	Venturesome: accepts unaccustomed risks	Venturesome to conservative; accepts accustomed and unaccustomed risks	Primarily conservative; generally risk-averse	Conservative, risk-averse
Reward management	High base compensation to attract people; discretionary bonus	High levels related to job; incentives for building results	More average levels related to job; incentives for results above high goals	Average level: incentives for cost control
Know-how development	Know-how depth important near top; development needed to support expected expansion	Ever-broadening scope and increasing numbers of managers and specialists required	Development needs & know-how becoming specialised, static	Specialised depth and scope of know-how

SOURCE: taken from Nash (1983). pp. 33–4

strategies and tactics that should be followed. The nature of the signals from the contingencies are rarely absolutely fixed and determined, so that people can rarely categorically and universally perceive their nature. Indeed, they are often not fixed because they are subject to control and determination by people who are 'using' or reacting to them. People not only create the 'links' that exist between contingent factors and structure, but they are also the creators of the contingency factors themselves.

The discussion of technology and environment in Chapters 3 and 4 was replete with examples of how technical and environmental characteristics are the creatures as much as the masters and mistresses of people in organisations. For example, modern technologies are not only the creatures of their designers but they are also often highly flexible and can be used in a variety of different ways. Even with fairly traditional mass production equipment, developments at the Volvo Kalmar and Saab Scania engine plants in the late 1960s and early 1970s showed how technologies were not simply fixed constraints which had to be 'met' by a particular form of structure. Similarly, as Weick (1969) reminds us (see Chapter 4), people create features of their environment: for example, through mergers, joint ventures, advertising, marketing and lobbying. Just as in the 1960s the move was away from 'There's no best way to organise', so in the 1980s the message must be 'There's no one best fit between structure and context'. This is because of the heterogeneity of context and the fact that within the context, organisations and groups can both be pursuing a variety of conflicting objectives and, sometimes to the exclusion of such purposive action, reacting with increasing panic to the variety of signals they are receiving in the short term.

Problem area B: linkages between structure and performance

Multiple indicators of performance

Just as the links between contingent factors and appropriate structures are both more complex and much looser than an initial reading of contingency theory might suggest, so too with the links between appropriate structures and performance. To begin with there is the question of the choice of performance indicators themselves. The performance of a factory, a corporate group, a service enterprise, a social work agency or a school cannot simply be represented by a neat collection of weighted variables. There are many indicators, and to pursue some of them may lead to underachievement on others. Figure 5.7 shows the list of primary and secondary performance measures used by the Hay group, Philadelphia, and reproduced in Nash (1983). In one setting the main concern may be with the efficient use of input resources in terms of quantity and quality of output generated, and so a single index of rate of return on capital invested may be taken. But will this mean ignoring the effectiveness of meeting objectives relating to market growth, innovation quality and stability of workforce? And what about the short- and

FIGURE 5.7
Measures of Performance in an Industrial Company

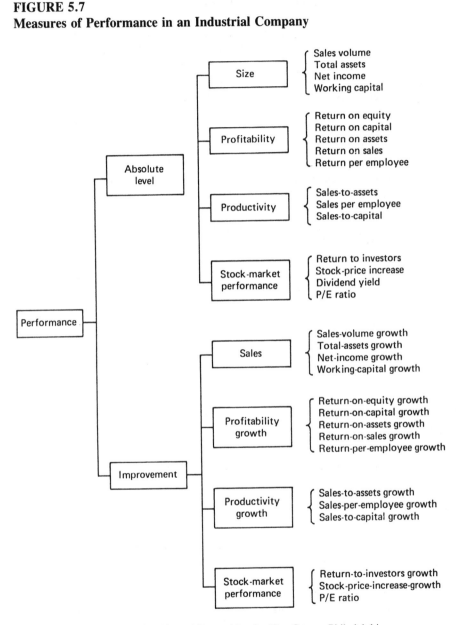

SOURCE: taken from Nash (1983), p. 118: used by the Hay Group, Philadelphia.

long-run aspects of efficiency and effectiveness? An appropriate structure for short-term efficiency may be disastrous for long-term innovation or growth. In another setting, a social work agency dealing in long-term family case work, the suggested indicator of performance may be the proportion of cases in which children are kept within the family and not taken into care. But how would it be weighted against the costs of the overall case-load, the number of families seen, or the proportion of children kept in families who were subsequently abused in some way?

Causality

Even if a link can be established between 'appropriate' structures and high performance, and conversely between 'inappropriate' structures and low performance, it remains to be determined which, if either, side of the equation determined the other. The issue of 'assumed causality' between structure and performance arises directly from the methodology of most of the early work which led to the development of a contingency approach. Most contingency research findings are based on cross-sectional rather than longitudinal studies. Associations between context, structure and performance are assumed in these cases to relate to a particular pattern of causality which was never proved. It is possible, for example, that as well as an appropriate fit leading to better performance, the reverse can sometimes be the case. Thus poor performance, for whatever reason, can lead, as Khandwalla (1977) suggests, to increased centralisation and the imposition of tight mechanical controls. In this way a dominant coalition may hope to run a 'tight ship' to keep everyone working to precise specifications and to maintain close financial control. This may, however, have disastrous effects, possibly because it is inappropriate to a context which requires high flexibility. A vicious circle of increasingly poor performance may thus be established. On the other hand, good performance may lead to a loosening of structural controls, and this in itself may be inappropriate and so lead to a downturn in performance.

Other influences on performance

The issue of the causality of any links between structure and performance is further complicated by the observation that performance is clearly related to many things other than appropriate structure: for example, interest rates, exchange rates, commodity prices, freak climatic conditions, industrial relations crises in another but linked industrial sector, and broader social and political changes. Some of these features are liable to influence people in the focal organisation, others less so. Some of them are arguably part of the 'contingent' environmental factors, but their impact on performance can be direct, regardless of any intervening effects of structure.

Problem area C: the overall concept: linkages between contingencies, structure and performance

A common theme has emerged from the discussions of the linkages between contingent factors, appropriate structures and performance: namely, that people tend to be underplayed in contingency approaches to organisation design. People's beliefs and actions are important not only in deciding and implementing structures, but also in making and implementing decisions about the 'contingencies' of technology and market developments. Sometimes, to be sure, these contingencies are constraints, but at other times and in other places they are subject to choice and modification by those in power.

Strategic choice

Child, in a seminal article on strategic choice (Child, 1972), was important in leading a major reappraisal of mechanistic contingency theory. In doing so he was prompted partly by Chandler's historical account of the development of different structural forms in the late nineteenth and twentieth centuries in America. Chandler's (1962) thesis was that the importance of changes in structure and indeed in the 'contingent factors' of size, technology and location, followed changes in strategy. More recently Chandler (1977) has continued his analysis and argued, in a similar fashion to Williamson's *Market and Hierarchies* (see Chapter 4), that the 'invisible hand' of market organisation between small and medium-sized firms exchanging intermediate products has been replaced by the visible hand of multidivisional corporations, owning and supervising transactions between the parts. To Chandler's mind the key factor leading to this change of strategy, and hence structure, is that the multidivisional organisation is appropriate for ensuring efficient co-ordination between the parts. One reason for this development is that modern technology is increasingly complex and ambiguous, and thus is difficult to manage in the marketplace. Chandler argues that the arts of successful management, especially for those involved in co-ordination across many stages of design, manufacture and delivery, are at a great premium and are best provided within a multidivisional form.

Child's emphasis on strategy and choice found resonance in the writings of commentators and theorists who claimed that contingency approaches had wrongfully obscured and negated the part played by people in creating the realities they inhabited. In the UK, Silverman (1970) was an early protoganist of this view, and it has subsequently been taken up by many other writers, such as Weick (1969), Pettigrew (1973), Salaman (1979) and Pfeffer (1981b). It becomes clear that even if the environmental features do (within a short time-span) largely 'determine' what happens and there is little room for exercise of choice, managers still have a symbolic role because people generally like to think that someone is 'in charge' (Pfeffer and Salancik, 1978, p. 263). A concern with the way people's perceptions and interests are crucial filters in any linkage between contingency factors, structures and levels of performance is linked to calls for an analysis of organisations as political economies (Benson, 1975, 1977a, 1977b).

Although Child took a leading role in emphasising the role of strategic choice in determining the content and form of both contextual and structural factors, it is interesting to note that he maintains a clear distinction between 'task contingencies' (the environment, diversity, size, technology and personnel) and 'political contingencies' (managerial preferences, market conditions and political context: Child, 1984a, pp. 218–33). The fact that this distinction is made suggests that task contingencies fall into an 'objective', 'out there' category. In contrast, this book suggests that both 'task' and 'political' contingencies are inextricably linked in that it is managerial preferences and political contexts which exert strong pressures on the choices made about technology, personnel practices and patterns of growth.

Social action and social structure

The area of debate about the role of action and choice as against structure and determinism has its roots in a more general problem for social science which concerns the balance and interrelationships between social action, human agency and social structure. The position taken in this text is that one should not incline either for practical or analytical purposes to either extreme, but see that both, within definitions of time and space, offer explanations of activities and outcomes in organisations. This is not the place to enter into a theoretical discussion of the issue, but it is so important to the general concerns of this book that the reader's attention is drawn to Anthony Giddens as a British social theorist who is perhaps most centrally concerned with bridging rather than widening the gap between the two philosophies. His recent work (Giddens, 1984) is in his terms an 'extended reflection' on Marx's proposition that 'men make history but not in circumstances of their own choosing'. This in some ways would be an excellent text for this book if it were not so grand in the expectations it raises.

Serendipity and whim

As well as the interdependence and yet separateness of 'choice' and 'constraint', there is also the 'non-rational' serendipity element of life in organisations which also cuts across any bald contingency explanation. Many activities and coincidences arise not because they have been consciously planned, either in respect of meeting contingencies or in terms of furthering self- or group interest, but because they follow from whims, fantasies and chance encounters which may not be consciously related to either contingencies or interests. Theories of psychoanalysis would have to be discussed if we were to go deeper into this aspect of life, but limits of space and maybe the interests of readers advise against this. The elements of serendipity and fantasy which interlace with the paradoxical interdependencies of constraint and choice should be remembered, however, until there is another opportunity to reflect on them in Chapter 8.

5.7   Concluding Remarks: And So . . . What of Contingency Theory?

The conclusion of this discussion of the problems and potential of contingency theory must be that for the analyst the picture created by contingency theory is too simple, too mechanistic and too neglectful of the role of human agency, power and interest. For the practitioner, however, one must conclude that contingency theory provides a limited basis for diagnosis and prescription of appropriate forms of organisation, albeit with associated costs as well as benefits. To get the structure 'right' in this way should help people to operate in particular technological and environmental contexts, but structure is not everything. Performance, however measured, is also going to reflect chance, or rather unpredicted happenings, whether they be in international politics, interest or exchange rates, climatic conditions, or scientific discoveries. Of particular relevance to the concluding section of this chapter, performance is also likely to be affected by the values, beliefs and qualities of the people involved. This is a factor which is not independent of structure but which must surely be subject to separate scrutiny. Hence the next chapter on culture.

Culture: Creature or Creator? 6

6.1 The Place of Culture in Organisational Analysis

The term 'culture' in organisational analysis refers to 'shared values and beliefs' which are seen to characterise particular organisations. Hofstede (1990) describes how in his terms people acquire 'mental programs' or 'the software of the mind', which create patterns of thinking, feeling and action. Culture is, then, in Hofstede's terms 'the collective programming of the mind which distinguishes the members of one group or category of people from another'.

Examples of key value dimensions through which culture is created concern beliefs about:

1. The nature of people (e.g. are they: (a) 'naturally' moral/immoral; (b) lazy/conscientious; or (c) fixed in their ways/open to development and change?)
2. The relationship between people and the natural world (is it 'naturally' harmonious, conflicting, dominating?)
3. The nature of people's relationshp to space and time (how is territory defined? How is time assessed? Are horizons for planning and action typically long or short term?)
4. The nature of essential, desirable or irrelevant behaviour (e.g. doing, controlling, being?)
5. The nature and implications of barriers between 'them' and 'us' (who is 'in' and who is 'out'?)

Shared values and beliefs are both created by and revealed to members of organisations and those with whom they interact. The term corporate culture

136

is often used to describe the values and beliefs which characterise a particular organisation.

The comparatively recent emergence of an interest in culture in organisations can be understood in terms of an acknowledgement of the limitations of structure in providing what was called, in the introduction to the previous chapter, the 'glue' which holds organisations together.

The tradition of work which has been the subject of previous chapters has focused on how to determine the most appropriate form of structure for organisations. The emphasis has been on the determination of roles and relationships, rules and procedures. These give the material base for control and co-ordination, and can be seen to have a concrete existence in organisation charts, rule books, job descriptions and committee terms of reference. Besides these more formal manifestations, there has also been a commentary on the importance of 'informal' organisation, which reflects the emergent procedures and relationships which are actually found rather than those which are formally specified (see, e.g., Dirsmith and Covaleski, 1985). Gouldner (1954) and Fox (1974) pointed out some time ago that the informal organisation may or may not be coterminous with the specified formal organisation. Where there is a discrepancy, there may be a degree of discomfort. This is relatively slight where the formal is simply ignored and people get on with operating in an informal way, but much greater where formal organisation is imposed over an incompatible informal organisation.

There has been a growing realisation on the part of organisational theorists as well as practitioners that structure – even with the additional consideration of informal structure – can only go so far in either providing the social mechanisms for co-ordination and control from a managerial perspective or in explaining human behaviour at work from a theoretical perspective. Structure, as it were, seems to provide the basic framework, but cannot either determine organisational life, or fully account for the 'effects' of the organisation on people's behaviour. Figure 6.1 provides an illustration of the way in which we can consider culture within the context of other aspects of organisation.

In the centre of Figure 6.1 there is a core of shared values, beliefs and assumptions. The issue of the extent of homogeneity or diversity of such 'shared' values will be discussed in subsequent sections. For the moment 'shared values and beliefs' are taken to exist at least to some degree. The relationships between the values people hold within an organisation and the organisation's practices, structure, technology and strategy are complex and interactive. Each of the outer rings in Figure 6.1 is the creation of people, the subject of decision-making, the result of actions taken or not taken. These actions or inactions are, we assume, to an extent reflective of values; hence the influence from the centre outwards. If there is value diversity within the organisation, it is unlikely that everyone's values will be equally represented.

The influences shown in Figure 6.1 are two way because each layer, once created, has an impact on the way values are subsequently developed.

FIGURE 6.1

A Map of the Corporate World: How Culture may be Revealed and Created in Organisations

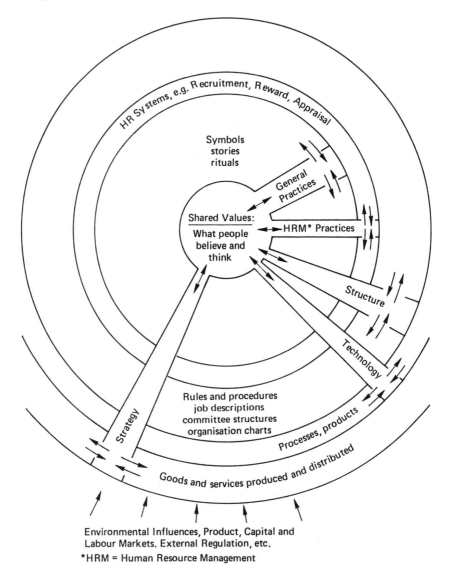

Environmental Influences, Product, Capital and Labour Markets. External Regulation, etc.

*HRM = Human Resource Management

Furthermore, Figure 6.1 represents an incomplete as well as an interactive set of influences. In reacting to, and anticipating, events outside the organisation, the actions and decisions of its members are not guided by values alone. There are often significant external environmental influences which largely dictate internal actions, although of course (as Chapter 4 has shown) there is also the possibility of the influence coming the other way, with organisations controlling aspects of their environment. Some examples to illustrate in words the relationships outlined in Figure 6.1 follow.

The first layer in Figure 6.1, labelled general practices, includes rituals, stories, language and symbols. Values are revealed in these symbols and yet symbols and practices also shape values. The search for an appropriate attention-catching logo or signature tune or a company song may easily lead to the encapsulation of a value which is either already dominant or else has been selected for serious promotion. The use and development of language reflects values: for example, Garscombke (1988) shows how, in adopting the language of militarism (e.g. defensive strategies, guerilla marketing and counter-offensive), managers are creating a militaristic culture in their organisations. The rituals associated with induction and retirement, with the Christmas Party, the Annual General Meeting or the annual cricket match, all reveal things about values as well as being the means by which attempts are made to engineer value changes. The internal and external designs and fittings of buildings, office space and recreation facilities, and the layout design and contents of the annual report are similarly both creatures and creators of corporate values.

Moving to the next layer shown in Figure 6.1, the focus shifts to human resource management practices. The operation and contents of rewards systems including pay, promotion and fringe benefits, appraisal and performance management, recruitment and selection, both reveal and shape values. It is often here that disjunctions between practices and values become apparent. On the one hand the company philosophy may talk of treating all employees equally, of placing high value on long service and loyalty, and yet employees may still find that separate dining and recreational facilities are maintained for different levels of the firm and that pay and promotion are geared to achievement of short-term performance targets. Similarly, disjunction can occur between expressed values (usually at the top of the organisation) and the next layer in Figure 6.1, the structure. High value may be placed on the maintenance of internal communication systems, the importance of encouraging risk-taking and the development of entrepreneurial flair, and yet procedures for authorising expenditure may remain bureaucratic and stultifying.

Handy (1985, 1989) a leading commentator on organisations in the UK, has described the close relationship which often exists between culture and structure. In describing four types of culture Handy refers not only to values but also to the shape of the 'host' structure. Thus his 'power' or 'club' culture, with its strong value element of 'watching the boss', is described as a network around a central point. His task culture, with values of 'all hands on deck', is described as an open network without a central point. His 'role' culture, with value placed on following the book/procedures, is described as a pyramid or temple. His 'person' or 'existential' culture, with value placed on human relationships, lacks any focus at all but is a collection of valued individuals or groups. Handy also finds different cultures as typical of different types of company: for example, he describes how small, family-owned firms and new start-ups often have a power culture; how a role culture is most often found in large organisations in stable environments, and the person culture in universities and professional practices of doctors and lawyers. The boundaries between strategy, history, structure and culture in this analysis become blurred.

Moving to other layers in Figure 6.1, we can also consider the relationship between values and technology (as evidenced in product and process developments) and strategy (as evidenced in the choices made about which goods and services to produce and sell). These decisions and outcomes may well embody and reflect central values, but equally they may reflect values held only by a minority. Indeed they may reflect opportunistic expedient and be thoroughly sensible decisions in terms of achieving strategic objectives, but these may not be in accord with values. For example, investment in new process equipment may facilitate lower unit costs and higher quality, and yet require some redundancies. What impact does this have on a cultural change programme which emphasises creating a caring, family-like atmosphere within the organisation?

Once established and revealed, culture is perpetuated or modified through intent and chance by the processes of socialisation, recruitment, and strategy formulation and implementation. In other words who (in terms of people) and what (in terms of practices and strategies) gets hired, who and what gets fired and who and what gets promoted.

Culture may, therefore, be the centre of an organisation, as much of the literature to be discussed in the next section often suggests, and Figure 6.1 gives it that prominence. However, such a view may be itself more symbolic than real. A good analogy is with medieval maps, which sometimes represented a 'view of the world' with Jerusalem at its centre with no regard to the 'rationality' of geographical analysis. So Figure 6.1 shows culture as the centre of organisation analysis. Sometimes culture may be the driving force exerting a major influence on all layers of experience and outcomes. Empirically one can find organisations where culture is of great influence to all the layers, and indeed subsequent sections will show how this is advocated by those who see developing appropriate cultures as an essential basis for successful organisational development. Sometimes, however, it would be more appropriate to draw a diagram with one of the other elements of organised activity in the centre, or indeed with all characteristics of organisations seen as largely responsive to the environment (see Chapter 4).

At a general level there is agreement that culture refers to collections of shared values and common assumptions. There is less agreement in organisational analysis about the definition of the 'collectivity' in which they are shared, the mechanisms and processes by which the values and assumptions are created or emerge, and the methodological issues of how 'shared values and beliefs' are revealed. These differences mean that there are several very different ways of approaching, defining and indeed using the concept of culture in organisations.

Why is culture now seen as important?

The roots of an emphasis on culture are several, from empirical research, from theory and from practice. The recognition of the limitations of structure as the social glue for organisations has already been introduced. Empirically, scholars who sought to operationalise variables to determine effectiveness had for some time devoted research to definitions and measures of 'climate', by which they meant the statistical construction of a profile of the values and attitudes which were held in the organisation (Payne, Pheysey and Pugh, 1971). In another area, discussion of power and conflict in organisations focused on the extent to which people's beliefs and interests underlay strategic and operational decisions so that, for example, there was discussion about 'organisations as technically constrained bargaining and influence systems' (Abell, 1975). In another area, anthropology had long ago recognised the concept of 'culture' as critical to the understanding of human behaviour. Douglas (1986) placed cultural analysis firmly on the agenda of organisational analysis.

Theoretical and empirical roots of a concern for culture in organisational analysis can thus be discerned, but it was Western observation of the Japanese 'economic miracle' which arguably stimulated most interest in culture in organisations. It has been argued that the secret of Japanese success lay in a homogeneous national and religious culture which was easily reflected in a corporate culture. Shared values of dedication, reciprocity, rights and obligations provided a cultural power house as one of the engines of corporate and national economic success. It was easy (but fundamentally misguided) to draw the conclusion that all that was required for Anglo-Saxon organisations was to find a way of recreating what was in fact a stereotypical version of Japanese culture in order to reap similar competitive advantage (e.g., see Thurley, 1984; Gow, 1986; and Wickens, 1987, for a critical discussion of such simplistic analyses). In practice, as we shall see, there are enormous difficulties in working out whether indeed culture can be 'created' and, if so, the extent to which 'homogeneity' and 'appropriateness' can be secured.

6.2 Different Perspectives on Corporate Culture

Consideration of these issues will be undertaken by a discussion on two themes. The first theme is the extent to which corporate cultures are more a reflection of external national ethnic or religious forces, or more a reflection of internal managerial, professional or 'business history' forces. The second theme is the extent to which cultural values and attitudes can be created or manipulated to reflect the will, interests and intentions of powerful and influential groups or, at the other extreme, the extent to which values are seen to be the outcomes of emergent processes which are not easily controllable or manipulable (at least not within the sort of timescales which are likely to be employed by executives within organisations).

The relationship between corporate culture and the culture of wider social groupings

The work of Hofstede (1980, 1985, 1990) in identifying what he calls national cultures is central to this discussion. He has conducted fifteen years of empirical research into differences in national work-related value systems, through paper and pencil questionnaires distributed to matched samples of respondents, originally in forty countries and subsequently in a further ten and three multi-country regions. From this data base, Hofstede has identified four value dimensions which he claims discriminate between 'national cultures'.

1. Power distance (i.e. the extent to which people accept that power is distributed unequally). High power distance implies a high acceptance of power inequalities.
2. Uncertainty avoidance (i.e. the extent to which people feel uncomfortable with uncertainty and ambiguity, and so seek to develop ways of working which limit their exposure to uncertainty and ambiguity).
3. Individualism (i.e. the extent to which there is a preference for membership of tightly-knit collectivities with strong bonds of loyalty and mutual care and support, or a preference for a more loosely-knit society in which individuals and their immediate family are far more independent).
4. Masculinity, by which Hofstede understands a preference for achievement and assertiveness rather than a preference for modesty and caring relationships.

Hofstede argues that the first two dimensions have the strongest influence on organisations and that different combinations of power distance and uncertainty avoidance imply different perspectives on organisations. High power distance and high uncertainty avoidance incline people to view organisations as bureaucratic pyramids typical, he claims, of Mediterranean countries. Low power distance and high uncertainty avoidance incline to a view of imperial bureaucracies or well-oiled machines (as, he claims, in Central Europe). Small power distance and low uncertainty avoidance values incline to a view of an adhocracy or village market, which he claims are typical of Great Britain and other Nordic countries.

The third and fourth dimensions of Hofstede's analysis, individualism and masculinity, reflect an individual's self-concept, approach to team work and relations with others. In describing a group of Mexican immigrant workers in a US shoe factory, Hofstede described how the US management was frustrated by aspects of the Mexican approach to work. For example, US managers found work groups of Mexicans to be reluctant to be regrouped and to believe that absenteeism to attend to family crises was normal. However, the management was pleased that in another display of local loyalty the workers were reluctant to join the US workers' union. In more recent work Hofstede has added a fifth dimension, 'The trade off between long term and short term gratification of needs' (Hofstede, 1990).

There are, of course, difficulties in generalising about whole nations from the mean tendency of individual replies. For example, some British readers reflecting on their experience of some large private corporations (such as BP before the cultural revolution of the present Chairman, Bob Horton) will feel they are not exempt from a view of organisations as a pyramid, whilst for others encounters with the Department of Social Security will have made many claimants feel as if they were dealing with an imperial bureaucracy.

Nonetheless, although there may be methodological difficulties with this approach, most students of organisations and practitioners who deal internationally with people from different countries all agree that there is a face validity to the view that the French and English ways of doing business are different, and that misunderstandings arise, for example, between Americans and Indians, or the peoples of East and West Europe. 'A German [well-oiled machine] is appointed to run a civil engineering project in Indonesia [family]. He will create rules and procedures, only to discover that nobody keeps them and that his personal presence is what gets the job done' (Hofstede, 1985). The work of Nancy Adler (1986) is also important in documenting some of these differences and developing practical ways in which they might be overcome.

The extensive empirical work of Hofstede on differences between national groups has suggested that there are fundamentally different ways of seeing work and organisation depending on one's geographical, ethnic and religious origins and experiences. Hofstede thus reveals the basis of difficulties which arise when any form of corporate activity requires cross-national understanding (for instance, negotiation of joint ventures, international trading relationships or simply individual relations between expatriates and 'host community' employees). The concept of corporate culture is seen in this context as predominantly derived from accumulated and shared social experiences and values from a wider social context.

In examining the relationship between national and ethnic cultures one needs to consider the extent to which national cultures are homogeneous. The greater the homogeneity within any one country the greater the likelihood that its effects will be strongly reflected in corporate culture.

The Japanese experience

The best and most celebrated example of a relationship between homogeneous national culture and corporate cultures is found in Japan. In discussion of Japanese organisational and working practices, emphasis is often placed on the values identified in Figure 6.2, which also shows the way they are said to be manifest in the company.

Ethnically Japan is a comparatively homogeneous society. This reflects careful control of immigration and multiple channels of reinforcement of dominant codes of conduct (e.g. through family, through school and through employment). The corporate culture in Japanese companies, which has not necessarily been created in any determined fashion, can be seen to have emerged from the corporations' strong roots in Japanese society.

The 'excellence' literature: create a 'strong' corporate culture

Perceptions of the Japanese experience (e.g. Abernathy, Clark and Kantrow, 1983), together with observations about what appear to be the secrets of success for large corporations in the USA, gave rise to much discussion within

---

FIGURE 6.2
Values Attributed to the Japanese and their Manifestation within the Company

Social Values	*Corporate Manifestation*
Stress upon vertical rather than horizontal relationships	Loyalty to company Loyalty to 'boss' Less loyalty to 'profession'/ occupational group
Stress upon consensus	Apparently loose and under-defined structures for decision-making from which consensus emerges
Stress upon rights and obligations in all relationships	Reciprocity between functional groups and between levels
Stress upon diligence, tenacity and responsibility	Pride in performance, quality and service
Stress upon distinction between insiders and outsiders	Company/group membership is all important and claims primary loyalty over other collectivities. *But* company looks after family, so there should be no conflict between company and family.

---

the USA and subsequently in Europe about the importance of developing what is often called a 'strong' corporate culture.

Table 6.1 summarises the eight attributes of 'excellence' which Peters and Waterman (1982) championed as the secrets to corporate success in their best selling management tract, *In Search of Excellence.* They deduced these attributes from a review of the practices and policies of forty-three high-performance American firms, including Hewlett Packard, Texas Instruments and IBM. Table 6.1 suggests that by 'strong culture' such commentators are not only looking for a strong value core but that the values themselves should

---

Table 6.1
Back to Basics: Eight 'Attributes of Excellence'

---

1. *Bias for action*: a preference for doing something – anything – rather than sending an idea through endless cycles of analyses and committee reports.

2. *Staying close to the customer*: learning his or her preferences and catering to them.

3. *Autonomy and entrepreneurship*: breaking the corporation into small companies and encouraging them to think independently and competitively.

4. *Productivity through people*: creating in all employees the awareness that their best efforts are essential and that they will share in the rewards of the company's success.

5. *Hands-on, value-driven*: insisting that executives keep in touch with the firm's essential business and promote a strong corporate culture.

6. *Stick to the knitting*: remaining with the businesses the company knows best. Decide what the company stands for and go for that.

7. *Simple form, lean staff*: few administrative layers, few people at the upper levels. One structural dimension: product *or* function *or* geography should have clear primacy.

8. *Simultaneous loose-tight properties*: fostering a climate where there is dedication to the central values of the company combined with tolerance for the idiosyncrasies of employees who accept those values. A paradoxical combination of central direction and individual autonomy.

SOURCE: adapted from Peters and Waterman (1982).

---

be particular in their emphasis, and that they should stress the importance of action and analysis, independence and autonomy and individual and group responsibility. In this sense 'strong culture' does not mean strength in just any values, but strength in these particular values.

The development of such a culture is seen to be part of a seamless web with attributes of structure, strategy and performance. Stress is also placed on a flat open structure characterised by high levels of delegation and discretion, open communication, the recruitment of a relatively large proportion of professional specialists and the careful development of humanistic employment conditions to provide a strong base for unobtrusive controls, supplemented by output rather than bureaucratic controls. The strategic aspect of this approach stresses customer care, quality and sticking to areas in which the company has a proven track record (see, e.g., Kanter, 1983, 1989). Corporate culture is thus viewed as the creature of senior executives and as a tool for achieving their purposes. It is seen as a basis for conveying a sense of identity to members, facilitating commitment to something larger than individuals and enhancing social stability.

Ouchi (1981), in a comparison of American and Japanese firms, reaches similar conclusions. His analysis suggests that American firms, especially those hitting hard times, are typically bureaucratically controlled, with specialised and fragmented groups held together 'as strangers' by contractual relationships which specify measurable, and often minimal, performance criteria. In contrast, he argued, Japanese firms are less specialised and show great concern for fostering commitment and loyalty to shared internalised values and common goals. Greater emphasis is also given to the long rather than the short term and to fostering co-operation rather than confrontation. Ouchi acknowledges that there are important differences between Japanese and American cultures, and that consequently Japanese forms cannot be immediately adopted in America. However, along with Peters and Waterman, he considers that American firms can and should foster loyalty and commitment and so dramatically shift their approach. Ouchi is particularly concerned with the way participation, egalitarianism, security of employment, honesty and clarity can provide a basis for such a shift. In this way American firms can, he claims, 'meet the Japanese challenge' and develop his 'theory z type of organisation'.

An emphasis upon strong and shared corporate values which emphasise and encourage individuality, risk and commitment have found a strong resonance with senior executives in the USA and UK. This resonance is shown in the publicity which accompanies programmes to change the culture of companies. Such programmes of culture change are often part of a programme of radical transformation: for example, to make British Telecom more entrepreneurial, to make British Airways more quality oriented, to make the National Health Service both more commercially sensitive and more patient-focused, or dramatically to change the style and internal communications of BP. Each of these exemplar organisations has mounted significant programmes of change with the avowed aim of ensuring a change in values or beliefs, in order that values which support and underpin the required changes of behaviour will become increasingly shared throughout the organisation. These programmes are predicated on the belief that the 'stronger' the culture in the terms described in Table 6.1, the less need there is for bureaucratic rules, procedures and systems to provide the 'glue' which will hold the organisation together.

In this perspective culture is the creation of senior executives and a tool for achieving their purposes: for example, to develop a sense of identity and focus for loyalty and commitment amongst members, and so to enhance social stability and cohesion within the organisation. The problematic relationship between created values and other aspects of organisational life, such as structure, strategy and technology, has already been discussed in the context of Figure 6.1. The companies cited by Peters and Waterman (such as RMI with its emphasis on the value it places on the happiness and smiling faces of its workforce, and McDonald's with its emphasis on 'Quality, Service, Cleanliness and Value'), were notable for the consistency they had developed between the values, practices, structures and strategies. However, Peters and Waterman only gave snapshots of successful companies, whereas evidence of disjunction between the levels is more likely to emerge from a longitudinal study. This is an issue to which we will return in the concluding sections on culture and performance.

But . . . can culture be 'taught' or can it only be 'caught'?

The 'excellence' literature and much contemporary management consultancy takes the view developed in the previous section: that it is a key management challenge to create a strong and appropriate culture which will facilitate both the development and implementation of a 'winning' strategy. But there is a counter-argument which claims that attempts at deliberate cultural creations are, in the long run, doomed to failure. Such a view is based on the assumption that the values people espouse are not open to relatively short-term manipulation. Smircich (1983), Clegg (1990), Turner (1990) and Anthony (1990) are proponents of this approach in which culture is 'caught', not 'taught'; in which underlying themes of 'organisational cognition' (Thompson and Wildavsky, 1986) shape the cognition of individual members of organisations in what are, to an extent, subconscious processes. Experience is gained and values are formed within the organisational arena. Executive policies and practices have an impact on cultural creations, but their impact is not subject to executive determination.

This perspective has become popular with theorists but, as one would expect from a view which denies the basis for deliberate manipulation, less popular with practitioners. Nonetheless one of the reasons for its development has been practitioner concern that attempts to create a Japanese-style situation in organisations in Europe or USA were easier said than done. Even though executives could identify the cultural results they felt were desirable, they have proved very difficult to recreate (Wickens, 1987).

The view of culture as emergent rather than prescribed can be most obviously supported in situations where there is a fundamental lack of consensus, as a result of what one might call chronic inequality or heterogeneity. Where there is no overarching value consensus it is easy to discern a variety of sub-cultures, wherein different sets of values and beliefs serve as 'sense making' devices for different groups of workers who co-exist within one organisation. The culture of waitresses in a cocktail bar described by Spradley and Mann (1975), or of slaughterhouse men described by Ackroyd and Crowdy (1990), are examples of sub-cultures. Such examples are often seen as peripheral 'curios', not as part of mainstream corporate life. However, other (less peripheral) groups have been graphically described, including the dealers on the floor of LIFFE portrayed by Caryl Churchill in her play *Serious Money*, or the clerks of public service captured years ago by Merton (1957) in his description of the 'bureaucratic personality', which give further evidence of heterogeneity and cultural diversity in one employment context.

In this perspective, values, myths and rituals are not independent artefacts; they are not creatable, but they are generative processes that yield and shape different meanings for diverse groups. Events, working practices, structures and strategies create the context in which these generative processes grow and develop, but they do not determine them. Thus, for example, a crisis situation where survival is believed to be at stake may generate cultural change, but whether this cultural change is seen as supportive or subversive towards executive action cannot be exactly determined. Thompson and Wildavsky (1986) assert that for every 'overground' (i.e. formal) structure there are any number of contradictory 'undergrounds' or 'ways of life', or, in the terms used in this book 'sub-cultures'. Once one becomes part of a culture one admits oneself to social constraint but, 'even so, the individual keeps testing the constraints, reinforcing them if they prove satisfactory in practice, modifying or rejecting them where possible, if not' (p. 276).

Which perspective should one choose?

The relevance of considering these different perspectives on corporate culture is that each of them has some empirical validity; one can find examples which fit with each. One can find corporate cultures of Canadian firms which exactly fit Hofstede's ideas of 'national' imprinting of values. One can find examples of Kanter's 'strong corporate cultures', and one can find examples of diverse and conflicting sub-cultures retaining their strong and individual identity in the face of efforts to transform them into something more amenable. This variety suggests that the term 'culture', and even 'corporate culture', is used far too loosely.

Which perspective one finds most useful depends, amongst other things, on the characteristics of the organisation with which one is concerned and the characteristics of the person who is making the analysis. For example, the following characteristics will influence one's approach.

Organisational characteristics
- homogeneity and ethnic composition of wider social culture.
- size of the company
- geographical dispersion
- degrees of consensus and conflict amongst different groups and stake-holders
- extent to which organisation is seen to be in need of revolutionary or evolutionary change

Characteristics of the analyst
- timescale of concern
- one's interest and stake in the organisation
- perceptions of crises/problems within the organisation

For example, if the timescale is at least medium term and the basis for consensus is present in a company's structure and history, it may be possible to create a strong corporate culture. If the timescale is either very short or very long, this may not be so feasible, particularly if there is a lot of heterogeneity in the company which may have its roots in the values of the surrounding society. Attempts to develop a strong consensual culture within such a company are unlikely to be successful and a variety of emergent sub-cultures are likely to flourish.

As a practitioner, the important point is to be able realistically to identify values which are held by organisational members and to assess the relationship between the cultural and other elements introduced in Figure 6.1. To make such a request is in itself paradoxical, for it is asking an 'objectivity' of the participant which in a sense is denied by the sort of cultural analysis implied in the last emergent perspective.

6.3 The Contribution of Culture to Performance

The practitioner's emphasis on culture has been strongly influenced by its presumed association with strong corporate performance. At a fairly simplistic level, two sets of relationships have captured the imagination: the first is the presumed association at a national level between Japan's industrial performance and its culture (this is then extended into the analysis of individual Japanese companies); the second is from the 'excellence' literature and is the presumed relationship between the cultural attributes listed in Table 6.1 and excellent performance.

Japan revisited

The outstanding growth and strength of Japanese industrial performance in the last two decades has inspired envy and emulation in the West. Japan does, of course, present a very different political, social and cultural context from that of Britain, and there is much discussion about the manner in which Japanese-grown social and managerial practices will transplant to British soil (see, e.g., Clark, 1979; Lambert, 1982; Thurley, 1981, 1984; Wickens, 1987). It is ironic that a return to an interest in 'people' in the USA has coincided with an emulation of Japanese methods, since it is highly likely that the meanings given by Japanese people (who have a strong internalised Confucian philosophy) to greater involvement and a higher emphasis on obligation and loyalty will be very different from those given by people in Britain or America, who have very different and more individualistic cultural traditions.

Futhermore, the celebrated Japanese industrial practices which foster autonomy, discretion and flexibility within and between work groups, a strong consensus on objectives and high levels of group loyalty and organisational commitment, are not characteristic of all Japanese employing organisations. They are mostly found in the larger enterprises, which also pay great attention to the provision of life-time employment, extensive social welfare and educational programmes for employees and their families, and a slow but sure ascent to the top of the organisation for sufficient of those who start at the bottom to give hope to them all. However, large numbers of Japanese people do not find employment, let alone promotion, in such organisations. Instead they are employed in small sub-contracting and supporting enterprises which exist on the 'breadline' of fluctuating demand for their goods and services. They are offered relatively poor employment packages and often move in and out of temporary employment, with little security and relatively poor working conditions.

It can be seen that there is a dual labour market and dual industrial structure in Japan. The professionally or technically qualified, who can attract good employment conditions, are in the primary sector. In the secondary sector are the relatively disadvantaged, who have erratic employment records, are largely employed in small enterprises, and are disproportionately drawn from minority racial groups, the old and women. Interestingly, it will be noted below that with the development of information technology processes and products, changes in industrial structure and economic recession, we may be witnessing similar labour market developments in the UK.

The argument, then, that cultural characteristics, whether imprinted from wider social contexts (as it is often argued in Japan) or developed and nurtured by management action, can determine or explain corporate performance (or even national economic and industrial performance) is gross oversimplification.

Figure 6.3 shows a view in which, at the national level, cultural values have a place; but it is only one place amongst many in explaining virtuous (or, in

FIGURE 6.3
Illustrating the 'Virtuous Circle' which underlies Japan's Industrial Performance

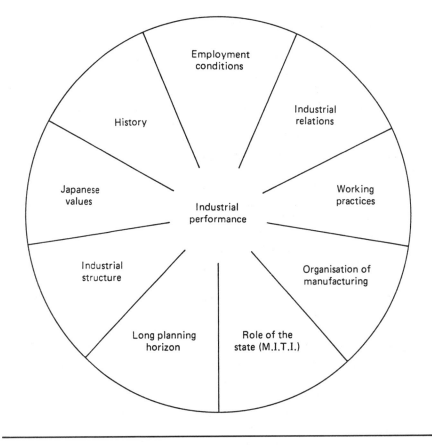

other circumstances, vicious) circles of economic performance. In Japan's case flexible working practices, bureaucratic and stable employment conditions, just-in-time manufacturing systems, long-range planning horizons, enterprise rewards, labour and capital market structures, sound macro-economic management and the role of the state in general, and of MITI (Ministry of International Trade and Industry) in particular, all have a place alongside culture in any explanation of industrial performance (see, e.g., Friedman, 1989; Okimoto, 1989).

Culture is only one of several human factors associated with organisational performance. Other human factors include staff capability, structure and human resource management practices. Furthermore, there are other factors deriving from technology, market position and national, global, fiscal and economic conditions which profoundly affect performance. The notion, then, that culture and performance are somehow bound together in a unidimensional way is unrealistic.

Universal characteristics of excellence or veiled contingencies?

New forms of organisation in the Ouchi (1981) and Peters and Waterman (1982) style are championed in the industrialised West because they seem to promise flexibility and innovation in technologies, together with high employee commitment and loyalty, while avoiding the rigidities of bureaucracy or the confusing and time-consuming complexities of matrix structures. This advocacy of flexibility is reminiscent of Hedberg's excursion into *Camping on Seesaws: Prescriptions for a Self-designing Organisation* (Hedberg, Nystrom and Starbuck, 1976). In this striking article the authors argue that residents of changing environments need to build 'tents', not 'palaces'. An organisational tent places greater emphasis on flexibility, creativity, immediacy and initiative than on authority, clarity, decisiveness and responsiveness. An organisational tent actually 'exploits benefits hidden within properties that designers have generally regarded as liabilities'. Hedberg is thus also for flexibility, risk-taking, action and adaptability, although he has more in common with March (1974) in stressing the importance of creativity, insight and action than he does with Peters and Waterman, who are more concerned with consensus and co-operation.

To what extent is the resurgence of interest in culture, people and values, flexibility and action important either to the practitioner or the analyst? Seeking to answer this question reveals some methodological problems. Curiously enough, some of them are shared with contingency approaches, since most protagonists of this 'new wave' base their assertions on cross-sectional data collection, and so encounter the same difficulties of inferring cause and effect relationships between managerial and structural characteristics on the one hand, and successful performance at a particular time on the other. Furthermore, there appears to be an overrepresentation of firms who were among the first to enter a new hi-tech field or to exploit a new market opportunity among Peters and Waterman's 'excellent' companies. It may be, therefore, that far from being 'universally good characteristics' from a management point of view, Peters and Waterman's attributes of excellence are those aspects that are most appropriate for the particular conjunction of technological and market conditions which characterise firms operating in the expanding markets of the late twentieth century.

Undoubtedly, aspects of the development of sophisticated technology for the transmission, storage, accessibility and complex analysis of information do call into question the necessity of complex formal structures. Child (1984a, p. 260) comments: 'As the inter-dependencies between financial activities are made more visible through integrated control systems and shared data services, so the logic of team-working and networks emerges as the natural basis of organization, rather than patterns of work and communication defined by departmental boundaries.' Similarly, vertical barriers may weaken with less emphasis on the middle levels of management, given the speed with which information can be generated or used at either the 'top' or 'bottom' of the organisation. Child speculates that the forecasts that were made about the first mainframe computer revolution in the 1960s will perhaps now be realised with present and subsequent generations of information technology hardware and software. He also speculates that dual-labour markets will become common, with an elite cohesive group at the top and a mass of people in secondary labour markets at the bottom. However, he enters a cautionary note about the rate of change, particularly in Britain where the rate of take-up of new technology is patchy and slow (Child, 1984a, p. 263).

Another possible explanation of the findings of Peters and Waterman is that the position of many of their firms in terms of technological developments and environmental changes may in itself explain their competitive advantage within national and international economies, and thus their relative financial success may be largely irrespective of the organisational forms adopted. After all, it was these factors in a previous age, when mass production and mechanical automation were dramatically changing the American industrial scene, that led the early so-called 'classical organisation and management theorists' (such as F. W. Taylor, Urwick and Fayol) to herald a bureaucratic administrative system and a hierarchical structure as the universal answer to all organisational and industrial problems. Their 'best' structure was then held together by a great deal of personal centralised control as well as bureaucratic and technological controls. Their technology and market policies gave the early mass producers, like the archetypal Henry Ford, a competitive advantage. People desperate for jobs got employment, and a bureaucratic hierarchy with close supervision appeared to be *the* prescription for success. With hindsight we now appreciate the complex economic, political and social factors that accounted for this success and subsequent demise, and can see how misplaced the faith was in bureaucracy as universally appropriate. It would thus be as well to maintain a healthy scepticism of any late twentieth-century 'universals' until we can be more certain about the cause-and-effect relationships and the importance of managerial choice reflecting aspects of the economic, social and political context.

In a sense, therefore, the universal theories of Peters and Waterman and others are beginning to sound increasingly like contingency ones, particularly as, with time, recipes for excellence are shown to be perishable. Slim consensual organisations of the future are probably applicable to firms employing professionals and technicians from the primary labour market in the development and operation of new technology or highly fashionable products and processes. They may, however, be less successful in other technological, product and labour market conditions.

Questions have been asked about whether the Peters and Waterman prescriptions could withstand the voyage across the Atlantic. In a debate reported in the *Financial Times* (26 November 1984) between Waterman and de Woot (the latter is a Belgian professor from Louvain who has published a research study into the competence of European management: see de Woot, 1984), de Woot questioned whether European firms were ready to embrace all the attributes of excellence. In response, Waterman stressed that he and his co-author had not seen people, innovation and values as alternatives to structural solutions, but that they were concerned to revive interest in the 'soft Ss' (style, skilled staff and shared values) on the assumption that the 'hard Ss' (strategy, structure and systems) were already well established as preconditions. De Woot's six-year study of management at all levels within subsidiaries, affiliates and head offices of nine French and Belgian corporate groups showed that in some large companies there is little concept or application of strategic management; thus de Woot argues that there is no basis for developing a Peters and Waterman-type scheme.

Notwithstanding the criticisms that have been made, there is no doubt that Peters and Waterman have struck a very popular note with practitioners. It is commonplace to hear of companies requiring all their senior executives to read and act on the book. Many in-company workshops and seminars have been organised on the themes of the book, and programmes to emphasise people rather than structure, action rather than analysis, etc., have been instiued far and wide in Europe and the USA. Frustration with complex structures, coupled with perceptions of the possibilities presented by information technology, has led to decisions in many companies to develop flatter, more compact structures of professional, technically competent managers bound together by common values.

Excellent companies can fall from grace

Two years after the publication of Peters and Waterman, articles were already appearing which suggested some of the 'excellent' companies were sliding from grace. The 'cover story' in *Business Week*, 5 November 1985, documented the difficulties which some of the hitherto excellent companies were then facing. Hewlett Packard was said to have fallen in the critical microcomputer and super mini-computer markets, and 'its technology-driven, engineering-orientated culture, in which decentralisation and innovation were a religion and entrepreneurs were the gods, is giving way to a marketing culture and growing centralisation'. Atachi 'was so out of touch with its market that it failed to realize its customers were losing interest in video game players and switching to home computers'. Interestingly, as their success begins to fade, far from emphasising their 'excellent attributes', those who face difficulties appear to revert to more conventional forms of centralised structural response. In such cases will there be a resurgence of centralised bureaucratic controls? This is what has happened in the past, although it must be added that there is no strong evidence that it has ever necessarily done any good.

When facing difficulties some organisations may 'revert' to 'traditional' forms, whereas others may cling on to following what they believe to be the secrets of their success. Miller (1990) develops this theme and illustrates how, in his view, companies which have experienced 'excellence' take their excellence characteristics to dangerous and counter-productive extremes. He talks in terms of four broad categories. 'Craftsmen' (such as Texas Instruments) degenerate from single-mindedly doing one thing well to becoming obsessive 'tinkerers' with technicalities, and their concern with quality and innovation becomes marginalised in an oppressive bureaucracy. 'Pioneers' (such as Apple) become 'escapists' chasing yet another break-through uncontrolled by the ultra-flexibility of their organisational forms. 'Builders' (such as ITT) become greedy imperialists, acquiring businesses that are difficult to manage effectively; while 'arch salesmen' (such as IBM) with high-profile brand names, may easily become 'drifters' so that it is difficult to determine where strategic decisions are being made and on what criteria. In each of these organisational pathologies, tunnel vision increases as organisational learning ceases.

Miller maintains that recovery is possible but it has to come from changes in the managerial process, greater flexibility and open-mindedness. Peters would now probably agree. The erstwhile champion of excellence has now moved on from prescribing universal recipes for success, having declared that 'the era of sustainable excellence is ended and that managers need to learn to thrive on chaos' (Peters, 1987). Having found one way to excellence they must learn that sticking to that managerial knitting will not necessarily stand them in good stead even in the medium term. It is no longer appropriate (if it ever was) to wait until natural managerial succession creates change. This is a theme to which we will return in Chapters 9 and 10.

Innovation and flexibility through 'neo-Fordism' or 'artisanal' organisation

Interestingly, Charles Sabel (1982), in quite another context, has come to similar conclusions about contemporary developments in organisations. Unlike Peters and Waterman, Sabel is not concerned with telling managers and owners how to succeed, but in documenting changes in work organisation. Nevertheless he reaches a similar destination, although he is less sanguine about its overall chances of long-term success and its general effects on social and political life. Sabel documents the origins and consequences of a crisis in 'Fordism', which is the name he gives to the form of organisation that is dominated by technological and administrative controls as a basis for facilitating the mass production of standardised goods for mass markets. The crisis arises because of technological, economic and social change in the global environment of the enterprise.

Sabel sees Western companies as beseiged by several important developments. To begin with there are production plants in low-wage areas which
increasingly challenge their traditional markets in terms of both imitative
mass production and developing their own technological and scientific base.
Second, raw material prices are subject to gross fluctuations which are beyond
their control. Third, environmental pressure groups and concern about
occupational health and safety call some of their activities into question.
Finally, some of their wealthier erstwhile customers now want something
different from the mass prodution items they have consumed hitherto.

Sabel suggests that, in the face of this crisis, senior people in large
corporations have a choice between two fundamental responses. One is a
protectionist, reactive response in which they aim for tariff barriers, marketing agreements, lobbies to ensure 'industry' is protected from 'hysterical'
onslaughts from community groups, and advertising to get customers to
continue to 'want' mass production goods. But, argues Sabel, this is a difficult
strategy to maintain, since it requires the continued coalescing of different
interests which are likely to break ranks. For example, while it is always a
good idea that other people's raw material prices are held steady, will you do
the same for yours? People want employment, but as consumers they also
want different products, and so on. Sabel is therefore pessimistic about the
long-term success of a protectionist policy, since it is likely that companies, on
a global scale, will fall behind and not catch up.

The alternative to protectionism is, Sabel argues, innovation – the creation
of specialised products and processes – which may lead to benefits for a
variety of interest groups. For example, he cites Abernathy and Ronan's
(1980) report on the Honda Motor Company's CVCC engine, which showed
that their new stratified charge engine both reduced polluting emissions and
gave more fuel efficiency. But the implications for organisation of any
innovatory stance are considerable, and require at least a re-interpretation of
Fordism. Instead of well-defined structures and jobs, there must be more
flexibility, so that the manufacturer can perceive opportunities within the
problems and needs of others and create new goods and services which in
themselves will stimulate their own demand. The movement is thus from
low-risk to high-risk forms of activity, and innovation rather than cost
minimisation has to be the dominant creed. This is reminiscent of some of
Peters and Waterman's prescriptions, notably 'stay close to the customer'
(p. 170) and 'autonomy and entrepreneurship to ensure motivation' (p. 208).
Sabel suggests that given these 'needs' (dare one say 'contingencies'?) created
by the desire to thrive in a changing political, technological and social
context, there are two ways in which people in organisations can seek to
foster innovation.

One way, which has a lot in common with the approach of Peters and
Waterman, Sabel called 'neo-Fordism'. This approach aims to make the
'large factory flexible enough to meet the demands of more articulated
markets without abandoning the central principles of Fordism' (p. 209). The

owners and senior managers try 'to have their cake and eat it too: to meet and create new demands for more varied products whilst holding fast to familiar principles of command and organisation'. But it inevitably requires a separation of conception and execution of tasks, which leads to the development of low-trust relationships within the enterprise and an inability to adapt quickly. Sabel, then, unlike Peters and Waterman, is pessimistic about large organisations in this context being successful in the long term. He does not consider the role that collective values, consensus and a caring emphasis on people can play. One presumes he would see them as irrelevant to an essentially antagonistic workforce, who, he thinks, will incline negatively to the introduction of flexible manufacturing systems.

Sabel's alternative to neo-Fordism is small-scale, decentralised, high-technology, cottage industry. Taking the pre-industrialised model of groups of artisans working in a 'post-industrial age', he calls this form of organisation 'artisanal'. He has found an area in the north west of Italy around Venice, Ancona and Bologna, where many groups of between five and fifty workers are joining together in the manufacture of a wide range of products, including textiles, agricultural machinery, machine tools, buses and knitwear. They share a concern to produce the special goods and services which individual customers request; furthermore, they join with the customers in trying to design a product which will satisfy a rather ill-defined need or solve a rather ill-defined problem.

Artisanal organisations, like Mintzberg's 'adhocracies', exhibit a lot of collaboration between levels and functions which Sabel feels can only be ensured in small organisations. He acknowledges that they do not face a lot of competition from large corporations in Italy, whereas similar artisanal organisations in the USA and West Germany tend to be swallowed up in mergers and acquisitions precipitated by the large companies which, through 'neo-Fordist' developments, have retained some flexibility. He also acknowledges that there are long-term problems for the Italian artisanal organisations. For example, there is always the temptation to move into mass production and lose flexibility, and there is a problem in securing skills training for the next generation since the present generation were mostly trained in large corporations which are now in decline. There is, therefore, a long-term need, Sabel argues, for co-operation between labour, the state and entrepreneurs to ensure common services and training, and he is doubtful whether this will develop.

6.4 Concluding Remarks

Culture captured the imagination and for a time appeared to promise the basis for a universally applicable recipe for success. A closer look at its definition and origins and presumed associations with performance, however, shows that conceptually it is so fuzzy that it is unlikely to be able to deliver success in these terms. This is not to say that values and beliefs are not important in analysing organisations: they are often central to our understanding of process and outcomes in organisations, but they have to be considered within the context of other characteristics, as Figure 6.1 indicated.

It is extraordinary that people over the ages, whether in Ancient Greece and Rome or more recently in the nineteenth and twentieth centuries, have known at one level that it is unlikely that simple linear relationships will apply in human systems. Yet it seems each generation has to learn anew that organisations are dynamic multifaceted human systems operating in dynamic environments in which what exactly suits at one time and in one place, however great its apparent success, cannot be generalised into a detailed universal truth, although it is hoped that general principles can be abstracted.

So with culture, as with each of the characteristics of organisations that have been discussed in the first part of this book, the conclusion is that a static model is an insufficient device for understanding organisations. There is a great need for an analysis of processes and it is to these we now turn in Part 2.

Part Two

Processes in Organisations

Power and Conflict 7

When someone is prevented from doing as they wish, they often talk in terms of power. They feel that in this situation or that decision they are powerless to alter things now and perhaps in the future. They complain of a lack of power in relation to both other people and what they see as 'the system'. On the other side of the coin people can be encountered boasting of the amount of power they do have over people or events. Power can also exist when no one speaks of it at all. This chapter begins with a few examples of different situations in which people are parties in power relationships, and then proceeds to analyse and discuss important aspects of power in organisations.

In the post office, a mother tries to obtain her child benefit and is told by the clerk: 'It's not my fault that you can't get your child benefit this week, it's just that your book has run out and your new book hasn't arrived yet. Probably that's because of the train drivers' strike delaying the post, but whatever the reason, I can't do anything about it; I've no authority to pay your benefit without a book.'

In an oil refinery, a maintenance fitter trying to service a poorly positioned valve complains to the shift supervisor about access. 'Don't blame me', says the supervisor, 'I didn't design the plant, I only try to see it operates efficiently. The designers never ask us operating blokes or you maintenance people what would suit us – they just go ahead and hand over the design. We've no power over them. But never mind all that, I need this plant fully operational within the next hour, so you'll just have to manage as best you can.'

The manager of a purchasing department of an electrical assembly factory complains to the sales representative of one of their suppliers about late deliveries. 'I'll see what I can do', says the rep. 'The problem is that we're retooling one of our production lines and production are in difficulties. I'll do what I can about your order but I can't promise anything in the immediate future. You see, production never consult us when they make changes and

161

we've no power to insist. They should produce a lot of stock before shutting down, but they don't want to increase their stock levels.'

A building materials firm has just borrowed heavily to set up an extensive export operation when a change in government monetary policy has the effect of making the pound increasingly strong. Interest owed on loans increases at an alarming rate, and it becomes particularly difficult to remain a strong competitor in export markets flooded with cheaper comparable goods from countries with weaker currencies. The export director, increasingly anxious and concerned, is especially frustrated since he feels his special venture is going to fail because of things over which he has no control. He tries to persuade the finance director to find additional sources of short-term credit but fails.

A design consultancy is moving into new offices; two engineers want the same office. They are equal as far as the organisation chart and job grades are concerned. They each try lobbying the senior administrator on the strength of their case. One succeeds partly because he hints that he will consider leaving the company if he is not given an office which he says will allow him the peace and quiet he needs.

The board of a large car manufacturing firm decides to invest heavily in automatic processes for its body and assembly plant. In the process the workforce is to be reduced by 20 per cent. Voluntary redundancy is being offered to the workers who are affected but, if this does not yield sufficient reductions, compulsory redundancies will be declared.

Each of these cases describes power relationships in which the desires, requests and interests of individuals or groups are frustrated either by the decisions or actions of other people or by characteristics of the technical and administrative system that has been created and developed in the past. The claimant is less powerful than the officer, who is less powerful than the administrative system when it comes to determining whether or not the mother gets her child benefit. The maintenance fitter is less powerful than the shift supervisor when it comes to determining working conditions. But in turn the shift supervisor is less powerful than design engineers when technical systems are being designed. The sales representative of the components factory is less powerful than the production manager over issues of inventory and production schedules. The purchasing manager of the assembly plant may have to bow to the suppliers in the short term, but in the long term he may well discover other suppliers and hence shift his power relationship with the components firms in a fairly dramatic way. The export director of the building materials firm is less powerful than the finance director in determining the company policy on credit, and both of them can do nothing, at least alone, to influence government and Bank of England monetary policy. The workers on the shop-floor can do little individually to affect the board's policy on technical innovation and consequent changes in the composition and size of the workforce. Collectively, however, they may be able to do something to affect the implementation, if not the overall content, of the policy.

7.1 Defining Power Relationships

This chapter will concentrate on power within organisations, although reference will be made to power relationships that are embedded in the environment (see Chapter 4). There are strong relationships between the political context inside and outside a focal organisation. At a simple level individuals and groups who hold strong positions in society are usually those who dominate in organisations. Other less obvious relationships may also be apparent. Where an organisation is preoccupied with political struggles in its environment, its internal political life may be relatively quiet, with few conflicts emerging. On the other hand, organisations which are dominant in their environment are often much taken up with interdepartmental political wrangles. An emphasis on political interactions and the pursuit of interest in organisations is found in several significant publications. Readers should see, for example, Pettigrew (1973), Abell (1975), Tushman (1977), Pfeffer and Salancik (1978) and Pfeffer (1978, 1981b).

Power as the pursuit of interests

Power is defined as the capacity to get decisions and actions taken and situations created which accord with, and support, one's interests. Interests may be reflected in expressed views about what should happen, but they are not always formally articulated. Putting this definition negatively means that a power relationship exists when the desires or interests of one party are frustrated by the actions or creations of others. The assumption is that positions adopted imply a view about what has happened and what should happen. Notionally these views derive from an interaction of perceived self-interest (what is best for me?) and altruism (what is best for the group or organisation?). However, life is not so simple; definitions of what constitutes self-interest and altruism depend on the level of analysis, one's value position, and the skill of the parties in finding an altruistic justification for the pursuit of selfish interests. In the redundancy case, workers fighting to keep their jobs argue for maintaining employment through high manning levels. According to management perceptions, such arguments may be seen as totally self-interested. However, if one widens the social reference to include issues of regional employment, one could argue that there were strong elements of altruism in the workers' postion, since they were fighting to maintain employment, which may be more in the general regional interest, at least in the short term, than is an isolated increase in one company's profitability. It is important, therefore, to look at different social reference points for an assessment of altruism and intentions.

Influence

Influence is defined as the process whereby one party changes the views or preferences of another so that they now conform to their own. In this way the exercise of power as such is unnecessary. For example, if a group of managers is discussing next year's budget and the technical director can persuade the personnel director that it really is in everyone's best interest to put more money into manufacturing technology than into office automation, then agreement is reached without any overt exercise of power. Subsequent discussion will show, however, that the distinction between power and influence is difficult to uphold since the exercise of power is often based on some prior exercise of influence, if only in terms of the general experience of socialisation that was discussed in Chapter 1. Accordingly, most of this chapter is concerned with power.

Power as a property of social relationships

Power is not a characteristic of an individual but is a property of relationships between people. Consideration must be given to the actions and reactions of all the parties, not just those who emerge as most powerful. Powerful relationships need to be specified as regards the subject area or domain in which they apply. For example, we can speak of A having power over B when it comes to the subject of C, but not for subject D. The finance director of the building materials firm is more powerful in decisions about where the company's export drive should be concentrated. The office administrator of the design consultancy has power over the unlucky design engineer as regards office location but not as regards the content of designs.

7.2 Conflict: A Precondition for the Exercise of Power

Power is only relevant to our understanding of behaviour and organisation when there is conflict. If there is genuine agreement on means and ends between people with interests in a particular decision or action, power becomes a redundant concept in explanations of what is happening, although influence may have been important in arriving at consensus. Chapter 2 demonstrated that differences reflecting external groupings, hierarchical level, functional membership, geographical divisions and personal character-istics are fairly commonplace in organisations. Even where coincidence of interest occurs, this may be the creation of power struggles and conflicts in the past.

Overt and covert conflict

Conflicts of interest will not always be manifest in open disagreement, seething arguments or contradictory actions, since existing power relation-ships may be such that conflicts are never openly aired. Table 7.1 summarises four conditions which describe different forms of covert conflict and power. These are compared with situations of overt conflict where the parties are

Table 7.1
Conditions for the Overt and Covert Expression of Conflict and Exercise of Power

Expression of conflict	Knowledge about issue over which there is conflict between interested parties	Action of interested parties to press own interest
Overt	Known to all parties	All parties press own interest
Degrees of covertness	Known to all parties	Some parties 'choose' not to press own interest because they consider they will be unsuccessful, or otherwise fear consequences
	Known to all parties	Some parties 'choose' not to press own interest because they consider the dominance of another partner is legitimate
	Known to some parties but not to others	Some parties excluded from pressing own interest
	Not seen as an issue, part of taken for granted world	No specific action

aware of the issue and consciously take action in pursuit of what they perceive to be their 'best interests'.

Fear of consequences

The first and most obvious covert condition is where some of the parties are aware of the issue and would like to push their viewpoint, but they make a conscious decision that the circumstances are not right for them to do so because they do not want to precipitate adverse consequences. There are four main reasons for adopting this approach: (a) they may consider they will lose anyway; (b) they may feel they will not be given a fair hearing; (c) they may fear that by speaking out they will jeopardise their personal position; (d) they may think that although they have a chance of winning, the 'loss of face' from losing will be more damaging than the benefits from winning. Thus workers who feel that they should have more say in decision-making may not press their claims to representation on key committees because they fear that to do so will lead to them being 'marked' men who will not be given the opportunity to advance their own position. In another case it might be well-known that the head of a small private engineering company is totally against losing the name and autonomy of the family firm. The fact that the production director feels that it would be best for the company and for himself to enter into some sort of merger with a larger company will thus be largely irrelevant, at least in the short term. Instead, the director will bide his time until a situation ripe for change has developed. In a larger company, engineers in the development department may feel that the future for their company lies in specialised, custom-made articles rather than the mass production range they are presently producing. However, the power of sales may be so entrenched and the structure of the sales and production operation so geared up for mass production that they, too, decide to opt for the quiet life and to concentrate their efforts on ways of increasing mass production yields and efficiency. In another situation a senior development engineer might tell a works supervisor to stop production in order to test a new set of switching procedures. The works supervisor may comply simply because the engineer is senior to him in the hierarchy and is known to have the ear of the managing director. His compliance was not because he felt that the engineer had made a legitimate request, but because he had alternative sources of power and support which the works supervisor decided not to challenge.

Ideas of legitimacy

The second covert condition is where some parties are aware of the issue and their relative disadvantage but do not push their own interests because they consider that the others are acting *legitimately*, and therefore that compliance is the appropriate response. Legitimacy derives from internalised norms which provide a broad base for domination and compliance. The norms may be based on wide cultural assumptions, on aspects of the particular culture and language of the enterprise, or on the acceptance of specific documents like job descriptions or instructions. For example, many articled clerks do not question the legitimacy of senior solicitors giving them instructions and criticising their work. Similarly, when a factory supervisor gives an operator his worksheet for the day, the operator generally complies with legitimate authority and does as he is instructed, in spite of the fact that he would rather be doing something else. However, it is unlikely that the operator would comply if the supervisor told him to vote for a particular political party in an election, or indeed, nearer the workplace, to vote for a particular workmate as shop steward.

The establishment of norms of legitimacy is closely associated with the forms of unobtrusive control discussed in Chapter 1. Blau and Schoenherr (1971) describe how 'insidious control' of groups and individuals at work can be achieved through the promulgation of bureaucratic rules and procedures which, once accepted, lay the ground rules for interaction and notions of legitimacy and so control behaviour without the need for any personal intervention. They comment: 'We today are freer from coercion through the power of command of superiors than most people have been, yet men in positions of power today probably exercise more control than any tyrant ever has' (p. 35). Similarly, Perrow has focused on 'unobtrusive controls' of personnel through selection and training programmes which build on the prior education and experience of recruits and seek to mould them into the organisation's image and authority structure (Perrow, 1979, p. 149). Clegg and Dunkerley (1980, p. 444) suggest that in all organisations there is a strong division between those who produce and apply knowledge, which then technically and socially ensures the maintenance of their dominance and the subordination of others. The former define the rules of the game of organisational life which generally support the established structures of power and domination, even if the individuals within the structures may sometimes change.

Continuing the theme of legitimacy and unobtrusive controls, Pfeffer (1981b) writes about 'critical forms of meaning – meaning which justifies and rationalises decisions and actions and which discredits the motivation or information of opponents' (p. 228). A crucial but often neglected part in the creation of meaning and of norms of legitimacy is played by the language that is used (e.g. the designation of all bosses as 'senior partners'), the ceremonies that are enacted (e.g. the firing of a scapegoat or the inauguration of his successor), and the symbols that are displayed (e.g. a new logo or a new organisation chart).

Exclusion of some parties

The third condition shown in Table 7.1 is found where some parties are actually excluded from the knowledge that an issue in which they have a strong interest is under discussion and liable to change. For example, the operatives in an aerospace factory may be profoundly affected by decisions about new technology, but they may not even be aware that decisions are being made until redundancies are announced. In this way they are excluded from having a voice. However, others who are adversely affected, such as the production manager, may have sufficient power to enter the decision arena, and may both 'leak' the information and support the operatives' cause.

Taken-for-granted assumptions

In the fourth covert condition the opportunity for outwardly pressing different interests may not be open to anyone. Unlike the second condition, where individuals are aware of conflicts but consider their subordinate place to be legitimate, and unlike the third condition, where some groups are excluded from an overt process, in the fourth condition the issue as such never comes up for discussion or note. It is accepted uncritically as part of the taken-for-granted world by all or some of the parties. Yet in the status quo there is an implicit conflict and dominance which is not yet recognised, although it may become an issue in the future. For example, the use of a toxic substance or a dangerous piece of equipment at work may not be seen as a contentious issue. Neither workers nor managers may have considered the question of whether exposure to such risks is acceptable, since the risks themselves have never been discussed. In such circumstances, where there is a lack of awareness of the issue, 'interests' of participants can only be defined by an external observer who knows that the state of affairs (a) is theoretically changeable (e.g. alternative substances or machines could be used), and (b) as presently constituted, acts to the benefit of one party (e.g. production or the board) and to the detriment of others (e.g. operatives). We cannot assert that such 'inequalities' will ever necessarily become voiced grievances even when they become known because they may then fall into one of the other forms of covert conflict: for example, the operatives may be prepared to trade risk of exposure to toxic substances for high pay.

Bachrach and Baratz (1962, 1963, 1971) refer to the conditions where parties are effectively excluded from pressing their claim or where the issue is never raised, as examples of 'non-decision-making', which is 'The practice of limiting the scope of actual decision making to safe issues by manipulating the dominant community values, myths and political institutions and procedures' (Bachrach and Baratz, 1963, p. 632). The study by Crenson (1971) of the approach to controlling air pollution in two similar cities in the USA, cited in Chapter 4, is an example of this form of non-decision-making. In this case the power of US Steel within the local political and social structure of one city was sufficient to prevent the issue of air pollution even being raised for many years after measures had been taken in the other city to control comparable pollution levels. Schattschneider (1960) made a classic statement on the inevitability of this form of covert conflict in political organisations: 'All forms of political organisation have a bias in favour of the exploitation of some kinds of conflict and the suppression of others because organisation is the mobilisation of bias. Some issues are organised into politics while others are organised out.' The existence or not of overt conflict cannot be taken as a sign of the importance of power. Indeed, the lack of overt conflict may mean that power is highly relevant, but the power differences are so large and so entrenched that the powerful maintain their position without outward sign. Often the overt display of conflict represents the tip of the iceberg of power in organisations.

7.3 Opportunity for Change or Choice: A Precondition for the Exercise of Power

Power relations extend throughout social life, but as we have seen they are not always visible even to the parties involved. The fourth condition of covert conflict and power must be noted as an essential aspect of organisation, but by its very nature it cannot be the subject of empirical study or practical comment. It does, however, provide the background against which issues and conflicts are identified and interests pursued. Power can only be seen to be exercised when there is opportunity for different interest groups to champion their viewpoints. This usually means that choices and changes are possible. A development engineer recently recruited into a newly designed and commissioned plant may disagree with the design principles and outcomes, but there is little he can do to change them. In the short term, at least, they represent constraints within which he must operate. If, however, he had been recruited at the beginning of the design stage with a very general brief, then there would have been opportunities for him to try to influence the design. Similarly, a newly recruited production supervisor might be very disappointed with the calibre of her work team. Apart from waiting for them to leave or trying to influence their behaviour and attitudes by a series of motivation exercises and training programmes, there is little she can do until she can have a hand in recruiting new workers. Although constraints change with time, at particular points they represent barriers which interested parties may be unwilling or unable to challenge.

The reader will note that constraints are being identified as particularly telling for the person newly entered into a situation, as those who have been in an organisation for some time may, depending on their relative power, have had the possibility of participating in setting the constraints. On the other hand, a new recruit who has a strong power base can often make dramatic changes, unhampered by existing debts, loyalties and history (see Pfeffer, 1981b, p. 254 for a discussion of the politics of 'executive succession').

7.4 Sources of Constraint

The main sources of constraint which limit attempts to exercise power in pursuit of interest are:

1. technological: the parameters set by the plant, machinery and equipment;
2. administrative: the parameters set by rules, procedures and formal structure;
3. ideological: the views of those who are already in strong positions of power concerning what is feasible and desirable.

It is not unusual, then, in contemporary organisations for at least one interested party in a conflict to be represented either through the rules, procedures and other elements of an administrative system or through the parameters of the technical and physical work situation (e.g. the plant, equipment and machinery). To return to the opening examples, the interests of the claimant seeking her child benefit and the craftsman attempting to service the plant are frustrated by aspects of the administrative and technical system which are not only beyond their control but are also beyond the control of the intermediary representations of the 'system' (the post office clerk and the shift supervisor) with which they are dealing.

7.5   Contact and Intention in Power Relationships

Administrative and technical systems do not, of course, just appear. They are created and developed by people. It is therefore analytically possible for one to look at their creators and modifiers as parties to a power relationship with the clerk and shift supervisor as well as with the claimant and maintenance engineer. Certainly their actions in designing and developing the systems have a profound effect upon the capacity of the clerk, supervisor, claimant and maintenance engineer to pursue their own interests; but the designers may have been quite unaware of some of those particular effects. It is appropriate, then, to consider power being exercised in an unwitting and unintended way, particularly where the parties are only 'connected' over considerable time lags? The lack of intention in one party does not alter the profundity with which the effects can be felt, but they do alter the nature of the power relationship. For example, the export director of the building materials firm is at the mercy of the Treasury and the Bank of England, and they in turn are responding to the government's policies. Certainly it is extremely unlikely that their policies are in any way designed to have a precise effect on a particular man, who is probably known to no one in the government, Treasury or Bank of England. Nonetheless, they are greatly affecting what he wants to do and thus can be said to be exerting considerable power over him. Similarly, it is doubtful that the striking train drivers particularly wished to delay the delivery of child benefit books, but this was an outcome of their actions. Table 7.2 illustrates how power relationships vary according to the nature of the contact between the parties and whether the effects on the less powerful were intended by the more powerful.

7.6   Zero Sum or Open Exchanges

Issues about the nature of contact between parties in a power relationship form part of a debate about whether power is always exercised in what is called a 'zero sum' way. This means that if A wins, B loses. The extent to which interests are consciously pursued and outcomes are seen clearly in terms of a 'win-lose' framework depends in part on the cultural background and ideological constructs of the parties involved, including the observer or researcher. Individuals incline to views of the status quo in which they or others are 'objectively' disadvantaged either fatalistically ('It's not good for me/them but I/they can't do anything about it') or happily ('This is my/their

Table 7.2
Contact and Intention in Power Relationships

Extent of intention	*Nature of contact between parties in power relationship (where A is more powerful than B)*			
	1. Direct contact between A and B	2. Indirect contact between A and B who are aware of each other's existence	3. Indirect contact between B and administrative system created by A	4. Indirect contact between B and technical system created by A
A intends effect on B				
Effect on B unintended by A but results from A's action				

Note: Power relationships may be classified as appearing in more than one cell within either of the rows, but they cannot be classified in cells in both the intentional and unintentional rows.

proper place in society or at work and I/they accept it') or radically ('It's wrong and I'm going to try to change it').

Theorists of different complexions acknowledge the importance of a common value base in maintaining social life, but they differ over the answers they would give to the question of how a common value base emerges. Does it arise from a natural identity of interest, or does it derive from an established structure of domination and subordination based on a prior and continuing exercise of power, force, coercion, extortion, etc.? If you see a natural identity of interest, then the exercise of power can be viewed as a facilitating process: the means of ensuring that things (which ultimately are in everyone's interests anyway) get done and the system is nurtured and maintained. There may be some 'temporary' or 'subsidiary' conflicts over distribution in the short term but no fundamental conflicts in the long term. The writings of Tannenbaum (1968) on power in organisations are centrally within what is known as the 'functionalist' tradition in which the various parts of a social system are seen ultimately to contribute to the survival of the whole.

Williamson (1975) and his fellow institutional economists would argue that consensus is ultimately secured through a common interest in efficiency, at least in private sector organisations. Thus the organisational form adopted in the long term is that which provides all parties to transactions with the greatest efficiency in effecting the transactions rather than (as, e.g., Perrow, 1981, Turk and Willman and Francis, 1983 argue), the form which best secures the interests of those in power so that they can retain and strengthen their dominance. Williamson's long-term thesis appears at first glance to imply a consensual view of organisation. However, a question remains, even if one accepts the long-term thesis about whether the 'path' to greater efficiency in every case is uniquely determined. Such simplicity in complex social organisations seems unlikely. The choice between alternative paths is likely to be affected by the pursuit of different sectional and individual interests which may well relate in a zero sum way.

If one inclines wholeheartedly to a zero sum view, then cultural and social structures are themselves the result of the exercise of force and domination in organisations in which there is a fundamental conflict of interest, although this may be obscured from the participants precisely because of the conditions of covert power and conflict. The writings of Clegg alone (1975) and with Dunkerley (1980) illustrate this viewpoint.

Even an apparently 'consensual' issue reveals zero sum characteristics within organisations where people are concerned about the distribution of scarce resources between different activities. For example, issues of health and safety at work are often cited as the epitome of matters in which there is a 'natural identity of interest' (Robens Report, 1972). Yet they often reveal a competitive rather than consensual view of organisations in which power is important. On a general level no one wants accidents and ill-health to result from work activities, but their prevention often makes calls on scarce resources of finance, staff time and interest, materials and plant. Thus when it comes to decisions or actions that are likely to result in a reduction in workplace hazards, differences of interest between the operators most affected, their managers, other managers, shop stewards and safety specialists often become apparent (Dawson *et al.*, 1983, 1988).

7.7 Strategies to Secure and Increase Power

The underlying principles of power relationships have been discussed and note has been taken of the established patterns of domination and subordination, in society generally and in formal organisations in particular, which are extremely resistant to change. The status quo is embodied in a massive array of technological, administrative and above all ideological constraints. In examining how some groups and individuals in organisations acquire and use power one must remember, therefore, that one is only looking at the tip of the iceberg. It is here that different interests are articulated and people try to secure the acceptance of their views through three main strategies: through persuasion and influence to change people's views, which will be discussed in Chapter 9; through bargaining over scarce and valued resources, which is the main subject of the next section; and through the blatant use of force, threat and fear, which will also be briefly discussed in this chapter.

The control of scarce and valued resources

Core activities in organisations, concerned with the production and distribution of goods and services, always involve the acquisition and deployment of a diversity of resources and the generation and disbursement of others. Organisations can thus be viewed as arenas for the exchange of valued resources. As Table 7.3 suggests, resources can be grouped into three main categories: human, financial and physical. The physical and financial resources are fairly easy to identify: they include capital and revenue, plant, tools, equipment, buildings, energy, and so on. Human resources are more nebulous. At the more obvious end they include definable skills and knowledge, but they also encompass individual charisma, personal reputations and influential connections, which are often highly valued by others and hence become scarce resources which can be used in bargaining.

The exchange and bargaining relationships between people associated with any organisation are rarely symmetrical. Although one party, A, may require a resource from another, B, B may receive in exchange resources from yet another, C. A series of interlocking exchanges is thus created, as illustrated in Table 7.4. Starting with the 'requirements' of the boards of directors, third-party suppliers of these resources are identified together with the fourth parties who might be responsible for providing resources to the third parties. For example, if the board's strategy requires the application of technical knowledge, they will employ professional engineers whose salary will be partly determined by the board in accordance with general personnel policy, but will also be influenced by their superiors. Similarly, their immediate superiors will mediate their access to more or less interesting work. Another resource required by engineers is the acquisition and maintenance of appropriate equipment, which will be partially dependent on the approval of the finance director, who will in turn depend in part on the recommendation of the technical director. The maintenance of the equipment will depend on technicians and craftsmen who, in their turn will look to the engineers for good appraisals and interesting work. Development engineers may turn to university consultants as a source of research and development knowledge, and these consultants will then expect payment from the finance director. In this way a professional engineer both gives and takes resources to and from a range of different individuals and groups in a firm.

Table 7.3
Organisations as Arenas for the Exchange of Valued Resources

Resources taken into organisations	*Resources generated within and taken out of organisations*
Human	*Human*
Manual skills and abilities	Skills, qualifications and experience
Personal reputation and charisma	Personal reputation
Technical knowledge and	Promotion, job security
intellectual ability	Praise, support, fulfilment
Administrative knowledge and	Identification with well-known
expertise	company or people
Access to influential people in	Services
government and the market	Information about performance
(lobbying capacity)	Strategy
Information about the market	
Financial	*Financial*
Financial capital	Dividends
Financial revenue	Wages and salaries
	Interest
Physical objects	*Physical objects*
Materials, components	Product goods
Plant, equipment, machinery	New technologies
Energy for heat, light, power	

Exchange, dependency and power

Any partner in an exchange is also party to some form of dependency. The degree and direction of dependency of each party on others will be based on the availability of satisfactory alternatives for each party (i.e. the ease with which substitute resources can be found from another party), and the importance or centrality of the desired resources or commodities to the fulfilment of their needs, goals and objectives.

The extent to which resources are substitutable varies considerably both over time and place. The degree of substitutability of the human resources of labour, skills and knowledge reflects the extent and nature of an individual's education, training and experience, as well as labour market characteristics. Graduates, who in the early 1960s in Britain were in short supply, were

Table 7.4
Examples of Suppliers and Recipients in Exchanges of Resources in an Industrial Organisation

Resources required by board of directors	Third-party suppliers	Resources required by these third parties	Fourth-party suppliers
Manual skills and abilities	Operators	Wages Job security Training	Production managers First line supervisors Personnel department
	Craftsmen	Wages Job security Tools and equipment	Engineering managers Workshop supervisor
Technical knowledge	Professional engineers	Career promotion Salary More interesting work Well maintained equipment Source of new ideas	The board Superiors Personnel directorate Workshop University consultants
Administrative capacity and knowledge	Managers	Salary Job security Career development	The board Personnel directorate Technical directorate
Capital	Bank shareholders	Interest	Finance directorate and other functions
Income	Customers	Products	Production and sales
Materials, components machinery	Other firms	Money Continuing secure markets	Production directorate Development directorate

quickly snatched up into employment. Now their successors with the same qualifications several years later are quite likely to join the dole queue. The substitutability of physical resources depends on the availability and distribution of raw materials and energy over the earth's surface and technical knowledge, which can facilitate the use of more easily obtainable substitutes or the development of new forms of plant, equipment and machinery.

The more individuals and groups are parties to exchanges in order to secure resources which are highly central to them and for which there are few substitutes, then, all other things being equal, the relatively less powerful and more dependent they are on their present suppliers. Sometimes 'other things' are not equal, and the power afforded by the control of scarce and valued resources may be offset by what is happening in other areas. Furthermore, patterns of exchange and dependency may change over time with the market of supply and demand and as the parties change their preferences.

Emerson (1962) argued that where there are imbalances in exchange relationships, the party with least power and greatest dependence will seek to alter the situation. For example, it may change preferences to reduce the resource's centrality; find alternatives; withdraw from the exchange; or, through collective action, secure a coalition of weaker parties against others. the preparedness of people to use an 'exit' option, or to stay and 'voice' their grievances in the hope of securing change, or to stay and accept the status quo with 'loyalty', is the subject of discussion by Hirschman (1972) under the title of *Exit Voice and Loyalty.*

Few people feel they have complete freedom of movement, although no one is absolutely forced to exchange their commodities with others (except perhaps in prisons or other custodial institutions). Nonetheless, many feel they have little alternative but to comply with the demands placed upon them because their dependence is high and their power is low. For example, a machine tool manufacturer may supply a large proportion of his output to one large conglomerate. If he cannot find alternative purchasers, the survival and growth of his business depends on his ultimately accepting the best terms he can get from his main customer. Similarly, a qualified development engineer whose family commitments make geographical mobility difficult, will be relatively bound to his present employer who operates the only high technology plant in his area. In such circumstances the resources as required by the machine tool manufacturer and the development engineer relate to highly central preferences, which are difficult to satisfy through other suppliers.

Issues and outcomes cannot be viewed in isolation; they are usually related to one another even across different domains. Some cautious people never accept a proffered favour, whether a free lunch or a day's outing, for fear of the *quid pro quo* which might be expected later. Similarly, there is always the possibility that one might 'win the battle but lose the war'. It is thus always important to take a series of issues and exchanges over a period of time if one wants to make judgements about the relative power of different groups.

Discretionary control of resources

The power afforded people through their control of resources is not, then, simply a matter of ownership but of being conscious of having discretionary control over their availability and use. For example, anaesthetic equipment in hospitals is usually owned by the state, but it is the anaesthetists who use the equipment and who make it available to surgeons and patients. If for some reason there is a shortage of anaesthetists in a hospital, they will be in a relatively strong position in relation to other specialists and will be able to dictate not only which equipment is used, by whom and for what purposes, but they will also be able to press some more personal claims about their working conditions. The importance of discretionary control has been demonstrated in a study of power relations in prison workshops (Dawson, 1975). Although the workshops were endowed with considerable resources, the industrial supervisors did not have discretion over their use and so could not use them in their relationship with the inmate workers. Since they were not in a position to offer the workers anything they really valued, the supervisors had very little power and were often unable to ensure workers' co-operation. A similar situation was found by Bennis *et al.* (1958) in their study of supervisory power in 'ordinary' factories. They found that where the rewards for the workers, especially promotion, were not influenced by supervisors, their power and influence were considerably impaired.

Similar problems have been encountered with attempts to promote dual career ladders for professional scientists and engineers working in industry (Gunz, 1980). This is a device for trying to keep good scientists in research and development work rather than automatically promoting them out of science and into management. Two promotion ladders are established, one for conventional managers with increased rewards for more responsibility, and one for specialist scientists with rewards for expertise. In spite of considerable support (e.g. Moore and Davies, 1977), a major criticism (Goldner and Ritti, 1967) is that it does not provide status or power equivalent to that on the managerial ladder since 'it does not provide the power to allocate limited resources or to pursue alternative goals, and this power is intrinsic to traditional prestigious and successful professional performance'. This argument bears upon this discussion in two important ways. First, scientists on the scientific ladder are not sufficiently rewarded and hence, all other things being equal, will look elsewhere for rewards or status. Second, one reason their status is not improved is because they do not have sufficient control of discretionary resources in order to pursue their own interests.

Groups as well as individuals can exercise control over resources. This has been documented by Hickson *et al.* (1971), who have focused on the control of 'strategic contingencies' as a basis for group or departmental power in organisations. Crozier (1964) explained the power of maintenance men in a French factory in terms of their power to handle technical breakdowns, which were a major source of uncertainty for senior managers. Following this line of explanation, Hickson *et al.* (1971) argued that the division of labour in organisations created interdependent departments whose major efforts are directed towards 'coping with uncertainty'. Those units which are better able to cope with the more important sources of uncertainty and whose work is difficult to substitute emerge as the most powerful. Thus the power of work groups is seen to be much influenced by their position in the production flow, their irreplaceability, and their uniqueness within the organisation. Salaman (1979) uses this analysis to explain why senior organisational members are often keen to limit the discretion available to lower level groups by routinising their work. In this way the substitutability of their work is increased and the senior's dependence on the junior's control over uncertainty is decreased. But it is not possible to eliminate discretion entirely; areas of uncertainty remain, and indeed are created by participants wishing to retain a 'special position'. The exercise of discretion cannot then be totally eliminated, and it sometimes falls on people who are formally low in the hierarchy and in the most unfashionable of specialist departments.

Mechanic (1962) described in a classic article how 'lower participants' could exercise power in some domains of organisational life. If, like Crozier's (1964) maintenance men, they have skills, knowledge or information that are needed by their superiors, they can extract a harder bargain in terms of their own pay, status and work style than can other groups. Mechanic described how hospital orderlies took advantage of the doctors' dislike of administration to take control of aspects of the administration until they had sufficient power effectively to control the operation lists. Developments in microprocessor technology and the surge of interest in seeking applications in many fields has meant that good software engineers are in extremely short supply. They are consequently able to command more favourable terms and conditions of employment than colleagues who have the same level of qualification and years of experience, but who are in a more established field where good engineers are relatively abundant. It is likely that the 'power' of software engineers, deriving from their employment market position, will extend beyond their ability to secure favourable personal terms of employment to a more significant place in decision-making on items as various as the company's future product strategy, a proposed restructuring or the training programme for users of new information technology.

But . . . remember the formal hierarchy and emotional attachments

One should not, however, be too captivated by the idea of the power of lower participants. It is noteworthy because it is the exception rather than the rule, and even in the exceptional cases one is usually talking about fairly well defined issues or domains in which it is possible to use 'negative' power to prevent rather than 'positive' power to promote. In general, the formal structure that was discussed in Chapter 5 provides the basic scaffolding on which power in terms of the control of scarce and valued resources is generated and used. Furthermore, as Zald (1970) and others have described, people accept subordinate positions not simply because of their relative position in the formal strucure, but also because of 'promises of values fulfilled and promises of friendship and prestige', as well as the established and accepted norms and rules which create the fabric of unobtrusive control.

Collective control of resources

It is often the case that people do not individually have control over scarce resources valued by others, but that as part of a collectivity (like a trade union or professional association) they have considerable potential power. The difference between individual and collective forms of power is that the potential in the latter is not as easily transferred into action as in the former. Collective action requires some form of mobilisation and shared consciousness amongst the group if it is to achieve unity of behaviour and become a genuine force within the enterprise. The relevance of collective consciousness in work group power is demonstrated, for example, by the work of Marchington and Armstrong (1982, 1983) on shop steward organisation and work group power. If collective consciousness is not forthcoming, the role of the shop steward is often vital in raising issues which then form the focus for a collective realisation of both interests and sources of power. If, however, the steward is unsuccessful and collective consciousness is not forthcoming, work groups which might be 'expected' to be most powerful in terms of their position and role in fact often have little influence on matters which affect them as a group.

A fairly mundane resource like that of the ability to operate a lathe, which is shared by thousands in a person's immediate labour market, can become a significant and scarce resource if all the other 150 operators doing similar work in the factory agree to strike in support of better terms and conditions. The strike at Ford's Halewood Plant in July 1983 was the result of a dispute with a handful of security officers and firemen, but their activities were so central that the plant had to close. In the long coal miners' strike in 1984–5 the position of the pit deputies' union, NACODS, was critical. Whereas the National Coal Board was not moved to find a settlement with the National Union of Mineworkers, it was determined to maintain the co-operation of the key men in NACODS.

Force and coercion

Power through the use of force, punishment or negative sanctions is in some ways the mirror image of power through the use of valued resources or positive rewards. It could be argued that withholding scarce resources from another party (for example, when bonuses are withheld or promotion is not given) is a form of punishment which occurs as part of exchange and dependency. At a formal level employment legislation and company rule books establish rights and procedures for the parties involved in disciplinary or dismissal cases. Dismissal is a strong means of coercion, especially at times and in places of high unemployment. In general, such exercises of power may well be successful in terms of ensuring minimal compliance from subordinates, but they rarely lay the basis for inviting extra effort and co-operation unless the punishment is seen as fair and legitimate for some misdemeanour.

7.8   Concluding Remarks

The language of this last part of the chapter has reflected a market model in which there are sources and rates of supply and demand for some resources which are subject to more or less tight constraints. But the image of a marketplace for power cannot be left to dominate this chapter. Certainly it is a good image of the tip of the iceberg which displays the overt and observable aspects of power in organisations, but the market operates within the technological, administrative and, above all, ideological constraints that were discussed in the first part of the chapter. Covert power and conflict, reflecting underlying social and cultural structures, often make any more obvious manifestation of power unnecessary or misleading. Such situations may appear to be deceptively 'free' from the exercise of power, and yet in many ways it is here that power differences are strongest and most deeply ingrained. Such a paradox means that any analysis of power in organisations needs to be done with great sensitivity and awareness of different levels of meaning and experience. The fact that this is a difficult task does not mean it should be neglected, since the acquisition and exercise of power is one of the main processes running throughout organisational life, and a basic understanding of it is relevant to the other areas discussed in this book.

With the hope of contributing to a more sensitive analysis, this chapter concludes with a checklist, presented in Table 7.5, which can be used by those who are prepared to attempt the daunting but highly important task of analysing power relationships in organisations. Situations vary in the extent to which any of the elements in Table 7.5 can be more or less well defined. In the most obvious power relationships there are clearly defined issues (for example, which of the design engineers should have the 'better office'). There are clearly defined parties: in the above case, the two engineers and the senior administrator. Interests are also fairly clear-cut: the two engineers want the same office and the administrator wants to maintain a stable and high quality team of consultants. Each party can call upon the scarce resources they command and their personal standing in the company as the basic 'weapons' in the fight. Lastly, there are clearly defined outcomes in terms of who wins or loses, and slightly less clearly defined but nonetheless discernible overall effects on the morale and turnover of the engineers as a whole. Other outcomes for the individuals may also follow (e.g. in terms of effects of their

Table 7.5
Checklist for the Analysis of Power Relationships in Organisations

1. *Parties* in the relationship: who are they?
2. *Domain*: what are the issues or subjects?
3. *Interests*: what are the interests of each of the parties in this domain?
4. *Consciousness*: to what extent are the parties conscious of their interests?
5. *Willingness*: to what extent are the parties willing to pursue their interests?
   (a) If unwilling to pursue: to what extent is this for practical reasons (fear of consequences, etc.); to what extent is this for ideological reasons (beliefs in legitimacy, taken for granted assumptions, etc.)?
   (b) If willing to pursue: what resources and weapons are available to them, and do they use them?
6. *Influence*: to what extent have the parties' views changed as a result of interaction with other parties?
7. *Outcomes*: how are the issues resolved?
                effects on issue?
                effect on main participants?
                other effects?

overall status in the company or in terms of their willingness to co-operate with the office administrator over other issues). Regardless of subsequent ramifications, the main elements of this power relationship are fairly easy to see. Often power relationships are not so easy to analyse, even for the parties themselves, let alone for some external observer or analyst, but it is in such situations that an analysis of power is likely to be most fruitful.

Communication and Decision-making 8

Organisational activity revolves to a great extent around the outcomes of a galaxy of decisions more numerous than could ever be counted or identified. Grossly simplifying, Table 8.1 provides a list of six main subject areas in which decision-making plays a vital role. Each of these areas is often seen as the special province of particular parts of the organisation. Thus decisions about strategy are usually seen as the responsibility of those at the top, operating decisions about how best to utilise resources are seen as activities for the middle line, and decisions about the procurement of physical and financial resources and technical innovation are strongly associated with technical support staff. Decisions about administrative and personnel requirements and industrial relations issues are seen as variously concerning both specialist and line staff. The sixth subject area in Table 8.1 is more general. Given the name 'social fabric', it is included to emphasise that decision-making in organisations is not only concerned with task-related matters but also has strong symbolic significance. It is one of the ways in which social bonds are created, strengthened and broken as coalitions and alliances flourish and die with different issues and in different contexts. Decisions also have ritualistic and symbolic purpose in justifying and legitimating past, present and future activities. For example, a manager who feels that his position is being undermined by an influx of bright new graduates may issue decisions which serve only to provide a symbol of his formal position of authority. Alternatively, two departmental heads who have argued over budget allocation may both agree to support a project in which they have little direct interest but which will allow them to show all concerned they are still the best of friends. The way decisions are made as well as their content have importance in the creation of corporate culture (see Chapter 6).

Notwithstanding the identity of decision areas with particular groups, however, each set of decisions is in fact usually influenced considerably by

Table 8.1
Subject Areas in which Decision-making is Important

Subject area	*Main concerns*
1. *Strategy* (the objectives pursued within the organisation which define the overall task)	• what to produce • how to produce it • what resources are required
2. *Day-to-day operations* (the utilisation of the assembled resources)	• production rate and schedule • monitoring short-term targets • schedule and organisation of maintenance • stock levels

3. *Procurement of resources*
  (a) physical materials, objects and energy
  (b) financial
  (c) personnel
	• securing supply of appropriate quantity and quality of physical resources
	• securing supply of capital
	• maintaining cash liquidity
	• recruitment, training and promotion of workforce
	• maintenance of morale, motivation and commitment
	• industrial relations

4. *Administration*	• set up and maintain appropriate administrative information and planning systems • set up and maintain appropriate organisation design
5. *Technical innovation*	• how can performance be improved? • what new products or processes can be developed?
6. *Social fabric*	• justification of past • legitimation of present and future plans • expressions of friendship and trust • expressions of enmity and distrust

information and opinion from other interested parties. For example, the selection of problems to be tackled by development engineers may ultimately be made by the board in response to a paper prepared by the technical directorate. But this decision will crucially depend on information from sales and marketing about forecast changes in customer requirements, on more or less informed guesses about what competitors are doing, on information from production on current and forecast bottlenecks and problems, on information from the development groups themselves about technical feasibility and from finance about the availability of cash and expected rates of return. Each set of information is the outcome of judgements made by other people, who in turn will often have made decisions in the light of information gathered by yet other people. Thus information passes from customers to sales, from suppliers to materials management, from operatives to their supervisors, and so on, and may be incorporated into decisions at many different points. Figure 8.1 provides an illustration of some of the sources of information that are likely to be relevant to the selection of development tasks. It shows the involvement of a variety of different interest groups in transmitting and receiving information and illustrates a general principle: that decisions are made on the basis of information communicated between groups, each with variable knowledge and sources of power and influence. Information, communication, interest and power are thus the raw materials of decision-making. Interests and power have already been discussed in Chapters 2 and 7. Consequently the first main section of this chapter is devoted to a discussion of information and communication; the second section provides an analysis of decision-making in organisations.

8.1   Information and Communication

Communication is defined as the sending of information (a message) and its receipt. It is assumed that the transmission of the message will lead to some 'change' in the receiver. At a minimum she will acquire an additional piece of information, which may reduce uncertainty and increase levels of knowledge, capacity to act, or understanding. How the message is received is as crucial a part of the process as how it is transmitted. The communication cycle is sometimes completed by feedback from the receiver to the sender.

Communication is a vital process in every organisation. Kar (1972) estimated that between 40 and 60 per cent of work time in a typical US manufacturing plant involved some phase of communication, and Beach (1970) estimated that top and middle-level executives devote 60 to 80 per cent of their total working lives to communication. The generation of information and its communication is particularly important in those parts of the organisation which deal with the uncertainties and complexities that originate both within and outside the organisation. Where there is more certainty and predictability people can rely on standard communication procedures. This at least would be the 'rational' approach. However, this is but another instance where the 'rational' response, assuming consensus and systematic analysis, is not always in evidence.

Even without considering differences of interest, people are by definition ignorant of what they do not know and thus may be unaware of new products,

FIGURE 8.1

The Interaction of Information, Opinion and Decisions in the Development of Detailed R & D Workplans

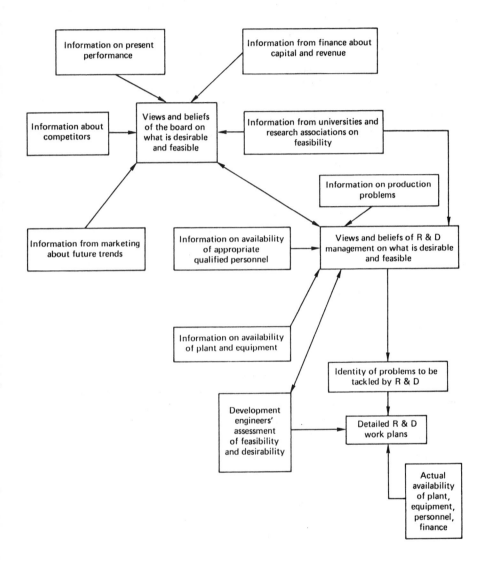

Note: this diagram is deliberately selective. Other sources of information, influence and feedback will be important.

processes, market opportunities, shifts in social attitudes and public opinion and changes in industrial structures. They may therefore misguidedly concentrate all their attention on ensuring effective communication within a technological, market and industrial relations strategy which is fast approaching obsolescence. Furthermore, ignorance is often compounded by fear of change, obsession with secrecy, defence of interest, and established patterns of friendship and animosity. Not surprisingly, therefore, many estimates suggest that much communication in organisations is largely ineffective and that vast tracts of information are ignored. For example, Davis (1961) estimated on the basis of American evidence that out of information communicated by top management, two-thirds of it was understood as intended by vice-presidents, 40 per cent of it was understood as intended by middle managers, 30 per cent by foremen and 20 per cent by production operators.

The impact of information technology

Significant developments in information technology now facilitate the speedier and more complex analysis and distribution of information. Some of the effects of these developments have already been discussed in Chapters 3 and 5. For example, it has been suggested that simplified management structures and more systematic approaches to planning, control and evaluation will become more common with the introduction of sophisticated information technology. However, conclusive evidence on such trends is not available and, given the arguments presented in Chapter 3 that technology can be created and used in a variety of ways, it is unlikely that any one pattern of effects will necessarily emerge.

The hardware and software of information systems are intendedly designed for specific purposes. They embody assumptions about the nature of organisations, the relative place and contribution of different groups, and the characteristics of appropriate planning systems. As Hedberg and Mumford (1975) illustrate, all those who specify, develop, implement and operate these systems do so in response to their views about the purposes and characteristics of the systems and their assessment of their own relative power and influence in effecting system design and operation. There is little, if anything, about the information technology itself which makes inevitable the spread of organisational forms in which a strong central core of professionals, drawn from the primary labour market, control peripheral activities, which are largely undertaken by people drawn from the secondary labour market. For example, Hedberg (1977) suggests that technology may be used to facilitate quite different developments in industrial democracy and 'organisational learning'. He cites developments in West Germany and Norway in 'workers' information systems', which use a similar data base to 'management information systems' but put the systems to different purposes, such as worker self-management of production control and scheduling. He complains that there is generally very limited feedback from the analysis of collected information in many formal organisations, so that learning circles are incomplete and people are denied the opportunity of seeing the results of their activities. Once again this bias is not inherent in the technology, but is a characteristic designed into it. Why not, he asks, provide more feedback and give the opportunity for greater autonomy and discretion on the shop-floor? The answers to these questions have little to do with technical issues as such, but a great deal to do with social issues of power, control and interest.

The massive information technology explosion which characterises the mid-1980s cannot in itself guarantee to eradicate basic communications problems in organisations since these largely originate in characteristics of social organisation and human behaviour rather than the nature of specific technologies. Nonetheless, its capacity for speedier generation and more complex analysis of information, within the limits imposed by social organisation, is likely to affect communication significantly.

Why are there so many 'problems' with communication?

Five characteristics of an ideal communication process can be identified.

1. Accuracy: message clearly reflects intention and truth as seen by sender and is received as such.
2. Reliability: diverse observers would receive message in same way.
3. Validity: message captures 'reality', is consistent, allows prediction and incorporates 'established knowledge'.
4. Adequacy: message is of sufficient quantity and appropriate timing.
5. Effectiveness: message achieves the intended result from sender's point of view.

There are many reasons why communication often falls far short of these ideals. A basic problem which faces all participants in organisations is how to get 'appropriate' information to the 'right' place at the 'right' time so that it has the intended effect, particularly when the complexities of life often make it difficult to determine what the 'right place', 'right time' and 'right information' actually are. An examination of some of the reasons underlying these difficulties with communication will be made through a discussion of the general issues summarised in Table 8.2.

Quantification

Information varies in the extent to which it is quantifiable. For example, the number of qualified people or the amount of money available for development engineering in any one financial year can be quantified, whereas the benefits and costs that have accrued from new personnel policies or from reorganisation may be more difficult to quantify. Many people are so

---

Table 8.2
Information and Communication in Organisations: General Issues

---

1. *Quantification*: (a) information varies in the extent to which it is quantifiable;
   (b) quantifiable information is often given precedence over non-quantifiable information in decision-making.

2. *Verification*: information varies in the extent to which it can be subject to external verification.

3. *Neutrality*: information is rarely used in a completely neutral way

4. *Scarcity*: information is a costly and scarce resource.

5. *Formal and informal communication networks*: hierarchies often emerge even if they are not imposed on communication networks.

6. *Gatekeepers* control access and interpretation of information across physical, social and technical barriers.

7. *Partiality*: information held and transmitted by people is often partial and reflects their interests and resources.

8. *Suppression*: some information may be consciously or subconsciously excluded from consideration if it questions or counters the dominant view.

---

attracted by harder, more quantifiable information that they concentrate their attentions on these matters to the neglect of others which are sometimes more important, particularly when one realises the 'imprecise' nature of many of the so-called 'facts' one is considering. This emphasis on the quantifiable can present particular problems in relation to control systems. Where there are several aspects to a job, a control system which provides data on the easily measured to the neglect of the more ephemeral may lead to poor overall performance. For example, if records of social workers' activities only include numbers of clients seen, and if social workers feel that importance is attached to these records, they are likely to make contact with as many clients as possible, perhaps to the neglect of the quality of their interactions with individual clients. Similarly, if a development engineer feels that his work is evaluated in strict 'cost minimisation' terms, which are easily quantifiable, he may neglect areas of work that could lead to significant developments. In another context, budgetary systems that concentrate exclusively on keeping 'in the black' may stifle initiatives which are critical to long-term survival.

Verification

Information varies in the extent to which it can be subject to external verification: for example, the price of a piece of equipment, the expected response of a shop steward to a proposal for changes in working practices, or reports on the number of applicants for a job are all open to some degree of verification by checking back with another person: in these cases, the supplier, the shop steward and the personnel officer. Additional checks can sometimes be made of records or documents, as in the case of the job applications and equipment price. Some information, however, especially that which comes under the guise of 'expert' or 'informed' opinion about the feasibility, desirability or consequences of suggested actions, is much less open to external verification. Even if information can be externally verified, there are no necessary grounds for believing this will always be done or, when it is done, that it will be done accurately and reliably.

Neutrality

Information is rarely used in a completely 'neutral' way; it does not and cannot 'speak for itself'. It is sent and received by people who may have different interests, opinions and assumptions. It is subject to many social influences and indeed is created as part of a social process. Even with so-called 'facts', and certainly with 'opinions', there are many ways in which their presentation and receipt can be altered.

Scarcity

Information is a costly and a scarce resource. Its collection, dissemination and receipt takes up time, equipment and materials. As a scarce resource it can be an important base for power and influence. This is graphically illustrated in Pettigrew's study of the decisions associated with the purchase of a new computer installation. He observed the way in which different groups of programmers, administrators and systems specialists used their access to scarce information as an integral part of their struggle to influence the final purchasing decision (Pettigrew, 1973). Its scarcity means that issues are often raised about whether additional investment of time and money in communication is likely to be worth the benefits that may accrue.

Formal and informal communication networks

Many laboratory experiments have been conducted into the effectiveness of different forms of communication networks (see, e.g., Katz and Kahn, 1966, pp. 237–8). In the main three networks are usually compared: a wheel in which people on the periphery communicate only with the person at the hub;

a circle in which everyone can communicate to their two immediate neighbours; and an 'all channel' network in which everyone can communicate with everyone else. Efficiency is defined in terms of speed of arriving at a correct solution to a problem. Repeated experiments show the wheel pattern to be most efficient. Furthermore, informal hierarchies usually emerge in the other two patterns before solutions to complex problems are found. This is of great relevance to our consideration of organisations since it suggests that whether communication is upwards, downwards or across, hierarchies will emerge, usually reflecting the relative power and interests of the parties involved. Where the communication channels do not follow those specified in formal organisational arrangements, 'informal networks' are said to exist. For example, two superiors in different departments may communicate directly with each other, rather than through their bosses. It is misleading to see the formal and informal systems as completely distinct; rather they should be seen as interdependent.

Gatekeepers

Gatekeepers control access and interpretation of information across physical, social and technical barriers. Some people in positions of strategic importance in communication channels have a special advantage in being able to open or close access to information for other people. For example, a personal secretary often acts as a gatekeeper for information into, and sometimes out from, her boss. The barriers which the gatekeeper occupies can sometimes be physical ones: the secretary's office may be between that of her boss and the rest of the organisation. Alternatively, the barriers can be social: it could be said that police officers and prison officers act as gatekeepers between 'criminal' and 'respectable' social groups, since these two groups rarely come into direct contact. Lastly, barriers can be ones of technical knowledge: the scientist who has a gift for communicating with lay people can act as a 'gatekeeper' between scientific and lay communities.

Gatekeeping is thus to some extent endemic in any complex organisation or society that is inhabited by groups of different interests, habits and knowledge. Nonetheless, individuals who perceive the strategic advantage that can accrue from their capacity to control and interpret information may exaggerate the extent to which gatekeeping is inevitable. In this way they are taking full personal advantage of the fact that information – like money and skills – is a scarce resource required by others in the organisation.

Partiality

Information held and transmitted by people is usually partial and reflects their own interests and resources. Total information on many subjects is rare in that there are still some things about these subjects that have not yet been discovered. Other information may be known to some people, but the people in whom we are interested may be in one of three states. First, they may be unaware that they could know more and are hence oblivious of the possibility of improving their information base. Second, they may realise that more could be known but consider themselves to be so lacking in areas of education, training or experience that they think they would not understand the information even if it was made available to them. Third, they may consider that more information could possibly be collected but are unable or unwilling to afford the time, energy or money necessary to acquire it.

Simon's (1957) concept of bounded rationality, particularly as it was developed by Thompson (1967), is related to these general points. It is based on the assumption that in complex situations individuals cannot know everything and that they will operate with a view of the world or 'rationality' that is bounded or blinkered by their knowledge, assumptions and interests. Since organisations are usually composed of a number of different interest groups, it would be very surprising if they all shared exactly the same rationality. Consider, for example, the problem of a fairly dramatic fall in productivity of one work group. The works manager may see this as a clear case of one newly recruited 'bad apple' affecting the work and motivation of others. The industrial relations manager may point to the fact that a recent pay settlement was a great disappointment to this group. The maintenance manager may emphasise that his planned maintenance schedule is being frustrated by production refusing maintenance access to lines because of 'rush' jobs and that consequently there are a lot of small daily problems with the machines which are reducing production rates overall and creating dissatisfaction among the workers. The development manager says they should have automated this part of the plant long ago and dramatically changed working practices. The shop steward says the problems arise because supervisors are clamping down on minor unofficial perks and keeping tighter control of time-keeping, and that this, coupled with a disappointing pay settlement, means that the group has lost its commitment to the company. In this way the accounts multiply in form, content and meaning. Each has a significant but different point and each holds it with conviction.

Thompson and Wildavsky (1986) develop a cultural theory of organisations which is predicated on the statement that 'organization is bias. For there is no way to look at all data from all directions . . . There are only partial ways, selecting some phenomena in and rejecting other bits outside of organised perception.' They suggest there are four general styles for rejecting information.

1. Risk absorption, whereby people regard life fatalistically like a lottery and hence do not seek out new information.
2. Networking, whereby people push out information to the periphery of their network so that they can concentrate on what is really important.
3. Paradigm protection, whereby people subtly reject information which fundamentally threatens their taken-for-granted sets of views and assumptions.

4. Expulsion, whereby far less subtly than the previous style, strong barriers are erected to preserve views and assumptions against new and threatening information.

Examples of the last two strategies are graphically provided in Johnson's (1987) study of change in Fosters Clothing Company, where a market research report which had unequivocally identified a serious problem was discredited by senior managers because it questioned basic assumptions and posed a serious political threat. It was reinterpreted in terms of accepted wisdom and thus an important imperative for change was overlooked.

Suppression

Information which questions or counters accepted viewpoints, or 'conventional wisdom' as it is sometimes called, may be excluded from consideration by the power processes which were discussed in Chapter 7. The suppression of, or at least failure to call up, conflicting information may be done subconsciously. Those involved may be so concerned with their own definition of the problem and possible solutions that they may not search for different definitions or solutions. For example, a maintenance fitter and his mate may be so sure that the problem with a gravity flow chemical plant lies with a faulty pump that they concentrate all their attention on the pump. In fact, the problem may have arisen because of the interaction of two incompatible valve systems creating flow problems which the pump cannot properly accommodate.

At other times the suppression of counter-information can be the result of conscious and purposive action on the part of some participants, which may mix with subconscious suppression by other parties. Janis (1972) describes situations of 'group think', wherein all parties suppress their doubts about the way an issue is being tackled and hence effectively suspend their powers of critical judgement. His most celebrated account is of President Kennedy and his advisers in the run-up to the Cuban Bay of Pigs fiasco. In the full flush of their relatively unexpected electoral victory, the group shared illusions of invulnerability and unanimity. They were profoundly influenced by CIA (Central Intelligence Agency) interests whom they did not wish to antagonise and orchestrated by group 'mindguards' and 'gatekeepers' who ensured that counter-information and doubts were deliberately excluded. Their ill-conceived plan was for the USA to spearhead a revolution in Cuba against Castro so that, once alight, the flames of revolution would quickly spread. Once committed to this road, they disregarded all contrary evidence, and indeed mostly omitted either to seek for verification on the 'facts' they were given or to call for new evidence. From this blinkered position, in which the expression of different points of view was both obviously and unobtrusively discouraged, they embarked on a disastrous course of action.

Explaining 'distortions' in communication

Effective communication can be said to exist when the sender's message is accurately received and has the desired effect on the receiver, which is conveyed through feedback to the sender. The eight general points discussed above provide explanations of why the sender may not have accurate and full information to start with, why it may be distorted from the sender's intentions when it is received, why it may be omitted and never transferred or received, and why feedback may not occur. It must be noted that 'distorted' or 'effective' communications are not, of course, absolute concepts; they depend very much on the views and interests of those involved (hence the use of inverted commas to indicate their relative definition).

Another way to understand the reasons for 'ineffective' communication is to look at the message, individual and organisational characteristics which explain the direction that 'distortions' take.

First, message characteristics, in terms of the qualities of transmission, receipt and feedback, may present problems. The telephone line may be 'crackly', the writing may be illegible, or the printout machine may be suffering from chip failure and give erroneous output.

Second, individual characteristics such as education, experience, social relationships and interests have a profound effect on people's views of the world and hence their interpretations of received information and their role as senders of information. The receiver may respond to cues which the sender regards as irrelevant; her own needs, values and interests will affect her interpretation of the message, which will also be influenced by her perception of the sender. A number of other processes have been noted by social psychologists as affecting communication. Stereotyping, for example, occurs when one party to the communication treats the other(s) as though they conformed exactly to their image of 'all people who belong to this recognisable category'. Some people have a generalised and often wholly inaccurate picture of 'all' trade unionists, financial controllers, social workers, and so on. Rather than stereotyping people into generalised categories outside oneself there is the opposite phenomenon known as 'projection', in which one assumes that the other party to the communication has the same characteristics as oneself. Communication is also affected by 'the halo effect', where only one or two pieces of information are used to generalise about a larger situation. As individuals are inclined to look for consistency, they are likely to try to make new information consistent with their existing conceptual framework when they encounter messages that are inconsistent with their established views and positions. All these factors explain why the message according to the sender is often very different to that received.

These personal experiences are found in all communication. Where it takes place in organisations, however, the situation is made more complex and thus provides the third group of impediments to 'effective' communication which derive from the characteristics of an organisation. In particular, the two structural dimensions of hierarchy and division of labour, as well as the strategy, technology, environment and culture, will have a profound effect on how information is generated and used. As information is a scarce resource which symbolises status, enhances authority and is often seen to have shaped careers, either in terms of advertising successes or concealing failures, deliberate omission of information in upward communication is often found. A subordinate is likely carefully to censor information which reflects badly on his activities and he will be helped in this if his boss feels overburdened with information. Wildavsky presents strong arguments about why, 'looked at in the large, organizations exist to suppress data . . . Organization is bias. Organization necessitates selectivity' (Wildavsky, 1983, p. 29).

Information in organisations is thus hoarded, ignored and used for personal and group interests as well as in relation to core activities and objectives. Ironically, many of the structural features such as matrix organisations, systems of accountability and performance appraisal, which were designed in part to unblock horizontal and vertical channels, may in fact cause further barriers to 'effective' communication. For example, departmental jealousy and fragmentation can lead to a situation of 'pluralistic ignorance' in which diverse specialists each cherish their piece of unco-ordinated information so that the whole picture is never revealed until some sort of disaster precipitates unwelcome knowledge. Wilensky's (1967) discussion of these blockages is extremely interesting and relevant, and readers are particularly recommended to his analysis of the relationship between American military leaders and intelligence officers in the period immediately prior to the Japanese invasion of Pearl Harbor (p. 44).

Any concept of perfect effective communications is thus utopian. Social psychology explains that communication between individuals suffers from omission, distortion and overload, and we know that these tendencies are exacerbated in organisational settings. Our understanding of communication must be placed within the context set by our discussion of power and interest, but having done that there are obviously strategies that can be adopted, from different viewpoints, to try to make communications to and from a particular interest as accurate and reliable as possible.

Beware the view that 'poor communication is the biggest problem in our organisation'

Although the existence of perfect communication and consensual rationality can never be guaranteed, it is misguided to see 'poor communications' as the single main source of problems for organisations today. It is too often suggested that 'if only communications were better everyone would understand each other and get on much better together'. In fact 'misunderstanding' and 'poor communications', far from the latter being the cause of the former, often stem from a common root: namely, the fact that organisations are arenas in which different interest groups collect for the pursuit of objectives which, although sufficiently compatible to encourage their participation in the first place, nonetheless are normally sufficiently divergent to ensure a degree of conflict. In such situations communications cannot as such serve to reconcile interests, although they may lead to people changing their views and positions to some extent. On the other hand, excellent communications may really lay bare the extent of divergence and conflict and thus from some points of view actually exacerbate deeper problems. Chapters 9 and 10 return to this theme in a discussion of change.

8.2 Decision-making

A decision-making process is defined as the thoughts and actions associated with a sequence of choices as well as the choices themselves. These thoughts and actions include becoming aware of a problem or issue and are often themselves the outcomes of communications and other decisions. For example, the final decision on the contents of a production schedule for a manufacturing plant may be taken in the light of the following factors.

1. Information from sales about decisions they have made about guaranteed and forecast demand for the coming periods.
2. Information from maintenance about decisions they have made about their schedule of routine maintenance, together with additional information on likely problems.
3. Information about the workforce, including the incidence of sickness, planned holidays and willingness to work overtime.
4. Information from materials management about decisions they have made on the factors affecting the supply of components and raw materials.

The choices made involve commitments to action. Decision-making is thus a vast subject. It is evident in all social groupings but, as we are concerned particularly with organisational analysis, our main concern in this section is to identify a limited number of important issues (summarised in Table 8.3) which should help to explain patterns and outcomes of decision-making in organisations.

Six main themes were outlined in the introduction. The sixth was that everyone faces a degree of constraint in which they have an element of choice. Decisions are made both to create, or to respond to, choice opportunities and to respond to perceived needs to accept, circumvent or conquer constraints. The extent to which people have prior knowledge of the constraints or opportunities that prompt decisions obviously has a bearing on the amount of information that can be assembled.

Table 8.3
Decision-making in Organisations: General Issues

---

1. Decision-making encompasses both 'rational' activities in respect of perceived opportunities and constraints and 'irrationality', insight, serendipity and symbolism.

2. Decisions vary in the extent to which they are programmable and amenable to standardisation.

3. Decision processes revolve around perceptions of issues, objectives and means.

4. Information is selected for inclusion in decision-making. The conditions governing the likelihood of information being available, being included, being considered and being given more or less weight were summarised in Table 8.2.

5. Complete agreement between different parties on objectives and means is rare.

6. Complete knowledge and information on objectives and means is rare.

7. Different patterns of agreement and knowledge about ends and means in decision-making provide a typology of decision processes.

8. This typology has implicatons for the decision-making strategies that are likely to be followed:
   (a) the rational logical approach;
   (b) compromise, bargaining and disjointed incrementalism;
   (c) judgement and research;
   (d) inspiration, anarchy and the 'garbage can' approach.

'Rationality' and 'irrationality' in decision-making

There is a tendency when thinking about decision-making in the abstract to imagine a rational process in which the parties involved agree on objectives, search for alternative means of satisfying them, evaluate the means according to agreed relevant criteria (e.g. cost, quality, other consequences), select the most appropriate means and implement the resulting decision. Given this operational definition of rationality, irrationality represents significant movement from this model. Examples of 'irrational' aspects of a decision-making process would include the following.

1. Impulsively deciding on a course of action without analysis of consequences in terms of objectives.
2. Neglecting to consider and state objectives but concentrating on symbolic
   impact.
3. Responding to intuition, taking a chance and unexpected opportunities.

In practice there are lots of reasons why the 'rational' model is often difficult
to discern in organisations and why significant displays of apparent 'irrationality' as well as 'rationality' are found in decision-making. Some of the
underlying reasons for this are:

1. Uncertainty and confusion amongst the participants about objectives and
   alternative means, which may reflect
   (a) shortage of resources to enable adequate search for relevant informa-
       tion;
   (b) location in an environment or with a technology which is so complex
       or new or turbulent that relevant information is not forthcoming;
   (c) inability to understand the nature of the issue.
2. A ritualistic observance of traditional ways of doing things without
   questioning their 'rational' utility.
3. Positive reinforcement for people who act on intuition, inspiration and in
   creative ways.
4. A power structure which stifles access to information which is a prerequi-
   site to rational action.

The twin edge of rationality and irrationality in decision-making is a theme
which relates to many of the other issues to be discussed. The list of factors
given above shows that there are characteristics of situations, such as the
availability of knowledge and information and the prevailing communication
and power structures, which incline people to follow what appears to be a
more or less rational approach.

However, beyond all these factors, although no doubt related to them, are
the individual quirks and predispositions which incline some people to revel
in ambiguity, chance, insight and serendipity, while others are never happy
unless they can feel themselves to be part of some rational plan. March
(1974), in an aptly titled article, 'The Technology of Foolishness', suggests
that goals are often discovered once participants become involved in decision
processes for other reasons. He argues 'human choice behaviour is as much a
process of discovering goals as of acting on them'. Together with Weick
(1969) and his co-authors Cohen and Olsen (Cohen, March and Olsen, 1972).
March is a protagonist for randomness, equivocality, ambiguity, playfulness
and hypocrisy being included as central features of organisation.

This theme has been developed by Brunsson (1982, 1985) who, through
considering decision-making theory in the context of action theory, has

concluded that what may be 'rational' decision-making may lead to 'irrational action' which is counter-productive for executives. The rational process may consume too many scarce resources and lead to missed opportunities and demotivated participants. Czarniawska-Joerges and Wolfe (1987) show how relative are the definitions of action and decision with significant variations occurring, depending on whether one is concerned with organisations in the private or public sector and those within and outside Scandinavia.

The programmability of decisions

Opportunities or constraints can be presented to participants in highly standardised and expected ways: for example, in terms of the requirements to undertake annual reviews of staff performance and to fix departmental budgets. Alternatively, people can be taken unawares and presented with situations with which they are unfamiliar and which elicit non-standard forms of response. Decisions that can be presented in standardised formats with clear objectives and means to their achievement and can be performed routinely by participants are said to be programmable. The parameters are well-known; it is merely a question of filling in the present values, following established rules and procedures and churning out a clear response. There are considerable savings of time and money if little search is required and standardised decision rules can be followed. Disasters are likely to occur, however, when participants wrongly assume that a decision is programmable when in fact there is considerable uncertainty about the nature of the issue, the rules that would be appropriate or the objectives that are implied. For example, a doctor may assume a patient has a common 'flu virus and proceed to make a number of programmable prescriptive decisions. Further search and a more open mind might have revealed, however, that he was suffering from Legionnaires' Disease, which required more careful consideration and complex decision-making.

Issues, objectives and means in decision processes

In making decisions participants make their own definition of the issue, situation or problem and then are more or less motivated towards certain means and ends which they regard as appropriate. All other things being equal, their definition of the situation is at best likely to be partial and reflect their own position in terms of their interest and access to information. There is always a tendency to latch on to one or two characteristics of a problem, possibly to the neglect of others. We see this even in respect of a relatively factual problem where the parameters could be fairly easily verified. For example, a maintenance fitter may proceed to rectify a faulty electric motor, convinced that the motor itself had failed (perhaps because this is usually the case) without noticing that some of the wiring into the control panel has been reversed. The tendency to make a hasty and 'wrong' diagnosis is even stronger where the subject is not so easily open to verification. Even if the issue is accurately diagnosed, it could be that 'causes' or 'reasons' are beyond the control of those who identify them. As well as thinking about a solution they will also try to persuade others to perceive the problem in their terms. This is rarely easy. For example, in a decision about the order schedule for components in a batch engineering firm, materials management are motivated by objectives of maintaining service to production, but since they are charged for stock, they are also reluctant to increase their inventory; thus for them the issue is one of running as tight a schedule as possible. Production, who have all the benefits and none of the costs of high stock levels, want stock levels to remain high. The clerk involved in filling out the order does not really care which set of objectives predominate, except that he has a marginal preference to support the position of his boss in materials management. His main concern, however, is ritualistically to fill out the forms on time.

The selection of information for consideration in decision-making

Information is selected by participants for inclusion in decision-making. The conditions governing the likelihood of information being available, being considered and being given more or less weight were discussed in the first part of the chapter and are summarised in Table 8.2. Once information has been selected it tends to fill a notional 'space' around the issue, such that it is often difficult to insinuate new information. Some people, following de Bono (1967), have advocated that people become more skilled in 'lateral thinking' such that they can unlock themselves from the 'bounds' of their own particular rationality. Our discussion of individual behaviour in Chapter 1 suggests how difficult this is likely to be.

Agreement on ends and means is rare

Parties in the same decision process often have different ends, although with luck they may each be satisfied by the same decision. For example, a job applicant and a personnel officer may seek different objectives in a recruitment decision, but both sets may be satisfied by the decision to appoint the applicant. In circumstances which were described in the previous chapter as involving zero sum power relations, the ends may not be so easily reconcilable. For example, the size of pay increases may be decided against a backcloth of the competing objectives of management and trade unions. Management may have the objective of settling for as little as possible, while at the same time wishing to introduce a pay structure that will encourage employees in declining skill areas to undergo retraining. The trade union representatives, on the other hand, may be looking to achieve as high a settlement as possible and reluctant to accept that some skills are in fact declining.

Even if they are seeking reconcilable ends, the parties to a decision may have very different views on the best means to achieve a decision. For example, the managers of sales, development and production may all agree that the use of a particular heat-sensitive raw material in a complex process causes quality, cost and delivery problems with the final product. How the material could be pretreated, however, or whether an alternative could be found within the cost and time parameters set for the projected life of the product may be the subject of fierce disagreement. The extent of agreement between the parties about the nature of the issue, the ends being sought and the means for their achievement can give rise to variations between decision processes. These were discussed in detail by Thompson and Tuden (1959).

Complete knowledge and information about objectives and means is rare

The amount of information and knowledge possessed by the parties to a decision process can be considered in respect of three things: (a) their understanding and definition of the issue; (b) their identification and understanding of proposed other responses to the issue; (c) their understanding of the consequences of each option. Taking variations in each of these three dimensions, it is possible to typify a continuum spanning conditions of certainty, risk and uncertainty under which decisions are made. The first condition of certainty is characterised by a well-defined and understood problem and a clear identification of available alternative solutions which are known to lead to specific consequences. The second condition of risk is characterised by an approximately defined problem and an understanding of alternative solutions to which probabilities of consequences may be attached. The third condition of uncertainty is characterised by poor problem definition and understanding of alternatives, with a lack of knowledge about the consequences of some or all the alternatives.

Where people are concerned about their lack of knowledge, they are likely to search for information. Paradoxically, when the need for more information is greatest, the cause of the problem, ignorance, may preclude the parties from realising that this is the case until too late. There are situations of 'false knowledge' in which the parties, oblivious of their ignorance, think they know all the parameters of a decision process. Dawn raids through the stock market to effect a takeover of the ownership of a company are graphic examples of such cases. Directors at one moment are sitting down to plan their next five years' marketing strategy and the next are leaving the keys to the company's Jaguar on their desks and looking for another job.

There is evidence to suggest that in times of crisis and threat, people in formal organisations display increasing rigidity in their responses, and they are more likely to restrict information or to concentrate on what is well-known and well understood rather than to search for new data or understanding. This is often coupled with an increasing emphasis on the importance of central hierarchy and close social links (Staw, Sandelands and Dutton, 1981).

A study of the US *Saturday Evening Post* provides such an example: Hall *et al.* document how this newspaper continued printing and raised prices even though it had no money and circulation was falling (Hall *et al.*, 1977). Staw, Sandelands and Dutton comment that while there is a tendency to centralise in the face of crisis within formal organisations, local and national communities, informally bound together, show a tendency to decentralise to relatively autonomous groups in the face of national disasters. Interestingly this means that in formal organisations change and experimentation are more likely to come in the wake of success than in the wake of failure, when they may be vital to survival.

A typology of decision-making strategies based on different patterns of agreement and knowledge

The two previous points have identified the extent of agreement and the extent of knowledge as important sources of variation between decision situations. It is interesting to note that they do not always relate to each other in the same way. One might think that where there is less knowledge there will always be more room for disagreement, but life is not so simple. Where the definition of ends reflects differences of interest, increasing the amount of knowledge or information available may be counter-productive for a solution. In some cases of pay bargaining, more information as such will not resolve conflicts over the distribution of scarce resources. In another case supervisors in both maintenance and production may agree on the objective of securing a schedule of planned maintenance to reduce fire-fighting crisis maintenance, but they may strongly disagree about whether this is best done by permanently dedicating one fitter to a group of machines or by maintaining a flexible crew across a number of different machines. As each group provides figures and other information to support their point of view, the conflict may increase rather than lessen.

The typology of decision strategies represented in Table 8.4 can be constructed by relating the two dimensions of agreement and knowledge to each other. This is a useful scheme for analysing decision situations and considering, as a participant, how one might seek to improve the process in any particular context. Limitations of space do not allow a detailed consideration of all the sixteen cells in Table 8.4. The discussion will focus on four different patterns of consensus and conflict over ends and means, largely taking all the A cells together, all the B cells together, and so on. The variations within the letter groups, that is between A_1, A_2, A_3 and A_4, between all the Bs, and so on, relate to different levels of knowledge and understanding which are discussed earlier in this chapter and in Chapter 4.

There is some confusion in the literature on decision-making about whether models are proposed as descriptive (what decision-making is actually like) or prescriptive (what decision-making should be like if it is to be 'effective') or both. Confusion is compounded because sometimes prescription is ill-

Table 8.4
A Typology of Decision-making Strategies

Participants' views on *means* to achieve ends		Participants' views on *aims* in decision situation			
		Agreed		*In conflict*	
		Well defined	Not well defined	Well defined	Not well defined
Agreed	Well understood	A_1	A_2	B_1	B_2
	Poorly understood	A_3	A_4	B_3	B_4
In conflict	Well understood	C_1	C_2	D_1	D_2
	Poorly understood	C_3	C_4	D_3	D_4

SOURCE: adapted from Thompson and Tuden (1959).

considered, while at other times description is inaccurate. Consequently one enters the area of decision-making strategies with some trepidation, uncertain about the path to take and the destination to be reached. But on reflection this is perhaps an appropriate stance to adopt in approaching the subject, since those engaged in decision-making are often in identical positions!

The rational 'logical' approach

The A cells in Table 8.4 describe a situation for which the rational model is a rough approximation. There is a view implicit in many discussions amongst students and practitioners that the ideal model of decision-making is one which conforms to a logical and rational pattern. The basis of this pattern is the following sequence:

- perception of problem or issue
- identification of objectives in respect of problem or issue
- comprehensive search for alternatives to achieve objectives
- identification of possible alternative courses of action as solutions
- evaluation of each alternative

- judgement on the best solution for securing objectives in most satisfactory way
- implementation of chosen course of action
- monitoring of effects in light of achievement of objectives
- if problems occur which reduce effectiveness of chosen solution, further search to refine problem definition, choice of solutions, methods of implementation, and so on

Many practitioners feel that they should attempt to follow this approach as it is advocated in many management texts. In fact it is only really applicable for the minority of routine and consensual issues where conditions of cell A_1 in Table 8.4 are satisfied, with all parties agreeing on an objective they wish to maximise, being completely informed on all alternatives and being capable and equipped to choose the 'best' one. If there is less than full knowledge and agreement on both objectives and means, then insight, impulse, ignorance, instinct, creative thinking and political activity will all be important facets of the decision-making process even though they do not feature within the rational model.

Even if it is possible to achieve full knowledge and agreement, people may be unable or unwilling to spend the necessary time and money on securing them. In other situations full knowledge or full agreement may simply not be possible given the array of different interests represented and the level of knowledge presently available. Where there is conflict or ambiguity over objectives, the participants must make decisions about procedures as well as substantive issues. For example, they may decide to seek more information and/or agreement. The latter is a feasible strategy if the differences of interests appear to be ultimately reconcilable within the existing framework, as in the following example.

The Tom Corporation is a large conglomerate where relations between divisional operating companies and headquarters were just emerging from a period of strain. Analysis revealed that the directors of individual operating companies had systematically overestimated their profits in their annual reports to headquarters, believing that this was necessary if they were to obtain the budget they felt they needed to function effectively. Consequently every year the corporate HQ had less funds available than anticipated for its centralised R & D functions. In the long term this situation rebounded on the individual companies, whose management then felt that people in headquarters were antagonistic to them and would not give them the R & D support they needed. A great deal of distrust built up, with the directors in the operating companies feeling that people in headquarters would never be sympathetic to their 'real' situation; hence they continued to paint it much 'rosier' than it really was. This strategy worked at first, then created suspicion and finally caused a great furore within the company. External consultants were given the remit of establishing why the operating companies were systematically underachieving their own targets. The reasons soon became clear, and through a programme of management and organisation development the parties involved moved to a position of greater mutual knowledge and understanding such that they all approached the budget-setting process in a more open way. Accordingly the decision situation of budgeting in this corporation moved from category B towards A, although the nature of the forecasting activity meant that it would never fully enter into cell A because, although there was a higher level of agreement, there was still uncertainty about appropriate goals and means.

On other issues (e.g. redundancies and office relocations), while a fuller disclosure of information can achieve a degree of increased understanding, the interests of the parties often remain in conflict and cannot be resolved. In such cases it is pointless to expend resources on attempting to achieve consensus. Instead each participant is likely to seek to negotiate the best bargain they can get.

Compromise, bargaining and disjointed incrementalism

Situations in which the ends remain ambiguous or the subject of conflict, but where the means are fairly well understood and agreed, fall into the B cell of Table 8.4. In such cases the decision-making style usually adopted is that of making a series of successive limited comparisons and so 'muddling through' in what Lindblom called a disjointed, incremental way. Rather than clarifying objectives, marginal alternatives are chosen to satisfy powerful interest groups. Lindblom (1959) and Braybrooke and Lindblom (1963) discussed this strategy, which they contrasted with accounts of rational decision-making. Like earlier advocates of the rational model, they wrote about disjointed incrementalism in a way which suggested that they saw it as both a descriptive and a prescriptive model. Critics, while agreeing that it may be a good description, argue against it as a prescription because of its lack of direction and inherent conservatism (Etzioni, 1973). Etzioni followed his criticism with the development of a *mixed scanning model* in which participants are urged to search widely to identify the main issues and formulate objectives and then focus on priority issues in more detail. This prescriptive model encourages a broad first stage of analysis and a detailed second stage, each with different implications for information collection and resource allocation.

An example from cell B is of a company in which management, facing a short-term cash crisis with a relatively sparse order book, were seeking ways to cut their financial outgoings in the short term. Trade unions, on the other hand, not fully aware of the company's financial problems, were sufficiently aggrieved over a recent pay offer to threaten strike action. The parties thus had very different objectives, but for different reasons were ready for a strike. In another case a personnel manager was very keen to send middle managers on a three-week management development programme run by a business school. The production director wanted to remove a somewhat irascible production manager temporarily from the scene while some changes were made. It suited their very different purposes for the manager to attend the course, although the production director had little hope that it would actually result in a different management style.

Judgement and research

In cell C of Table 8.4, where there is agreement on the objectives but a lack of knowledge and agreement on the means, the participants will probably put a great deal of effort into research on alternative means and use what is sometimes called a 'judgemental' strategy. With a technical issue R & D will be emphasised, as it is in many fairly new, small, specialist companies producing high technology processes or products. Fairly cohesive groups of professionals can agree on goals but often encounter considerable technical difficulties in the production areas. Accordingly, they put a lot of effort into R & D and problem-solving. With an efficiency issue in which the division of views reflects different departmental interests, an interdepartmental working party to 'brainstorm' on possible solutions would be a possible response. Another example is of a company, embarking on the manufacture of a new product range, which is facing a lot of uncertainty about the best way to retrain its workforce, although there is general agreement on the sort of workforce they wish to establish. In this case they may put a lot of resources into their training department to experiment with different ways of achieving the agreed ends.

Behavioural theory of the firm

Cells B and C can be understood to a large extent within a framework developed by Cyert and March (1963), called 'behavioural theory of the firm'. This theory is proposed as a more apt description of decision-making in firms than a more straightforward economic theory, which would assume that all situations could be treated as falling into cell A_1, where firms would operate in the market with perfect knowledge and with agreement based on a common commitment to maximise profits. Behavioural theory holds that these are not often valid assumptions, and that the dominant coalition (a concept which itself acknowledges different interests within the company) seeks solutions which 'satisfice' on a number of criteria rather than optimise on any of them. Furthermore, Cyert and March acknowledge that search procedures are often decentralised and conducted within sets of assumptions held by sub-groups which may differ from those held by other groups.

On the basis of their analysis, Cyert and March suggest that decision-making often has four important characteristics. First, they argue that search is often limited and problem-oriented, with alternative strategies and solutions only being sought when events create problems. In this way decisions tend to be made reactively rather than proactively. Second, they note that conditional commitments are often made before detailed analysis: for example, decisions are made to build new manufacturing plants without a detailed analysis of whether the supporting market evidence is really conclusive. Third, they identify feasibility as an especially important supporting and evaluating criterion. It is often not so much a case of 'Is it the best?' but 'Will it work?' Lastly, they note that the original problem is often 'solved' when the differing requirements of the interested parties are met, and so there is a 'quasi resolution of conflict'. Short-term and more quantifiable criteria tend to squeeze out longer-term and less quantifiable criteria and participants proceed as if uncertainty does not exist or, at least, can be avoided. There is interaction, although rarely in a logical fashion, between definitions of the problem situation, data collected, expectations formed and past experience. In the course of experiencing these complex interactions people in organisations learn and adapt, and so their priorities, definitions of problems, expectations and procedures shift and change.

Inspiration, irrationality and the 'garbage can' approach

The fourth group of D cells in Table 8.4 are ones where everything is in a state of flux and uncertainty. In D_4 there is neither agreement nor knowledge about either ends or means. This situation has been described by Cohen, March and Olsen (1972) as the 'garbage can' model. Organisations are described as 'organized anarchies' or 'collections of choices looking for problems, issues and feelings looking for decision situations in which they might be aired, solutions looking for issues for which they might provide an answer and decision makers looking for work'. In such situations, they suggest, there are four fairly independent streams of

- problems, arising for all sorts of reasons
- participants, who come and go
- choice opportunities when decisions are expected (e.g. annual budget time)
- solutions or answers looking for questions or issues

Cohen, March and Olsen argue that each of these four characteristics becomes arbitrarily attached to the others with surges of activity. In this way, solutions are often fairly arbitrarily selected.

Cohen, March and Olsen developed their model through studies of public sector organisations, where it could be argued that conflicts over ends are especially noticeable, since in the final analysis objectives sought and measures of performance used are subjects of political, moral and social debate. For example, consider the criteria for a public housing policy. Should a local authority build for sale or rent or not at all? How many units and of what size? Should they be flats, maisonettes or houses? Disagreement about objectives is unlikely to be reconcilable between different political viewpoints. In contrast, in the private sector, maintaining solvency is sometimes the final arbiter of survival. In spite of the diktat of liquidity, however, examples of the 'garbage can' model can also be found in the private sector, at least in the short term. For example, in the mid-1970s managers in a company manufacturing microchips were locked in profound disagreement about whether the company should aim for the high volume market of standardised mass produced chips or whether it should concentrate on customer-specific high quality chips. At the same time there were considerable problems with the process and great difficulties in increasing the yields of each production batch. Everything seemed uncertain, and the production managers who felt they were in the middle of the problems were much attracted by the garbage can model as an apt description of their situation. They were therefore particularly interested in the answer to the question: can anyone get out of the garbage can or is entry on a one-way ticket?

The answer is provided by returning to the axes of Table 8.4, in which the garbage can is at the extreme negative end for knowledge and agreement. One strategy would therefore be to concentrate resources on improving available knowledge so that the participants become more fully aware of how to achieve certain ends and the consequences of pursuing some ends rather than others. Another strategy would be to concentrate on increasing agreement, either through getting some participants to change their minds or through exercising power to enforce one line of activity rather than another. It is often the latter that happens. For example, in local and central government it is the leadership of the dominant political party that more or less dictates policy, and in private enterprises it is the board or the bank which often has a final say. Rather than emphasising the requirements of consensus, a *multiple advocacy approach* builds on internal disagreements within the group as a prelude to decision-making. If participants are relatively equal in terms of competence, power and entrepreneurial skills and have time for debate, then the quality of decision-making can possibly be improved through the approach.

The further a situation is removed from cell A_1, and in particular the nearer it is to D_4 where decisions are essentially unprogrammable, the more participants rely on intuition, faith, chance and perhaps on tradition to lead to a decision. Decisions reached often do not directly provide solutions to problems. Cohen, March and Olsen found in simulations of eight decisions that the outcome which they called 'long-term resolution' was less common than two other sorts of outcomes. One they termed 'oversight', which occurred when a solution or action emerged by 'default' as part of a set of relatively distant decisions and actions. The other they termed 'flight', which they said occurred when the problem of 'issue' got attached to a new choice so that its definition changed. Such a sequence is easily understandable as complex organisations often face many problems but in fact have few solutions available. This relates to an earlier point that change is often stimulated by success whereas failure results in rigid retreats to established practice. Cohen, March and Olsen also found that the chances of reaching any solution were directly related to the load on the system: that is, the more issues there were, the fewer were solved.

8.3 Concluding Remarks

Communication and decision-making are inextricably linked in organisations. They feed each other, and as central processes in organised activity provide the basic framework for the generation of organisational and individual outcomes. Simple and yet widespread assumptions that they are generally conducted in conditions of certainty, rationality and consensus have to be dispelled. The sources of uncertainty, irrationality and dissensus have been discussed, and their impact on the accuracy and validity of communication and alternative decision-making strategies illustrated.

Just as people in the past have argued for complete rationality, some are now espousing models of anarchy. In accordance with the 'middle road' followed in this text, the reader is urged to see the context and implications of both rationality and irrationality and to realise that both have a place in discussions of what does and what should happen. The art is to make the right decision! It is hoped that the framework given in this book provides guidance to this end.

Managing Change: Implementation, Learning and Creativity 9

Organisations are never static; something about them is always changing. For example, there is turnover in the membership, new administrative procedures are introduced, or a new customer arrives on the scene. None of these events is completely self-contained; each has implications for other aspects of organisational life. Some of them obviously result from decisions made within the organisation, some of them originate with decisions outside, and others just seem to happen. The common factor is that when something changes, whether or not it has been planned or decided by organisational members, it will have repercussive effects which will be variously welcomed, discarded or ignored by people within and outside the organisation. Their reactions will in turn affect other things.

Life in contemporary organisations is thus often complex and frequently unpredictable. As March (1981) put it, organisations change but they rarely do what everyone, or even some people, intend. For example, senior executives in a firm may decide to make extensive investment in a new production planning and scheduling system. However, if they do not look beyond the technical possibilities inherent in developments in hardware and software, they are likely to be frustrated when they find that the new system does not have the desired results of reducing rates of component obsolescence, streamlining the production process, and improving performance on delivery dates. One reason for this will be that they did not pay sufficient attention to their marketing strategy with a view to improving the accuracy of sales forecasts and introducing greater product standardisation; neither did they think about how to develop the organisational context to accommodate the significant growth in the systems analysis group.

9.1 A Model of Change in Organisations

Students of organisations who are interested in understanding as a basis for practical action are often drawn to start with a rational model of cognition and action: that is, with a model in which decisions are made on the basis of what they presume is the best and most appropriate information and analysis available. Such decisions are then implemented and put into practice and the discussion focuses on the challenges and problems associated with ensuring effective implementation. However, the discussions in previous chapters have already indicated that such a rational model is often not an accurate representation of what happens in organisations, and neither is it necessarily desirable to hold it up as an ideal model. In this chapter organisations are regarded as arenas in which a variety of activities, interactions and processes – notably physical labour, search, communication, power and influence and decision-making – mediate the effects of a collection of individual, organisational and social characteristics and result in a stream of outcomes, of which particular policies, plans and work practices are examples. As plans and decisions are made, whether loudly and clearly or quietly and vaguely, change does not occur immediately. Work activity carries on, and the extent to which the work actually done contributes to the fulfilment of any plan is always an open question. Outcomes are those event points at which the observers or participants can choose to take a snapshot of these processes and call the picture they 'capture' an outcome. Their choice, which will reflect their interests and timescale, effectively dictates what are seen as antecedents and what as outcomes in the process of change.

The main aim of this chapter is to present a model of change which reflects scholarly work and, at the same time, provides a realistic basis for action. As such the model needs to respond to what many contemporary commentators (for example, Kimberley and Quinn, 1984; Peters, 1987; Kilmann *et al.*, 1988; Quinn, 1988; Pascale, 1990) now regard as imperatives in the management of change. These are summarised in Table 9.1. The first imperative derives from discussions in the previous chapter on decision-making, where we saw both the need for and the inevitability of elements of irrationality entering the decision-making process. The second imperative in Table 9.1 concerns the need to have some interaction between decision and action, so that one does not feel that there is an imperative in managing change to make all the decisions 'first' and then set about implementing them 'second'. There are often strong reasons why theories of provisional decisions are 'tested' in action and the processes of decision and action are run together. Just as this imperative refers to the notion of relaxing distinctions between categories of decision and action, so the third imperative refers to the need to relax distinctions between those in the organisation who are the decision-makers and those who are the implementers. The fourth imperative concerns the need to include processes of learning, creativity and development as well as of implementation in managing change. Each of these imperatives has a

Table 9.1
Imperatives for a Model of Change in Organisations

1. To include elements of rationality and irrationality.

2. To include iteration between decision and action.

3. To include variable participation in decision and action from people in different positions in the structure.

4. To include processes of learning and creativity.

common theme: it is difficult, and indeed perhaps undesirable, to think of change in organisations as simply the rational revelation of a sequence of decisions being translated into a separate sequence of actions or outcomes.

The development of a model that will facilitate the analysis of the wide-ranging and ill-defined sets of variables which are involved in change in organisations is extremely difficult and can only be undertaken at a very general level. The ideal model would embody a full explanation of the determinants of different characteristics of organisation and their interrelationships, but we know from the previous chapters that such an ideal cannot be met. However, on the basis of the material presented in this book, a model shown in Figure 9.1 has been constructed to illustrate how changes may be precipitated and developed and thus can be analysed. Breaking into cycles of mutually interacting variables and choosing to identify precipitating factors and specific outcomes amidst the processes involves somewhat arbitrary decisions, since the same 'things' (such as people's skills, technology and markets) are both precipitators and outcomes.

Two points need to be made about the construction of Figure 9.1. First, the list of items under each of the main headings is intended to be illustrative of important factors rather than exhaustive and the items need to be seen as both precipitators and outcomes. Second, no satisfactory way could be found to include the words 'power' and 'influence' in the diagram. However, as Chapter 7 showed, their importance at every stage in change processes must not be forgotten. Indeed, it is the starting point for the analysis.

Felt need for change

People in organisations who have sufficient power and influence take action to institute change because they feel the need for change. This need is often expressed in terms of changes to produce desired results (in terms of 'better' financial performance, say, or of improving their own position). People become involved in decisions and actions with results which may or may not be intended by the participants. These outcomes in turn feed back into the

FIGURE 9.1
Change Processes in Organisations

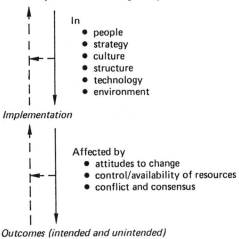

Precipitating factors

Changes in or uncertainties about
- people
- strategy
- culture
- structure
- technology
- environment
- indicators of performance

Members' felt need for change

Views on why change is necessary
- to improve performance?
- to maintain/improve own position?
- blockages to change
  - it's not necessary
  - it's impossible

Decisions/plans for instituting change

In
- people
- strategy
- culture
- structure
- technology
- environment

Implementation

Affected by
- attitudes to change
- control/availability of resources
- conflict and consensus

Outcomes (intended and unintended)

Manifest in
- people
- strategy
- culture
- learning
- structure
- technology
- environment

Feedback (including evaluation)

What are the costs and to whom do they accrue?

Chance
Serendipity/
creativity
learning
intuition

organisational system and may precipitate further changes. Thus one answer to the question, 'What generates organisational change?', is that it is the desire by members to improve organisational performance and their own position within the organisation. Chapter 5, however, has already discussed the reasons why such an apparently simple statement is problematic.

First, organisational performance is not a unitary concept. When people talk of improving organisational performance they can be referring to any one of a number of aspects, including effectiveness (goal attainment), efficiency (amount of resources used to produce a unit of output), productivity in terms of quantity or quality or timing, indicators of morale, and capacity to adapt and change to cope with the unexpected and unpredictable. Consequently, one change sequence which may be designed to improve effectiveness may not be very efficient, while another which improves efficiency may have a disintegrative effect. Second, organisations are composed of a variety of interest groups, and while one group may wish for a particular change, another may be against it. For example, the establishment of a computerised information system may be supported by the specialists who will design it and the superiors who expect to have greater knowledge of their subordinates' work, but may be resisted by local, relatively autonomous work groups. Notwithstanding these difficulties, however, nearly all proposed changes are justified in terms of improving organisational performance and are couched in terms of the need to 'do something' about one or more of the key characteristics of organisations which were discussed in Part 1 of this book, notably people, strategy, technology, environment, structure and culture. An outline of an approximation to a 'rational' model of managing change in organisations can thus be established, and this is shown on the left-hand side of Figure 9.1.

However, as Table 9.1 indicated, the model of change also needs to take into account the irrational, the creative and the intuitive aspects of cognition and behaviour. These facets of life are often as crucial in initiating, developing or blocking changes as is purposive action, but by definition they are difficult to subject to systematic study or analysis. Take, for example, the idea of 'serendipity' or chance events which unexpectedly open up new opportunities or reveal new threats. Their importance in understanding change is precisely in their unexpected nature, and it would be misleading to search for 'reasons' for chance happenings, and thereby return the analysis to purposive or rational action. Even if people attempt to introduce changes that will secure better adaptation to a changing world, a problem remains that messages about and from the world are often confusing, and people do not really know what they are seeing. Indeed, it is often as appropriate to say 'I'll see it when I believe it' as it is to say 'I'll believe it when I see it'. On the other hand, it may be helpful to spend some time seeking to understand the reasons for events so that a response can be planned and those involved can learn from their experiences.

The balance between rationality and irrationality is indeterminate. It is important that participants and observers are cognizant of both the left and the right side of Figure 9.1, and see the creative and intuitive interwoven at all stages.

Precipitating factors

The evidence and arguments assembled in support and criticism of contingency theory in Chapters 3–6 are of relevance to this part of the model. Grossly simplifying, it is argued by many that the increasing complexity and turbulence of organisational environments and the increasing sophistication of modern technology require many changes which can only be guaranteed with the development of 'organic-adaptive structures' which are 'adaptive, rapidly changing, temporary systems of diverse specialists linked together by co-ordinating and task evaluating specialists in an organic flux' (Bennis, 1966). Arguments such as these underlie the proliferation of theory and practice in the field of organisational development (OD), which is concerned with the deliberate formulation and implementation of programmes of planned change. These programmes are designed to increase the effectiveness of the organisation through such things as the introduction of better systems for communication, problem-solving, decision-making and conflict resolution. Clark and Krone (1972) describe the effective OD practitioner as one 'who enables an organization to develop the attitudes and processes which will allow it to integrate proactively with its environment' through the introduction of matrix-like organisation structures and other strategies for coping with turbulence and complexity. This relates to the discussion in Chapter 4 of Galbraith's (1973) analysis of the way people in organisations adapt their structures and strategies to handle the information processing requirements which derive from the degrees of uncertainty that arise from environmental, structural and technological complexity. Another factor influencing people in organisations is their size, as we saw in Chapter 5. For example, Pugh and his colleagues, through their Aston programme of research, identified strong relationships between the size of organisations and elements of their structure: 'size causes structuring through its effects on intervening variables such as the frequency of decisions and social control' (Pugh, Hickson and Hinings, 1969a). It is suggested that the sheer growth in such things as numbers of employees and asset value, although obviously not unrelated to technological and environmental factors, are in themselves important triggers to change.

Contingency theory has been important in debunking the idea that 'there is one best way to manage all organisations', and has encouraged practitioners to consider aspects of their environment, technology and size as a basis for deciding on appropriate paths of change. However, as Chapter 5 showed, it has been justly criticised for its deterministic assumptions about the nature of change in organisations, inadequate appreciation of the role of strategic choice, beliefs and power, its simplistic assumptions about organisational performance and effectiveness and its neglect, *inter alia*, of the fact that organisations are collections of diverse interests. These criticisms do not, however, require that we should completely reject the idea of there being environmental, technological and size factors that induce changes in other parts of organisations. But they do mean that organisations cannot be seen as mechanical structures in which there are automatic adjustment mechanisms which take account of change.

It cannot be said, therefore, that changes in technology or markets will cause predictable changes in organisations, but we can say that participants' felt need for change can be precipitated by perceived or anticipated changes in the six characteristics which form our model of organisation. On the technological front, the development of a new process or product may prompt a reappraisal of the way innovations are incorporated into regular production. This may lead to the establishment of 'operational task forces' as an accepted feature of structure and lead to the development of a new career path for engineers, which in turn has ramifications for personnel policies and the attitudes of different groups to work. In the environment, occurrences as diverse as lowering tariff barriers, changes in commodity prices and suppliers' policies, a major advertising launch by a competitor, or a change in government policy towards the regulation of prices and incomes, are all examples which, if they happen or if people think they are going to happen, are likely to precipitate a sequence of changes. As a result of their study of factors which promoted successful innovations, the Project Sappho team stressed the importance of being in touch with market and technological developments and having a better understanding of user needs (Project Sappho, 1972).

On the strategic front, and of course not unrelated to developments in the other part of the model, opportunities to expand or contract activities in a particular market, to pursue the acquisition of another company or to mount a major programme of management development will also act as precipitating factors for a ricochet of changes in other areas. Changes in structure and people are similarly extensive in their effects. A problem of the overload of senior mangers, the recruitment of a new chief executive, an escalation in the conflict between two specialist divisions, the formation of a management information division, or the contraction of the workforce by 25 per cent, are all examples of fears, hopes and realities which are likely to precipitate far-reaching change.

Sometimes people's views change less because of their direct experience and more because of an outside influence. Indeed, books such as this and teachers of management are not irrelevant in precipitating change! Organisation theory generally and management courses in particular have been instrumental in alerting practitioners to the relevance of monitoring technological and environmental change, and thus in themselves have generated change. Most practitioners have many ideas about the best way to manage their organisations (e.g., that 'growth is good' or 'small is beautiful'), and these may motivate them to introduce changes irrespective of market considerations of their experience of technology. To take just one example, during the 1960s there was great support for the belief that structures which facilitated consultation, participation and widespread employee involvement were a better basis for management than more authoritarian structures. These beliefs are not unrelated to considerations of how to cope with environmental or technological change, but they were also formed on the basis of humanitarian beliefs about participation.

There may also be a bandwagon effect. For example, people may decide they must try out a new machine or a new management practice simply because they hear of other companies doing so. Dodgson (1985), in a study of the use of CNC machines in forty small establishments, found this to be a more common basis for buying the machines than was any careful analysis of the costs and benefits.

The 1980s have been the decade in which commentators have stressed the importance of generating an appropriate culture to secure a strong sense of corporate identity amongst participants. In this way culture has often been seen as one of the precipitating factors in change programmes (Handy 1985), although there have been many warnings that this cannot be achieved quickly or cheaply (see, e.g., Burack, 1991).

Apart from, but related to, changes in the six main characteristics of organisation will be changes in the apparent performance of the company as measured in terms of financial indicators, pattern of growth or record of industrial relations. Relevant indicators here might be a loss in market share, drop in profits, or creditable forecasts of long-term recession in particular industrial sectors. Such things will often in themselves be significant in instituting change. There are situations where, in spite of 'objective' evidence for the need for change, participants do not perceive the evidence in this way. Hence blockages arise so that the precipitating factors do not, in fact, precipitate any change at all. The common types of blockage are identified in Figure 9.1. The first is that 'we do not need to change'. Here people may acknowledge that some indicators of performance are slipping but they do not feel in any danger, hence they carry on as before. They are often supported by a feeling that other performance indicators are still good, or that their customers or clients have no alternative source of supply for their goods or services. Monopoly providers of public services, like health and education, are often thought to fall into this trap. The development of an internal market for health care in the UK in the 1990s is an example of the government seeking to expose service providers to greater competition and thereby somehow force them to be more responsive to needs for change.

The second blockage identified in Figure 9.1 is 'we cannot change, it is impossible for us'. This reminds us of some issues, discussed in Chapters 1, 5 and 6 concerning people, structure and culture, which suggest that sometimes people are hampered by the structure and unsupported by the culture. Experience of this blockage points often to the need for radical change, possibly spearheaded by a new leader. This is given further consideration later in the chapter.

Decisions and plans for instituting change

Whatever the precipitating factors, and regardless of whether they are hopes, fears or hard reality, 'organisational change' rarely just 'happens'. Whether it originates inside or outside the boundaries of the organisation, it is shaped by the decisions and actions of powerful and influential individuals and groups who have their own particular interests to pursue. Once sufficiently powerful people feel, for whatever reason, the need for change, decisions and plans are made which inevitably involve changes in one or more of the component parts of the organisation: its people, strategy, structure, technology, culture, or environment. Thus these factors are both cause and consequence of change in organisations. The wavy line of irrationality which runs throughout Figure 9.1 adds further complexity. The paths to and from decisions are likely to be characterised by irrationality, serendipity and foolishness, as well as rationality and purposive action. Chapter 8 describes how sometimes 'solutions' or 'decisions' go in search of 'problems' to which they may be attached rather than vice versa. Plans are often made on the basis of relatively poor information in a more or less 'illogical' and unsystematic fashion and in the face of poor agreement between the parties involved.

9.2   Implementation and the Generation of Outcomes

A major skill in initiating change is to anticipate its ramifications by predicting the outcomes – both beneficial and adverse – of any decisions. Once again, these will be manifest through complex interactions between the six aspects of people, strategy, technology, structure, culture and environment. Implementation will be much affected by who controls relevant resources, their attitudes to change and their relative positions in terms of power, conflict and consensus. Feedback, through the filters of particular interest and partial information, may occur at every point in the process, but the greater the time-lag between initiation and evaluation, the more problematic any evaluation becomes.

Consideration of implementation thus brings together many ideas which have already been discussed in previous chapters. This section highlights a number of important issues which are summarised in Table 9.2. Whenever one chooses to take a 'snapshot' of organisational life one can identify many 'outcomes'. Broadly, as Table 9.3 suggests, these outcomes can be considered in two separate but related categories. These are characteristics of the organisation, such as policy statements, productivity, profitability or quality records, and characteristics of individual members, such as feelings of security or satisfaction, or receipts of pay and fringe benefits.

Table 9.2
Implementation: General Issues

1. Implementation reflects a dynamic interaction between elements, resulting in the generation of outcomes.

2. Outcomes are definable at the individual and organisational level.

3. Not all outcomes are those that are intended by the people involved:
   (a) the effect of 'outsiders';
   (b) unintended consequences;
   (c) variation and conflict between different intentions;
   (d) the effect of coalition formation.

4. Intentions change after plans have been formulated.

5. Activities involved in generating outcomes take up valuable resources and place requirements on those involved which may not be met.

6. The relative power of the parties involved may vary at different stages, notably between planning and implementation, which can lead to the 'practical subversion' of planned intentions.

7. Rational planning for implementation may not be the most appropriate guide for activity.

8. People's attitudes are vital to any analysis of change:
   (a) understanding resistance;
   (b) changing attitudes;
   (c) consultation and participation.

9. Compromise, bargaining and compensation are important aspects of implementation.

Not all outcomes are as intended

At one level of analysis, organisational and individual outcomes result from the activities, interactions and decisions of people. But actions and decisions are heavily constrained and influenced by features of the wider social structure which in themselves are creatures of activities and interactions and, once established, in turn present constraints and opportunities for further action, and so on. A complex picture emerges which is reminiscent of sets of Russian dolls, nested inside one another, in which the central actions and decisions of people are shaped by their encapsulating social structures. However, just as with a set of Russian dolls, the observer is not certain

Table 9.3
Outcomes of Activities and Interactions in Organisations: Some Examples

Outcomes as organisational characteristics
* policy statements detailing objectives and how to achieve them

* financial performance as measured in terms of:
rates of profit
rates of turnover
return on capital invested
liquidity and cash flows statistics

* characteristics of product and production system in terms of:
quality of goods and services produced
rate of production of goods and services
efficiency of production system
working practices of operatives and maintenance workers

* record of competitiveness and innovation in terms of:
market share for products
rate of change of products
rate of change of process

* record of industrial relations in terms of occurrence of different types of industrial action

* the formal structures for authority and reporting relationships

Outcomes as individual characteristics
* level of pay
* extent of job security
* degrees of status in enterprise and in the community
* sense of satisfaction and fulfilment from work
* opportunities for promotion and advancement
* opportunities for congenial social contact

whether the outer casing or the centre dictates the shape of the others. This book favours significant influence from the outer social casing, but also emphasises that there is room for some degree of independence between the layers, as well as for influence in the reverse direction. There are four main reasons for differentiation between the layers of our Russian dolls of intention and outcome.

The effect of 'outsiders'

The outcomes that occur in any one organisation may result from actions initiated by individuals or groups who have no direct association with the organisation. For example, the Bank of England may raise interest rates and so have a profound effect on a firm's export programme, such that all the plans and decisions taken with a view to one set of outcomes are completely negated.

Unintended consequences

A second and related differentiating factor is that actions may not have the results intended by their perpetrators and they will certainly not reflect all the intentions that were associated with the translation of the original idea into a practical outcome. In a fascinating discussion of changes that had taken place in the BBC over a ten-year period, Burns (1977) notes:

> The biggest change in the BBC between 1963 and 1973 was not, I believe, the reconstruction of top management, the institution of stricter financial budgeting and surveillance, the increase of the powers of Managing Directors and the Controllers over them, or the depletion of the 'baronial' powers of heads of groups and heads of department, nor was it increase in size or increased union militancy or the appearance of a 'radical underground'. What did make the difference was the breakdown of the ordinary institutions of social interaction between the variety of people engaged in programme production – i.e. the unanticipated consequences of these changes, which did more to alter the internal working of the organisation than the intentional changes effected by management. (p. 272)

These unanticipated consequences were such as to increase the segmentation between traditionally rival groups so as seriously to undermine the overall commitment of employees and to exacerbate feelings of insecurity and anxiety.

Dawson *et al.* (1988) show how in studies of health and safety at work there are many examples where the outcomes of a set of activities, designed to secure an improvement in health and safety, have in fact had the opposite effect. At a simple level, many of the heat-resistant fire doors installed in buildings are made of opaque material. While they may reduce the risk of fire spreading quickly, they may also cause fairly serious injuries through being pushed open against an unsuspecting person travelling in the opposite direction. A more complex example is provided in the nuclear and chemical industries, where a technique of hazard analysis called 'hazard and operability studies' (HAZOPS) has been developed with a view to 'coping' with as many hazards as is feasible at the design stage. Like the fire doors, this development was expressly concerned to make work environments safer. However, in plants where HAZOPS have formed a serious part of new plant design or an operational review of existing plant, it was often associated with a fall-off in safety awareness and concern by people at all levels of the operational workforce. This seems to be because of a misguided view that there is no need to worry about safety any more, since the specialist engineers now take care of everything through HAZOPS. In fact, no analysis can predict all possible dangers, and even if predicted, the necessary remedial action is often not considered feasible because of expense or lack of available skills or material. One of the themes of Perrow (1984) is that specially designed safety devices sometimes interact with production systems in unintended and unanticipated ways so as to increase the overall level of danger for those working in the plant.

Variation and conflict between intentions

Every participant has a range of different interests and intentions, and often the realisation of one can affect the achievement of others so that compromises result. For example, a production manager in a batch engineering plant may intend to achieve his cost, quality and delivery time targets, but a 'flu epidemic among his staff and problems with one of his machines mean that he has to work unexpectedly high rates of overtime, thus achieving the delivery times, just satisfying the quality standards, but hopelessly exceeding his costs.

The variation of intention within one person is, of course, magnified enormously when considering variation between people. Given their different starting points in organisations and in society, not everyone is interested in the same outcomes, either for themselves or for the organisation. The development engineer may be most interested in creating a technically challenging work environment, the works supervisor in maintaining his job security, and the production manager in securing promotion. It could be that the coincident achievement of all three outcomes is possible, or that there is a degree of conflict. Similarly, there may be divergent views about the relative priority different individuals attach to organisational outcomes. For example, the finance director may be more interested in the annual rate of return on capital invested than in the detail of the new production schedules and shift rotas. The works supervisor may be more interested in the effects of the recent pay deal on productivity than in the new computer system being installed for administrative procedures. In the fullness of time, as the new shift system results in a decrease in effective machine utilisation, the finance director may well wish he had taken more interest in the activities that led to the new system being introduced. Similarly, when the works supervisor is inundated with additional paperwork, he may wish he had taken more interest in the computerisation of administrative tasks. We have already noted that everyone wears some version of 'blinkers' and tends to concentrate their attentions on those things which seem most pertinent to their position and present interests.

Outcomes vary in the extent to which they are compatible with one another. Taking individual and organisational outcomes as general types, four generic areas of conflict and consensus can be identified. At one end there is no conflict at all. For example, when there is a large increase in market share it may be possible for everyone within the firm to achieve the outcomes they intended for themselves and the organisation. Thus there is a total net gain within the organisation. But more often there is some conflict. This may occur in three guises. First, it might occur between the achievement of two or more organisational outcomes (e.g. the pursuit of increases in productivity may run counter to the pursuit of calm industrial relations). Second, conflict may occur between the achievement of one or more organisational outcomes and one or more individual outcomes (e.g. the achievement of a significant decrease in labour costs conflicting with individual job security). Third, conflict may occur between the achievement of two or more individual outcomes (e.g. where there is more than one contender for a single senior position). These three categories of conflict are not mutually exclusive and can be found in any combination.

There is a range of possibilities that arises from a collection of interest groups with varying intentions relating to a general subject area within a common time period. For each group their intentions can be 'realised' in one of the following four modes:

- the outcomes are realised as intended with no adverse side effects
- the outcomes are realised as intended but with adverse side effects
- the outcomes are realised, but not as intended
- the outcomes are not realised at all

The mode of realisation for one group may, of course, be different from that for others.

Coalitions and alliances

Where interests and intentions are different, 'unholy alliances' may be formed between groups who join forces to secure a change and then fight over its results. For example, a rumoured office move may win support from everyone who believes it provides an opportunity to improve their accommodation, even though it is obvious that some will be disappointed. More seriously, political revolutions often generate a great deal of support from a wide political spectrum of all who are dissatisfied. Together they concentrate their attention upon securing the removal of their opponents, temporarily suppressing thoughts about what will happen if their immediate intentions are achieved. The Islamic revolution in Iran saw a confederation of Islamic fundamentalists, communists and other disaffected groups in order to overthrow the Shah. But the Shah's demise was followed by a struggle for power in which the fundamentalists sought to purge the revolutionary hierarchy of all but their own followers. Coalitions formed at one stage for a particular issue will not necessarily survive to later stages of the same issue or for new issues. For example, production supervisors in a car plant may side with management over their decision to end 'washing up' time, but may then ally with the workers over the need to maintain overtime. Research and sales managers may push for product modifications which production wants to resist, but in other circumstances research and production may collaborate on securing process change which will improve the working environment but will temporarily upset sales by delaying deliveries.

Changing intentions

Notwithstanding the complex interrelations between intention and outcome and individual and structural characteristics, a heuristic model showing the way people's intentions can lead to activities and to outcomes is given in Figure 9.2. This emphasises that the ideas and thought processes which guide action are not only our original intentions but also reactions to perceptions of the 'created' context. In this way intentions are modified in the light of what we consider to be feasible as opposed to ideal objectives. A young development engineer may originally intend to persuade the board, through his boss, that the company should invest in the latest automatic manufacturing system. However, once he has learned more about the financial and market position of the company and the attitudes of the chairman, he may react and direct his efforts to making the present system more cost-effective.

Generating outcomes takes up valuable resources

It is always pertinent to ask whether the appropriate resources required by specific plans are actually available. Will the skills, finance, time, plant materials, etc., be forthcoming, and what costs will be incurred in their use? Furthermore, consideration must be given to who has control and discretion over the use of these scarce resources. A related point is the appropriateness of the main consituent parts of the organisation to secure the change. We have seen that organisational change cannot be represented as a simple linear change but is a mass of created interactions and outcomes. Some circumstances may be more appropriate to some points in the process than others. For example, in respect of technical change, Wilson (1966) has suggested that organisational characteristics such as plurality and diversity, which are favourable for the generation of new ideas, are not so appropriate for implementing the ideas into production, where he found centralisation to be more appropriate. This returns to the question discussed in Chapters 5 and 6 about the extent to which different departments in a firm should be differently structured to suit their particular context and objectives.

FIGURE 9.2
Relating Context, Intentions, Activities and Outcomes: a Summary

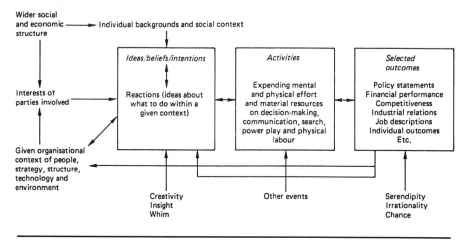

Power structure varies between planning and implementation

An important point illustrated in Figure 9.2 is that outcomes include both 'policy' and 'practice'. People's intentions may be largely realised as far as a policy statement is concerned, but they may find their intentions negated when it actually comes to practical outcomes. For example, Joan Woodward (1965) describes how in a reorganisation from a functional to a product structure, the purchasing managers fought a rearguard action which resulted in their department being the only one to retain an independent functional identity. The newly created product managers wanted to have purchasing together with other specialists within their direct spheres of responsibility, but as the reorganisation coincided with a drive to cut costs, purchasing managers were able to argue that independent product group buying would lead to increasing inventories of stocks, poorer negotiated discounts and confusion among suppliers who would be faced with four or five different purchasing points when previously they had good relations with just one. The suppliers informally supported their 'old friends' in purchasing, fearing to lose the goodwill and understanding that had developed to their mutual advantage. With both internal and outside support, purchasing ultimately won the argument and retained its independence.

Where a statement reflects the intentions of those at the top of the hierarchy and the practical outcomes reflect the intentions of those somewhere below them, 'control loss' is said to have occurred (see, e.g., Zald,

1970, p. 289). This form of 'subversion' of fo
policy goals is well illustrated by an account o'
1970s (Dawson, 1975). Policy-makers in the H
industries should be revamped in order to achi
(a) to give prisoners the habit of regular wor
the outside world as possible; (b) to make a f
net drain on resources; and (c) to offer wc
were taken in the face of some scepticism
officers. Nonetheless, plans were drawn
machinery bought, and premises identified and reiui..
image. Supervisors were recrited from 'outside' to complete the auuic....
of the experiment. However, once inside the prison and away from the
high-flown discussions of policy, the old guard was so strong that the
workshops could not operate in any way like 'outside' factories. The
supervisors had little discretion and much reduced means with which to try to
motivate and control their 'workforce'. The original intentions of the formal
policy-makers, so well enshrined in the policy outcomes, were largely
unrealised when it came to the outcomes of practical implementation, which
more or less ensured the realisation of the intentions of the 'old guard' which
had earlier been 'passed over'. As the old saying suggests, 'There are more
ways than one of killing the cat.' If groups fail at the policy stage, they often
have another go at the implementation stage.

Given the hierarchical nature of most organisation structures, with policy-
making at the top and implementation largely at the bottom, it is not
surprising that policy-makers often complain bitterly about 'subversion' of
their decisions. A more neutral way of expressing this is to see it as the
achievement (at last) of another group's intentions. From another perspective, reshaping outcomes in implementation can sometimes have unexpected
positive effects, even for the originally disappointed protagonists. For
example, it can be a way of securing innovation and change in highly
conservative organisations. But by the same token it can also have the effect
of reasserting the status quo, as it did in the example of prison industries. The
defeat of the intentions of policy-makers and the achievement of intentions of
those involved at grassroots level is especially likely to occur in organisations
where two conditions prevail: first, when they are highly bureaucratic and
formal, with little upward communication on the feasibility of proposals and
little downward communication or consultation on proposed policy before it
becomes a fully fledged and formal statement of intent; second, when there is
either little direct opportunity for close control or monitoring the work done
at grassroots level or great difficulty in identifying and agreeing performance
criteria. These characteristics are interlinked and are often at their most
obvious in people-processing, public service organisations. Nonetheless they,
and the 'subversion of implementation' to which they give rise, are also found
in manufacturing and private enterprises.

.nework for analysing the generation of outcomes summarised in
1–6 of Table 9.2 will be illustrated by looking at the installation of a
manufacturing process involving the purchase and use of automated
omputer controlled machinery. Table 9.4 identifies some of the key actors
involved and their intentions (i.e. what they attempted to achieve, secure or
prevent, through their involvement with this case). Their degrees of willingness and enthusiasm for the subject varied greatly. For example, the
development engineer who was likely to be promoted to be responsible for
commissioning the new plant was extremely enthusiastic and willing, whereas
the operator who thought he faced the prospect of learning new working
practices if he was lucky, or redundancy if he was unlucky, was less
enthusiastic. But whether enthusiastic or willing, these actors all had ideas
about positive and negative consequences for themselves and others and how
they would attempt to secure the 'best deal'. Their intentions were modified
in the light of experience and their assessment of changing circumstances. The
list of intentions in Table 9.4 is selective and yet highly varied. Some relate to
compatible outcomes which could be achieved together, but others are in
direct conflict. Some were achieved, others fell into abeyance. The production director's desire to stop aggravation from sales could be achieved
alongside securing the future of the works manager's production area and
giving younger workers the opportunity to retrain. But the maintenance
workers could not preserve existing working practices if the works manager
succeeded in changing them! Although technical difficulties with the machinery could have meant that the forecast production rates and quality were
never achieved, the production and maintenance workers could have become
well trained in the use and operation of new machinery so that they could
improve their job prospects in the open market. A lack of insight and
imagination from managers could have meant that opportunities for restructuring jobs and reorganising the department were lost so that the change was
less successful in terms of both productivity and employee morale than it
might have been. The development engineer could have achieved his dream
of commissioning an automated plant, but its lack of success on other fronts
may have meant that his next 'scheme' was less enthusiastically received. In
other circumstances fears about the new machinery may have led to a
dissatisfied and anxious workforce, but nonetheless, technically and financially, the scheme might have been a success.

The distinction between 'organisation' and 'individual' outcomes certainly
complicates evaluation, since the achievement of organisational outcomes
may be at the expense of some groups. For example, higher productivity may
be secured the same year as skilled workers' pay increases fail to keep pace
with inflation. The skilled workers' reaction will be heavily influenced by the
local economic and employment situation. Where unemployment is high, job
security is likely to be more important than pay levels to a man with extensive

Table 9.4
Actors and Intentions: The Comset Case: Planning and Implementing the Installation of an Automated Manufacturing Line

Selection of actors	*Selected intentions*
Finance director	• cut production costs • improve management information • increase strength of management control
Production director	• improve production performance • stop 'sniping' from sales about delays • avoid buying components which can be made in-house if production difficulties are overcome
Works manager	• remove 'dead wood' among employees • secure future of his production areas • create opportunity to renegotiate working practices with maintenance
Development engineer	• work with newer, more sophisticated machinery • increase staff in his department • excitement of commissioning new machinery
Shop steward	• secure a good deal on pay and conditions for new jobs • secure retraining for displaced workforce • opportunity to increase 'visibility' of role and increase union membership
Younger production workers	• opportunity for training in new technology
Older production workers	• secure promise of their continued employment or secure good terms for redundancy
Maintenance workers	• protect existing working practices • secure good deal for 'new work' involved in maintaining new equipment

domestic financial commitment. Although regretful of the depreciation of 'real wages', this may be overshadowed by the deduction that because of the productivity increase his employer is more likely to stay in business, and consequently he is more likely to stay in a job. In a more buoyant economic context his reaction and evaluation would be very different. In times of economic recession there is a tendency for people to group more closely together behind organisational objectives if they are seen as a route for individual objectives, since other opportunities appear to be extremely limited. If on the other hand, the route charted by dominant people in the organisation is seen as totally opposed to the pursuit of individual objectives, resistance and conflict are likely to be acute. The change in people's intentions over time introduces yet more complexity into the subject of planning and implementation. Whatever the process, however, several outcomes result, and once in existence they join the array of factors that are liable to affect the path of other changes. For some parties they will be seen as constraints, inhibiting the achievement of objectives; for others they may be seen as presenting opportunities.

9.3 The Limits of Rational Planning

To summarise, it is now possible to appreciate why the process of implementation, as the generation of practical outcomes from theoretical or abstract ideas, cannot be understood as a simple linear model even with just one set of concerns. There is always a multiplicity of parties and intentions and of technical, social, organisational and functional outcomes. The bridge between intentions and outcomes is formed by a range of activities and interactions involving search, communication, physical activities and decision-making. The actual course of events does not always follow a 'logical' sequence beginning with the identification of a problem, through the search and selection of a solution, to its planning and implementation.

If this 'logical' sequence had been followed in the Comset case, we might have expected the following to have happened. Sales would have reported an increasing level of customer complaints about quality, while production would also have been anxious about poor productivity rates, particularly in comparison with those of competitors. A range of solutions would have been considered: for example, changing maintenance procedures, extra training, rationalisation of production at another site, as well as the route that was finally chosen. The purchase of new equipment would have formed part of an overall change programme in which plans would have been drawn up to cover the technical and personal aspects of getting the new line fully operational.

In fact, however, the sequence was different. It was the availability of funds, not a quality or production problem, that prompted people to look for something on which to spend some money. This is likely to happen in two situations, both of which prevailed at Comset. First, managers feared that if they did not spend all their allocation in one year, their budget for the next period would be cut. Secondly, they wanted the status that was attached to being 'go ahead' and innovative managers. At the same time, a group of young development engineers were so taken with the idea of new equipment that they were looking around for an acceptable peg on which to hang a proposal to innovate. It was by chance that they met a group of salesmen in the canteen having their usual gripe about poor delivery times and quality from production. In fact, these had been sales grievances for years, but only when coupled with an engineering 'solution' and 'spare' production money were they taken seriously by senior management.

This case analysis of Comset should not be taken as a strange aberration from a usual rational mode of planning; on the contrary, it is indicative of the way things are more usually done. Furthermore, Peters and Waterman (1982) gave it their seal of approval with their emphasis on action in order to avoid 'analysis paralysis'. They stressed the importance of experimenting, of 'trial and error' and generating 'sufficient mistakes' in order to secure one or two great successes. Similarly, Quinn (1980a, 1980b) notes that many managers are finding that their elaborate and specialised planning staff and systems are counter-productive, since they result in elaborately analysed strategies which never seem to get implemented because strategy formulation and implementation are regarded as separate sequential processes. Those involved become frustrated and bewildered when their organisation does not respond *en bloc* to plans when they are dramatically revealed. In contrast to this approach, Quinn advocates a process which he has observed in a study of senior managers in ten large US corporations and which incidentally appears more realistic in the light of the general points made in the preceding discussion. He found that successful managers acted in what he described as a 'logical incremental' way. Thus they sought to improve the quality of their information, to work positively to overcome personal and political pressures resisting change, to create awareness, commitment and credibility, to amplify understanding and awareness, to search for and incorporate the views and knowledge of relevant people, and to reach and try out partial solutions, making use of flexible and slack resources. In this way, by the time the strategies are beginning to crystallise, parts of them have already been implemented and commitment to the rest is more or less assured. A lot of feedback and some shortcircuiting when crises precipitate action are important features of Quinn's scheme. At the end of any piece of strategic development which follows these precepts, senior managers, he says, know they have taken a strong leadership role, but they also know that the inputs from other people, in terms of both knowledge and commitment, have been profoundly important: 'Through the very processes they used to formulate their strategies, these executives had built sufficient organisational momentum and identity with the strategies to make them flow toward flexible and successful implementation' (Quinn, 1980b, p. 17).

It is in this context that we can understand the second imperative for a model of change identified in Table 9.1, namely that there should be interaction between decision and action and one should not see planning or decision-making as a separate activity undertaken by separate people from the activity of and participation in 'implementation'.

9.4   Transformational Leadership

In developing an approach to managing change, which involves interaction between decision and action, Schien (1985), Quinn (1988), and others have laid great emphasis on vision and leadership. Many commentators have described how, in order to 'transform', organisations need to make a significant break with their past to do what Kimberly and Quinn (1984) describe as restructuring, repositioning and revitalising. Tichy (1983) locates the mandate for such major transformation within a discussion of changes both externally and internally in three sections: the technical/economic, the political and the cultural/social.

Where it is felt that the need is for such dramatic and radical rather than incremental change, it is argued that the need is for transformational rather than transactional leadership. Burns (1978) coined these terms. Transactional leadership proceeds on the basis of exchange of punishment and rewards, whereas transformational leadership captures the hearts and minds of participants so that they 'buy into' a new vision and work to make that happen. There are strong elements of insight and creativity in this approach, both in terms of identifying the visionary goals and in developing means of pursuing them (see, e.g., Kimberly and Quinn, 1984; Schien, 1985; Tichy and Devanna, 1986).

9.5   Organisational Learning

Notions of radical change are often associated with what has become known as organisational learning. This relates to the proposition that, just as individuals can 'learn' new ways of seeing and doing things and 'develop' a sense of importance for new values, so organisations, being collectivities of people, can also learn and develop through the creation of new sets of assumptions, norms, histories and values (see, e.g., Hedberg, 1981; Martin, 1982; Fiol and Lyles, 1985; Senge, 1990). The outcomes of such organisational learning processes can be seen in terms of each of the organisational characteristics which have featured in this analysis, namely:

● strategy
● technology (new products or processes)
● environment (e.g. new markets)
● structure
● culture

The issue is, how do organisations 'learn through doing' and so create new ways of responding to difficulties as well as new products?

Schien (1985) after Argyris and Schon (1978) advocates an approach called 'double loop learning', which contrasts with single loop learning. Table 9.5

Table 9.5
Single Loop and Double Loop Learning

Features of single loop learning	*Features of double loop learning*
• Goals designed unilaterally, based on local information and reinforcing belief	• Individuals, groups, departments are open with data
• Emphasis on 'zero sum' games in which there are always winners and losers	• Data has 'ensured' yet 'questionable' integrity
• Individual/organisational objectives to be 'winners'	• Interests and understandings move beyond functional (and hierarchical) boundaries
• Information is a power resource and is kept 'close to one's chest'; little openness or sharing of information	• Decisions through participation not imposition
	• Norms and values open to change
• Emphasis on rationality and objectivity on the surface, even if it is clearly inappropriate	• Communality in values and perceptions an objective
• Conflict not confronted but smoothed over or postponed	• Shared 'ownership' and commitment
• Attractive in that it is familiar, measurable and reflects functional activities (e.g. engineering, accountancy)	• Policies and strategies seen as open and 'complex'

SOURCE: Derived from Argyris and Schon (1978).

summarises key characteristics of each approach. The double loop approach makes fewer assumptions, is more open to outside and countervailing influences and is less 'bounded' in its rationality. It fits well with an organic and open form of structure. It not only leaves the organisation open to the influences on the right-hand side of Figure 9.1, it positively encourages them to make their mark. In a similar vein Morgan and Ramirez (1984) write about holographic organisations which, in a constant state of flux around a few well-defined rules, are better equipped to learn and to develop new ways of seeing problems and issues as well as solutions. Senge (1990) makes a similar point when he writes about the need for corporations to focus on 'generative learning' (which is about creating and developing new ways of looking at the world) as well as 'adaptive learning' (which is about coping).

Schien's single loop approach and Senge's 'adaptive' learning is what one would find if one operated only with the left-hand side of Figure 9.1. This single loop mode of operating maintains existing assumptions and sets of rules and serves at each point of change to detect or correct errors only within the given frame of reference. Thus it emphasises structural divisions, 'local' goals and suppressed, restricted or filtered information. There is little incentive to cross boundaries, to share information or to 'brainstorm'. It encourages a self-sealing culture and a set of beliefs including that there is one right answer to be found within presently adopted and well-defined frames of reference. It is the antithesis of the 'open', searching, sharing modes of activities.

Protagonists for more openness also argue for a more open categorisation of the decision-makers and doers, and this was the third imperative for the model of change identified in Table 9.1. Participants throughout the organisation may at different times be involved in decision-making and/or implementation. It is argued that it is inappropriate to categorise people as being one or the other: they need to be both.

Justification for a more open approach to organisational learning and decision-making with its associated requirement to demolish boundaries between departments and levels is provided by a group of commentators who suggest that extreme pace and unpredictable directions of change are on the agenda of most contemporary organisations. There are choices to be made about the mix and nature of appropriate performance indicators and the social and economic means of achieving them. The context for organising is characterised more by chaos, turbulence and discontinuity and less by stability, continuity and incrementation. The once champion of excellence, Peters, declared that the 'era of sustainable excellence' was ended and that executives had to learn to 'thrive on chaos'.

This is not to argue for the suspension of all previous approaches, but rather that executives need to be critically aware of two of the basic themes of this book: namely, that there is 'no one best way to manage', and that there is an imperative for all senior executives to find ways of balancing conflicting demands and managing paradox. Executives, argues Pascale (1990), need to realise that organisations which once were great can ossify, and that the structures and cultures which once delivered them success may now be a recipe for decline. For example, Hewlett Packard at one time appeared locked into a consensus which had delivered it previous success but which was no longer timely. In contrast, Citicorp was locked into dissensus which had served it well in a previous era of operation.

There is now an emphasis on creative, open-minded, learning management styles, albeit coupled with the establishment of cost-saving and uncertainty-reducing administrative and technological controls, where appropriate. Three of Peters' guidelines for 'thriving on chaos' show how he feels appropriate managerial processes, cultures and structures can be developed. He advises executives to

- achieve flexibility through empowering people
- learn to love change and develop leadership in change at all levels
- build systems for a world turned upside down

The experience of the iteration between management theory and practice in the 1980s suggests that if such guidelines are appropriate, they will provide a bridge between an organisation and its environment so that winning strategies are likely to be developed. However, strategies which are picked as universal guidelines, like the two remaining in Peters (1987), are less likely to be universally applicable. He advises creating total customer responsiveness, and pursuing fast-paced innovation. But does the first not create the danger of becoming, in Pascale's terms, 'a drifter', and the latter the danger of becoming an 'escapist'? Such a paradox between high performance-driven incremental innovations and large-scale creatively-driven innovations is documented in Womack, Jones and Roos (1990) in their study of the automobile industry.

Acknowledging and living with paradox creates difficulties because there is no consistent paradigm. The appropriateness of many of our tools which are based clearly within one paradigm is called into question (Quinn and Cameron, 1988). Paradoxes arise in terms of both strategy – for example, should one consider competition or collaboration with key competitors (Brocklehurst and Francis, 1991) – and process – for example, should one encourage entrepreneurship or control within the company? The message is that by accepting tension and developing both sides of the paradox, by not seeking to ignore/bury one side, people in organisations grow to understand their position much better and are able to act more effectively. They will still need to accept some given assumptions for a time, but they will grow with these only as temporary 'stage props' which are reassessable, or indeed replaceable, when the next drama is anticipated. No executive should want to find out whether her present mind set is redundant as a support for the next drama. It is argued by advocates of greater involvement for participants in both decision-making and implementation that their involvement has an impact on people's attitudes to change and it is to this we now turn.

9.6   Attitudes to Change

Understanding resistance

Whether people are likely to be resistant, indifferent or supportive of change obviously relates, *inter alia*, to the extent to which the change process is seen to alter the content and structure of their jobs and terms of employment. For example, will it affect the intrinsic nature of their work? Will it affect the amount and direction of discretion, power and autonomy they have? Will it affect their terms and conditions of employment, particularly in respect of pay, promotion and security? Chapter 1 showed that people's reactions to these questions and the interpretation they put on the information they collect about the change will reflect generally on their social and work experience and their broad view of the world, including the relative importance of work in their lives. Their reactions will also reflect specifically on their particular organisational context. Is there, for example, a lack of trust between management and the shop-floor or between different functions? Are there strong fears about job security or further financial prospects? In Chapter 3 there was much discussion of the variety of effects that the introduction of new technology can have, both in terms of intrinsic and extrinsic aspects of work and people's attitudes. The role of management in pursuing particular sets of objectives through technical change (e.g. for control, for productivity, for long-term integration) and the manner of their pursuit were shown to be crucial in determining the way new technology was experienced or received.

It is clearly very important for the designers of change to be aware of the sort of reaction their innovations are likely to receive, and to bear in mind that it is almost universally and historically the case that change will be resisted by members who see it as a threat to their interests as represented in such things as intrinsic job qualities, money, status, professional integrity, location, security and promotion. No social group is immune to these feelings in the face of perceived threat. Resistance is likely to be stronger if people think that the costs of the change far outweigh the benefits, or that the proposed changes are unnecessary or that their success or failure will not be easy to determine.

Another reason for resistance may be that people are either simply set in their ways or so 'fed up with all this change' that they do not even consider whether the change is likely to be good or bad from their point of view before they adopt a hostile position to the proposals. Management must take some responsibility for generating these attitudes. Indeed, resistance may sometimes be the result of a self-fulfilling prophecy. Managers, expecting resistance and hostility, may adopt a defensive position which in itself invites hostility and suspicion. Another related point is that any change usually automatically involves an increase in the number and range of instructions that flow between people in different levels and departments. The visibility of power and authority is thus increased, and it may be this itself, rather than the substantive details of the change, that generates hostility. From the subordinate's point of view, proposals for change in one area may be an opportunity to voice grievances in other areas, as adjuncts to any discussions or bargains that are proposed. These 'side issues' may equally serve to exacerbate any resistance.

Acceptance of change, on the other hand, is likely to be stronger if the conditions discussed above are absent. Notably this means that vested interests are supported rather than threatened; benefits are seen to outweigh costs; the proposal is seen to be necessary and is justified in measurable terms; and people are relatively content with other aspects of work, or, alternatively, so bored with routine that they welcome the thought of a change.

In discussing managing change it would be foolish to see it simply in terms of group dynamics and to overlook the role that one or two outstanding individuals can play. There is a fair amount of anecdotal evidence to suggest that when change is greeted with inertia or resistance, the decisive push can come from the involvement of a new senior person of sufficient power, insight and commitment (the transformational leader discussed above). Such people can often take a fresh look at opportunities and problems, being unencumbered by existing loyalties, debts, plans and practices. They can also quickly signal their resolve and proposed direction of change by new appointments, the transfer of personnel, and the use of language, policy statements and general demeanour.

Individuals can also be important as third-party 'expert consultants' who may be brought in as 'change agents'. Although they often parade as 'neutrals' on the company ground, they are likely to be influenced by who pays them and by their commitment to particular styles of managing change. There are no universal laws to follow which will ensure the acceptance of changes, although there is a large number of consultants and theorists who suggest they have the answer. In Chapter 1 cognitive dissonance and persuasive communications were discussed as two approaches which have been advocated as means of securing changes in individual attitudes. A third approach is through participation and consultation.

Participation and consultation

The issue of whether or not participation and consultation are necessarily helpful in facilitating successful change programmes is one on which there is conflicting evidence and much polemic in support of at least three distinct positions.

First, there is the straightforward optimistic view that participation in the change process leads to genuinely better outcomes for all involved, since more information, knowledge, skills and insights are shared, and trust is built up between the parties. It is in this way that the transformational leader ensures that participants all buy into the dream and then the reality of change. Kanter (1983) is a strong advocate of participation and involvement as a basic precondition for effective change management: indeed, it is a theme of all those who in Chapter 6 were shown to be advocates for 'strong' corporate culture as a basis for generating commitment to shared values and thus an openness to consider and even to welcome changes in strategy, structure or technology in order to remain competitive.

The second view of participation is equally straightforward. It is the opposite of the first in that, far from giving all parties the opportunity to air their views on problems and contribute to the development of solutions, participatory schemes are designed to increase the acceptance of change among lower levels and peripheral departments, while basically leaving the structure of managerial power untouched or even strengthened. An example of this pessimistic view is Dickson (1981), who argues that far from helping people in lower levels to shape changes in their own interests, participation is really a means of increasing managerial control. This is accomplished through limiting the issues which can effectively be raised and the amount of influence that will flow upwards. In a study of thirty-one Scottish manufacturing plants Dickson found that participation was more likely where the organisation was formally bureaucratic and had a structured framework for participation which effectively retained and strengthened managerial control beneath a partici-pative façade.

Third, there is the view that participation will of itself neither necessarily increase the power of those at the top or at the bottom, nor necessarily make the acceptance of change more or less likely. This argument favours an 'it all depends' contingency approach. From a managerial point of view Vroom and Yetton (1973) provide a good example of this approach. They identify the following five management styles which are seen to be more or less appropriate in different contexts:

A.I *Highly autocratic*: manager solves the problem or makes the decision himself using the information presently available.
A.II *Autocratic*: manager solves the problem or makes the decision himself after he has obtained any necessary information from subordinates. Subor-dinates may not know the purpose of enquiry for information and play no part in defining the problem or suggesting solutions.
C.I *Consultative with individuals*: manager discusses the problem or deci-sion with individuals and gets their ideas and suggestions. The decision is finally made by the manager and may or may not reflect subordinates' influence.
C.II *Consultative with group*: manager discusses the problem or decision with subordinates to get their ideas and suggestions in a group meeting. The decision is finally made by the manager, and may or may not reflect subordinates' influence.

G.II *Group collective*: the problem or decision is shared with subordinates in a group; together the group generates and evaluates the alternatives and attempts to reach an agreed solution. The manager's role is that of a chairman, co-ordinating the discussion, who is willing to accept and implement any solution which has the support of the group.

Vroom and Yetton describe the context of decisions in terms of:

- quality (is the quality of the decision important?)
- information (how much is available?)
- structure (how structured is the problem?)
- acceptance (is subordinate acceptance of the decision important for effecting implementation?)
- prior probability (how likely is an autocratic decision to be accepted by subordinates?)
- conflict (is conflict between subordinates likely over preferred solutions?)

In order to match an appropriate style to the context, Vroom and Yetton suggest a series of questions, to which the answers 'yes' or 'no' will lead to the elimination of some styles. For example, in decisions in which the quality of the decision is important, if the leader lacks the necessary information and expertise to solve the problem by himself, and if the problem is unstructured, the method of solving the problem should provide for interaction among subordinates likely to possess relevant information. Accordingly, AI, AII and CI are eliminated from the feasible set. In this way Vroom and Yetton identify the conditions under which they consider it appropriate to consult members of a workforce individually or as a group (Vroom and Yetton, 1973, p. 36). Consultation is seen as having several guises; furthermore, there are some contexts where it is not the most appropriate style for management to adopt. In this way consultation and participation are seen as double-edged. From a managerial point of view it may be helpful in facilitating change if it allays fears and provides a forum for sharing information and beliefs in a context in which the represented interests are not diametrically opposed. It may, however, be counter-productive for managers if it only serves to lay bare the extent to which people's interests are in conflict and the extent of adverse consequences that are likely to be felt by some groups.

In a similar vein, Kotter and Schlesinger (1979) discuss the advantages and drawbacks of each of the following six approaches to change and suggest the type of situations in which they are most commonly used.

1. *Education and communication*, used when there is a lack of information or inaccurate information and analysis.
2. *Participation and involvement*, where the initiators do not have all the information they need and others have considerable powers to resist.

3. *Facilitation and support*, where resistance largely reflects problems of adjustment.
4. *Negotiation and agreement*, where one or more relatively powerful parties will clearly lose from the change.
5. *Manipulation and co-option*, where other factors will not work or are too expensive.
6. *Explicit and implicit coercion*, where speed is essential and the initiators have considerable power.

It will be noted that, in discussing strategies for change, we have once more returned to consider the importance of concepts of power and interest in explanations of organisational activity and outcomes.

9.7   Evaluation and Feedback

On the left-hand side of Figure 9.1, implementation is followed by an evaluation of outcomes in terms of original intentions and other objectives that have developed along the way. Even within a relatively rational model, however, the evaluative task is never easy. Problems are frequently encountered which, as Legge (1984) demonstrates, for the most part arise from the very nature of change. Nonetheless feedback is important, and information about the past (albeit partial and from different points of view in the present) can usefully be incorporated into decisions and actions. A degree of evaluation goes on all the time with the receipt and scrutiny of performance data. The extent to which it is important in the formulation of plans and in guiding future actions varies with the context as reflected in the present characteristics of the organisation (i.e. the interested parties and their relative power and influence, and their experience of present technological, administrative and ideological constraints). Interest in developing mechanisms and fertile conditions for organisational generative, as well as adaptive, learning are relevant here, since this allows the left- and right-hand side of Figure 9.1 to be brought closer together.

9.8   Concluding Remarks: The Rational Model Revisited

The implication of much of the discussion in this chapter is that a rational model of change is largely redundant. One will get full translation of plans as formulated to implementation as practised only when the following conditions prevail.

1. There is consensus at all stages between the parties involved, or there is a very strong power structure which stifles opposition in the long as well as short term.

2. There is complete knowledge of the cause and effect r
   in the generation of plans and their translation to p
3. There is stability in, or control over, all the variab

These conditions, as we have seen, are rarely achie
achievable is dangerous. This is because to achieve then.
organisations place fatal barriers against the right-hand side of Figu.,
so stifle learning, intuition and creativity. Diversity of interest is to an exte...
inevitable, and maintaining dictatorship or oligarchy is difficult and almost
certainly undesirable. Knowledge and information are scarce resources which
can rarely, if ever, be made fully available. Planning and implementation are
by definition dynamic political and social constructs; everyone involved may
have different interests and, moreover, will certainly have 'moved on' from
the point at which the processes started. It is, as Johnson (1987), Morgan
(1986) and Pascale (1990) insist, much wiser to see organisations as complex,
ambiguous and paradoxical rather than rational systems.

Consequently, getting to grips with the subject of organisational change is
an extremely difficult business, since there are potentially many variables
involved with an even greater number of possible patterns linking them.
Nonetheless, it is possible to analyse change in organisations in terms of four
dimensions, which should be considered in the context of the model presented in Figure 9.1.

The generation of change and outcomes

The interactive nature of organisational systems means that any decision on
the identification of precipitating factors for any one process of organisational
change is somewhat arbitrary. But it is important for practitioners and
analysts to understand the process and to identify the key organisational
features and people that are the dominant precipitators of change; to consider
whether changes were planned, anticipated or unanticipated; and to identify
the prevailing sets of assumptions which have an impact on the relative
importance of the left and right sides of Figure 9.1 in any particular context.
Similarly, it is possible to investigate which of the characteristics were
subsequently affected, and to identify a series of outcomes.

The degree of control exerted over the change process

Once the factors affecting, and affected by, change are identified, they can be
analysed in terms of the extent to which they are and were controllable by
people in the organisation.

Different roles in the changing organisation

Role analysis can be made on three dimensions: first, the degree of initiative
taken in precipitating, leading, acting and reacting to change; second, the

s of power and influence on the various aspects (planning, implementa-
n, feedback) of the change process; third, attitudes to and beliefs about the
changes, and the relationship between attitudes and behaviour.

Opportunity and constraint

Understanding organisational change requires an appreciation of three
contradictory forces: purposive action and choice, irrationality and foolishness, and constraint. Constraint cannot be absolutely defined; what is
perceived as irrevocably constraining by some people is seen as open to
change and negotiation by others (their experience of constraint and choice
being influenced by their hierarchical level or function in the organisation, the
economic context and general social background). All practitioners who work
in organisations are inevitably involved in reacting to change and may have
important roles to play in its precipitation and control.

The four issues suggested above, taken against the backcloth of the
preceding discussion, will provide guidelines on how people may become
more aware of the potential and the problems associated with change in
organisations. Practitioners should then be in a better position to decide on
their most appropriate strategy, both in reaction to change and in its creation.
Analysts should be aware of the complexity of the subject and the need to
conduct analysis at different levels and from different points of view.

Conclusion: Understanding and Managing Performance 10

This book has encouraged readers to make a journey through analysing organisations. The aim has been to develop a conceptual framework which is theoretically sound and practically relevant. In the conclusion we return to the theme of performance and effectiveness in organisations. What has been learned and can it be applied so that we can manage, as well as understand, 'good' performance?

Performance is no different from the other characteristics of organisations examined in this book, in that it is a social construct. Our understanding of the definition of key performance indicators and of the best ways to achieve sustainable high scores on these indicators varies with characteristics of our particular frame of reference. In Chapter 5 a variety of financial and non-financial indicators was discussed, and the point was made that one also has to look at different timescales.

Within any organisation one can find representatives of each and every function and level who will argue for their essential contribution to organisational performance. The designers of new products, those who directly service the customers, members of the board, the financial controller, and many more can each advance a case which suggests that, above all, *their* contribution to performance deserves special note and that it will be variously revealed in the short or long term in such things as market share, public reputation, unit costs or earnings per share. The criteria which are chosen cannot be exactly predetermined. Freeman (1984) and Fombrun and Shanley (1990) show how firms serve multiple stakeholders, with different interests, which inform the criteria they use in evaluating corporate performance. Variations occur over the timescale adopted and in the balance which is expected between, for example, financial, market and human resource indicators. Sometimes, particularly when organisations are subject to rapid change (either in growth or decline), criteria may not be explicitly identified

241

but may be indicated by the performance outcomes which result or emerge, given a set of constructed or emergent criteria.

Just as practitioners have their own special view of criteria and determinants of performance, so one can find theorists and analysts who advocate that their special area of study will contribute most to an understanding of corporate performance. In the 1980s advocates of the 'soft' inputs, the 'strong culture' brigade (e.g. Peters and Waterman, 1982; Kanter, 1983), and advocates of the ability to manage on the edge and balance between paradoxes (e.g. Pascale 1990) gained the ascendancy. But at other times and in other disciplines, competing commentators have focused attention on other things, such as appropriate structure (e.g. Woodward, 1965), securing the most appropriate source of competitive advantage (Porter, 1985), and determining an appropriate marketing mix (Kotler, 1989). Each practical and theoretical contribution can be justified and respected and it is important for the manager and the analyst to see the world from different perspectives. When it comes to understanding and predicting organisational performance, however, one needs to have a larger map than is supplied by any one perspective.

The performance of any organisation needs to be understood in terms of the activities, processes and outcomes which are internally generated within the boundaries of the organisation as well as in terms of activities, outcomes and processes in the environment which may have an impact almost *in spite* of what goes on in the organisation.

When students ask 'What is the point of organisational behaviour?' or, as termed in this book, 'organisational analysis', the implied question from the more commercially minded is, 'Has a company ever gone bust for failing to use this knowledge?' Certainly the most frequently given reasons are not failures in organisation, but such failures can often be seen to lie behind the stated reasons. For example, the reasons given for company failures are frequently inadequate investment (failure to secure resources), unexpected competition (failure of environmental scanning), a history of industrial relations disputes, poor morale, absenteeism and turnover (failure to create structures, cultures and develop committed people) and so on. Thus we can see that reasons for liquidation reflect process failures which are revealed in both problematic characteristics (e.g. inappropriate structures, subversive sub-cultures, inflexible technologies, overproduction of uncompetitive products and misguided strategy), and in the fit between the characteristics and the environment as implied in the words 'inappropriate' and 'misguided'.

The hope is that, having followed the discussion in the preceding chapters, the reader will be more aware of the contribution of analysing organisations to an understanding of why particular performance outcomes are achieved.

Figure 10.1 provides a summary illustration of the ways in which we can understand and manage performance in organisations. Each of the characteristics and processes identified in Figure 10.1 can receive bouquets for good performance or blame for bad performance. Each can and must be the focus

FIGURE 10.1
Understanding Performance

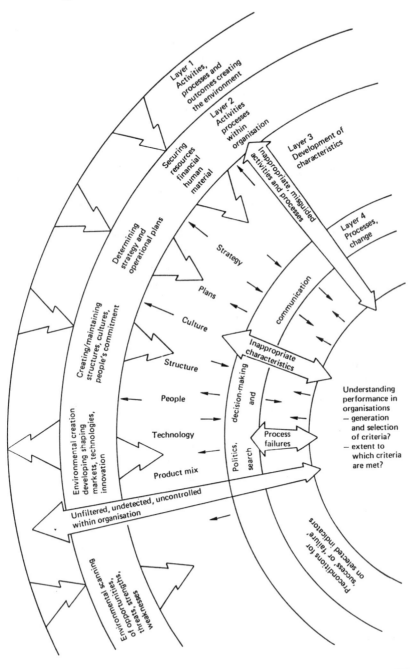

for special understanding or management, but each alone cannot be identified as the 'prime' reason for good or bad performance.

Each of the layers in Figure 10.1 may interact with the other layers and, whilst the interactions are usually between adjacent layers, they are not always so. Thus the activities and outcomes in the environment (layer 1) 'may' directly impact on core performance criteria if, for example, unexpected changes in interest or exchange rates occur or a competitor unexpectedly launches a new product. These are the 'unfiltered, undetected and uncontrolled' events in the environment shown in Figure 10.1. However, they need not necessarily be unfiltered and uncontrolled; more effective environmental scanning may have been possible. It is a reflection on organisation structure, work design and culture (layer 3) whether and how environmental scanning is carried out. In other situations, the company may have taken steps to 'hedge' against interest rate changes or to pre-empt competitors' moves; hence the interactions between the environment (layer 1) and core performance indicators are often mediated through the characteristics of layers 2 or 3.

Organisations are active in their environments in order to secure resources and then to deploy them (Pfeffer and Salancik, 1978), through developing and using social networks (Shrum and Wuthnow, 1988) and through media, PR and other forms of corporate communication (Salancik and Meindl, 1984; Steward and Dawson, 1991), so that a socially constructed reputation is created/emerges (Fombrun, 1986; Fombrun and Shanley, 1990). The interactions between an organisation and its environment are, as revealed in Chapter 4, two way. Powerful organisations can influence their environment: for example, through successful innovations of new products.

Internal activities and processes (layer 2 of Figure 10.1) may become manifest in internal characteristics such as structure, technology or culture (layer 3), or they may directly impinge on performance. For example, an informal working party may generate opportunities in new product development which have a greater impact on the views of institutional investors or fund managers and so on performance indicators and yet not to be reflected in printed strategy documents. On the negative side, a badly-managed conflict may lead to poor morale and lower commitment amongst key workers which also directly impacts on performance before it is discernible in such features of the organisation as its structure or culture.

In layer 3 of Figure 10.1 organisational characteristics are created through the activities of participants in organisations. We can discern structures, technologies, participants, etc.; in other words those characteristics which were the focus of discussion in Part 1 of this book. How these characteristics are developed over time is a reflection of the processes identified in layer 4 in Figure 10.1: that is, the processes of information search and communication, decision-making, power and politics and managing change, which were the focus for discussion in Part 2 of this book.

The interactions between and within the four layers and their outcomes as shown in Figure 10.1 create the preconditions for a degree of success or failure in the achievement of selected core performance indicators. This is not to say that the 'performance' core of Figure 10.1 is just a repository of effects. Trends in indicators feed back to all layers. An organisation will have more or less resources and confidence to pursue new programmes depending on its view of its own performance. Similarly key players in the environment – competitors, suppliers, customers and regulators – are much influenced by what they perceive to be an organisation's performance.

Thus at the heart of understanding performance in organisations is a realisation that the selection of criteria for judging performance, and the evaluation of the extent to which such criteria are met, are matters for human judgement. The outcome of such judgements will not necessarily be the same for all interest groups involved. They will be greatly influenced by the complex context illustrated in Figure 10.1.

The complexity of this highly interactive system is enormous, but so are the rewards (both practical and intellectual) of seeking to tease out the connections and interactions. This book is dedicated to increasing understanding so that these rewards will flow more readily to its readers.

10.1 Returning to the Main Themes

In the introduction to the book seven themes were identified in relation to the Elco case. They have been discussed and elaborated in the intervening chapters so that by now they should be accepted by the reader as justifiable principles which are invaluable to anyone interested in analysing organisations. They are merely repeated in bald summary here because they should now speak for themselves. If they do not, then the author has failed in her intentions; but out of that failure, of course, may come some unintended consequences which, in the spirit of this book, may have great import for organisations, for their analysis, and, indeed, for the author.

10.2 Summarising the Main Themes

1. Organisations are interactive systems, with change in one aspect having repercussions for others, sometimes in an unintended or unanticipated way.
2. Organisations are highly complex systems in which there is a great deal of uncertainty.
3. There is no one best way to act in organisations; an appropriate path should be taken through paradox and contradiction in a manner appropriate to the context.

4. Resources are always scarce, and any action is likely to have financial or social costs as well as benefits.
5. Organisations are arenas for the activities of different interest groups which are linked through patterns of conflict, consensus and indifference.
6. People in organisations perceive varying sources of opportunities for, and constraints on, possible action.
7. Activities in, and outcomes from, organisations can be analysed in terms of the level of the individual, group, organisation or society. It is very important to identify the levels that are appropriate to the problems, issues or opportunities with which any practitioner or analyst is concerned.

Bibliography

Abell, P. (1975) *Organizations as Bargaining and Influence Systems* (London: Heinemann).

Abernathy, W. J., Clark, K. B. and Kantrow, A. M. (1983) *Industrial Resistance: Producing a Competitive Future for America* (New York: Basic Books).

Abernathy, W. J. and Ronan, L. (1980) 'Honda Motor Company's CVCC Engine Report', DOT-TSC-80-3 (US Department of Transportation), cited in Sabel (1982).

Ackroyd, S. and Crowdy, P. A. (1990) 'Can Culture be Managed? Working with "Raw" Material: The Case of the English Slaughterhouse', *Personnel Review*, Vol. 19, No. 5, pp. 3–12.

Adler, N. (1986) *International Dimensions of Organisational Behaviour* (Boston, Mass.: Kent Publishing Co.).

Albrow, M. C. (1970) *Bureaucracy* (London: Pall Mall).

Alderfer, C. P. (1972) *Existence Relatedness and Growth: Human Needs in Organisational Settings* (New York: Free Press)

Aldrich, H. E. (1972) 'Technology and Organisational Structure: A Re-examination of Findings of the Aston Group', *Administrative Science Quarterly*, Vol. 17, pp. 26–42.

Aldrich, H. E. (1979) *Organizations and Environments* (Englewood Cliffs, NJ: Prentice-Hall).

Andrews, K. R. (1980) *The Concept of Corporate Strategy*, rev. edn (Homewood, Ill.: Dow Jones-Irwin).

Anthony, P. D. (1990) 'The Paradox of the Management of Culture, or He who leads is lost', *Personnel Review*, Vol. 19, No. 4, pp. 3–8.

Argyris, C. (1962) *Interpersonal Competence and Organisational Effectiveness* (Homewood, Ill.: Dorsey Press).

Argyris, C. and Schon, D., (1978) *Organisational Learning: A Theory-in-Action Perspective* (Reading, Mass.: Addison-Wesley).

Armstrong, T. B. (1971) 'Job Content and Context Factors Related to Satisfaction for Different Occupational Levels', *Journal of Applied Psychology*, Vol. 55, pp. 57–65.

Bachrach, P. and Baratz, M. S. (1962) 'Two Faces of Power', *American Political Science Review*, Vol. 56, pp. 947–52.

Bachrach, P. and Baratz, M. S. (1963) 'Decisions and Non Decisions: An Analytical Framework', *American Political Science Review*, Vol. 57, pp. 641–51.

Bachrach, P. and Baratz, M. S. (1971) *Power and Poverty* (London: Oxford University Press).

Barker, R. G. (1968) *Ecological Psychology* (Stanford, CA: Stanford University Press).

Beach, D. S. (1970) *Personnel: The Management of People at Work* (New York: Macmillan).

Bennis, W. (1966) 'Changing Organisations', *Journal of Applied Behavioral Science*, Vol. 2, No. 3, pp. 247–63.

Bennis, W. G., Berkowitz, N., Affinito, M. and Malone, M. (1958) 'Authority, Power and the Ability to Influence', *Human Relations*, Vol. XI, pp. 143–55.

Benson, J. K. (1975) 'The Interorganisational Network as a Political Economy', *Administrative Science Quarterly*, Vol. 20, June, pp. 229–49.

Benson, J. K. (1977a) 'Innovation and Crisis in Organisational Analysis', *Sociological Quarterly*, Vol. 18, pp. 3–16.

Benson, J. K. (1977b) 'Organizations: A Dialectical View', *Administrative Science Quarterly*, Vol. 22, March, pp. 1–21.

Benson, J. K. (1978) 'The Interorganisational Network as a Political Economy', in Karpik (1978b), first read as a paper to the 8th World Congress of Sociology, Toronto, Canada, 1974, and subsequently taken as the basis for Benson (1975).

Beynon, H. (1974) *Working for Ford* (Harmondsworth: Penguin).

Blackler, F. H. M. and Brown, C. A. (1980) *Whatever Happened to Shell's New Philosophy of Management?* (Farnborough: Saxon House).

Blau, P. M. (1955) *The Dynamics of Bureaucracy* (University of Chicago Press).

Blau, P. M. and Schoenherr, R. A. (1971) *The Structure of Organisations* (New York: Basic Books).

Blauner, R. (1964) *Alienation and Freedom* (University of Chicago Press).

de Bono, E. (1967) *The Use of Lateral Thinking* (Harmondsworth: Penguin).

de Bono, E. (1984) *Tactics: The Art and Science of Success* (Boston, Mass.: Little, Brown).

Bowey, A., Thorpe, R., Mitchell, F., Nicholls, G., Goswold, D., Savery, L. and Hellier, P. (1982) 'Effects of Incentive Payment Systems, United Kingdom, 1977–1980', Research Paper No. 26, Department of Employment, September.

Bradford, L. P., Gibb, J. R and Bennie, K. D. (1964) *Group Theory and Laboratory Method* (New York: Wiley).

Braverman, H. (1974) *Labor and Monopoly Capital* (New York: Monthly Review Press).

Braybrooke, D. and Lindblom, C. E. (1963) *A Strategy of Decision* (New York and London: Macmillan).

Bressand, A., Distler, C. and Nicolaidis, K. (1989) 'Networks at the Heart of the Service Economy', in A. Bressand (ed.) *Strategic Trends in Services* (New York: Harper & Row).

Brocklehurst, M. (1989) *Home Working and the New Technology: The Reality and the Rhetoric*, Personnel Review Monograph, Vol. 18, No. 2.

Brocklehurst, M. and Francis, A. (1991) *Some Paradoxes of the Management of Innovation: The Implications for Organisational Study*, Working Paper for 10th EGOS Colloquium, Vienna.

Brown, R. R. (1967) 'Research and Consultancy in Industrial Enterprises', *Sociology*, Vol. 1, No. 1 (January) pp. 33–60.

Brunsson, N. (1982) 'The Irrationality of Action and Action Rationality: Decisions, Ideologies and Organisational Actions', *Journal of Management Studies*, Vol. 19, No. 1, pp. 29–44.

Brunsson, N. (1985) *The Irrational Organisation* (New York: Wiley).

Burack, E. H. (1991) 'Changing the Company Culture', in *Long Range Planning*, February.

Burgleman, R. A. (1983) 'A Model of the Interaction of Strategic Behaviour, Corporate Context and the Concept of Strategy', *Academy of Management Review*, Vol. 8, pp. 61–70.

Burns, J. (1978) *Leadership* (New York: Harper & Row).

Burns, T. (1977) *The BBC* (London: Macmillan).

Burns, T. and Stalker, G. M. (1961) *The Management of Innovation* (London: Tavistock).

Burrell, G. and Morgan, G. (1979) *Sociological Paradigms and Organisational Analysis* (London: Tavistock).

Business Week (1984) 'Who's Excellent Now?' (5 November), pp. 46–8.

Butler, R. J. and Carney, M. G. (1983) 'Managing Markets: Implications for the Make-Buy Decision', *Journal of Management Studies*, Vol. 20, No. 2, pp. 213–31.

Cameron, K. S. (1986) 'Effectiveness as Paradox: Consensus and conflict in conceptions of organisational effectiveness', *Management Science*, Vol. 32, No. 5, pp. 539–53.

Chandler, A. D. (1962) *Strategy and Structure* (Boston, Mass.: MIT Press).

Chandler, A. D. (1977) *The Visible Hand* (Cambridge, Mass.: Harvard University Press).

Chase, R. B. (1988) 'The Customer Contact Approach to Services: Theoretical Bases and Practical Extensions', in Lovelock, C. H. (ed.), *Managing Services, Marketing, Operations and Human Resources* (Englewood Cliffs, NJ: Prentice-Hall).

Child, J. (1972) 'Organisational Structure, Environment and Performance: the Role of Strategic Choice', *Sociology*, 6, pp. 1–22.

Child, J. (1973) 'Predicting and Understanding Organisational Structure', *Administrative Science Quarterly*, Vol. 18, pp. 168–185.

Child, J. (1982) 'Professionals in the Corporate World: Values, Interests and Control', in D. Dunkerley and G. Salaman (eds), *International Yearbook of Organisation Studies, 1981.*

Child, J. (1984a) *Organization: A Guide to Problems and Practice*, 2nd edn (London: Harper & Row).

Child, J. (1984b) 'New Technology and Developments in Management Organization', *OMEGA*, Vol. 12, No. 3, pp. 211–23.

Child, J. and Mansfield, R. (1972) 'Technology, Size and Organisation Structure', *Sociology*, Vol. 6, pp. 369–93.

Child, J. and Partridge, B. (1982) *Lost Managers: Supervisors in Industry and Society* (Cambridge University Press).

Clark, B. R. (1956) 'Organisational Adaptation and Precarious Values: A Case Study', *American Sociological Review*, Vol. 21, pp. 327–36.

Clark, J. V. and Krone, C. G. (1972) 'Towards an Overall View of Organizational Development in the Early Seventies', in J. M. Thomas and W. G. Bennis (eds), *Management of Change and Conflict* (Harmondsworth: Penguin).

Clark, R. (1979) *The Japanese Company* (Yale University Press).

Clegg, S. (1975) *Power, Rule and Domination: A Critical and Empirical Understanding of Power in Sociological Theory and Everyday Life* (London: Routledge & Kegan Paul).

Clegg, S. and Dunkerley, D. (eds) (1977) *Critical Issues in Organisations* (London: Routledge & Kegan Paul).

Clegg, S. and Dunkerley, D. (1980) *Organisation, Class and Control* (London: Routledge & Kegan Paul).

Clegg, S. (1990) *Modern Organisation – Organisation Studies in the Post Modern World* (London: Sage).

Coch, L. and French, J. R. P. (1948) 'Overcoming Resistance to Change', *Human Relations*, Vol. 1, pp. 512–32.

Cohen, D., March, J. G. and Olsen, P. (1972) 'A Garbage Can Model of Organisational Choice', *Administrative Science Quarterly*, Vol. 17, No. 1, pp. 1–25.

Cotgrove, S. (1975) 'The Engineer, Professionalism and Society', *Birmingham: General Education in Engineering Project*, cited in Child (1982).

Cotgrove, S. and Box, S. (1970) *Science, Industry and Society: Studies in the Sociology of Science* (London: Allen & Unwin).

Crenson, M. A. (1971) *The Un-Politics of Air Pollution: A Study of Non-Decision Making in the Cities* (Baltimore, MD: Johns Hopkins Press).

Crozier, M. (1964) *The Bureaucratic Phenomenon* (University of Chicago Press).

Crozier, M. (1973) *The Stalled Society* (New York: Viking).

Cyert, R. M. and March, J. G. (1963) *A Behavioral Theory of the Firm* (Englewood Cliffs, NJ: Prentice-Hall).

Czarniawska-Joerges, B. (1991) *Reforms as the Last Hope of Control: On the Fate of Modernist Projects in a Post-modern World*, Working Paper Series, Institute of Economics and Management, Lund University, 1991/95.

Czarniawska-Joerges, B. and Wolfe, R. (1987) 'How we Decide and How we Act: On the Assumptions of Viking Organisation Theory' in R. Wolfe (ed.), *Organising for Industrial Development* (Berlin: de Gruyter).

Daft, R. L. and Weick, K. E. (1984) 'Toward a model of organisations as interpretation systems', *Academy of Management Review*, Vol. 9, pp. 284–95.

Daniel, W. W. (1970) *Beyond the Wage Bargain* (London: MacDonald).

Daniel, W. W. and McIntosh, N. (1972) *The Right to Manage?* (London: MacDonald).

Davis, K. (1961) 'Understanding What You Hear', *Nation's Business*, Vol. 49, No. 10 (October), p. 94.

Davis, L. and Cherns, A. (1975) *The Quality of Working Life*, Vol. 1 (New York: Free Press).

Davis, M. and Lawrence, R. (eds) (1977) *Matrix* (Reading, Mass.: Addison-Wesley).

Dawson, S. (1975) 'Power and Influence in Prison Industries', in Abell (1975).

Dawson, S. (1980) 'Natural Selection or Political Process; The Dynamics of Organizational Change', *Personnel Review*, Vol. 9, No. 1 (Winter) pp. 49–53.

Dawson, S., Poynter, P. and Stevens, D. (1983) 'How to Secure an Effective Health and Safety Programme at Work', *OMEGA: The International Journal of Management Science*, Vol. 11, No. 5 (February) pp. 433–46.

Dawson, S., Poynter, P. and Stevens, D. (1984) 'Safety Specialists in Industry: Roles, Constraints and Opportunities', *Journal of Occupational Behaviour*, Vol. 5, pp. 253–70.

Dawson, S. and Wedderburn, D. (1980) 'Joan Woodward and the Development of Organisation Theory', introductory essay to 2nd edn of Woodward (1965).

Dawson, S. J. N., Willman, P., Clinton, A. and Bamford, M. (1988) *Health and Safety at Work, The Limits of Self Regulation* (Cambridge University Press).

Day, P. and Klein, R. (1987) *Accountabilities* (London: Tavistock).

Deal, T. and Kennedy, A. (1982) *Corporate Cultures* (Reading, Mass.: Addison-Wesley).

Dennis, S. M., Gillespie, D. F. and Mornsey, E. (1978) 'Technology and Organisations: Methodological Deficiencies and Lacunae', *Technology and Culture*, Vol. 19, pp. 83–92.

Dickson, W..(1981) 'Participation as an Organisational Means of Control', *Journal of Management Studies*, Vol. 18, No. 2, pp. 1–18.

Dill, W. R. (1962) 'The Impact of the Environment on Organisational Development', in S. Mailick and E. H. Van Ness (eds), *Concepts and Issues in Administrative Behaviour* (Englewood Cliffs: Prentice-Hall), pp. 94–109.

Dirsmith, M. W. and Covaleski (1985) 'Informal Communications, Non Formal Communications and Monitoring in Public Accounting Firms', *Accounting, Organisations & Society*, Vol. 10, No. 2, pp. 149–69.

Dodgson, M. (1985) 'Work Organisation and Skills in Small Engineering Firms using CNC Machines', unpublished PhD thesis, University of London.

Donaldson, G. and Lorsch, J. W. (1983) *Decision Making at the Top* (New York: Basic Books).

Donaldson, L. (1976) 'Woodward, Technology, Organisational Structure and Performance – a Critique of the Universal Generalisation', *Journal of Management Studies* (October).

Dore, R. (1973) *British Factory, Japanese Factory* (Berkeley, CA: University of California Press).

Douglas, M. (1986) *How Institutions Think* (Syracuse University Press).

Downey, H. K., Hellreige, D. and Slocum, J. (1975) 'Environmental Uncertainty: The Construct and Its Application', *Administrative Science Quarterly*, Vol. 20, pp. 613–29.

Drucker, P. F. (1964) *Managing for Results* (New York: Harper & Row).

Drucker, P. F. (1989) *The New Realities* (London: Heinemann).

Duncan, R. (1972) 'Characteristics of Organisational Environments and Perceived Uncertainty', *Administrative Science Quarterly*, Vol. 17, pp. 313–27.

Edvinsson, L., Richardson, J. (1989) 'Services and Thoughtware: New Dimensions in Service Business Development', in A. Bressand (ed.), *Strategic Trends in Services* (New York: Harper & Row).

Edwards, R. (1979) *Contested Terrain: The Transformation of the Workplace in the Twentieth Century* (London: Heinemann).

Ehrenreich, B. and Ehrenreich, J. (1977) 'The Professional-Managerial Class', *Radical America*, Vol. 11 (March–April), pp. 7–31.

Eilon, S. (1962) 'Problems in Studying Management Control', *International Journal of Production Research*, Vol. 1, pp. 13–20.

Elger, A. J. (1975) 'Industrial Organisations, A Processual Perspective', in J. B. McKinley (ed.), *Processing People: Cases in Organisational Behaviour* (London: Holt, Rinehart & Winston) pp. 91–149.

Emerson, R. M. (1962) 'Power Dependence Relations', *American Sociological Review*, Vol. 27, pp. 31–41.

Emery, F. E. and Trist, E. L. (1965a) 'Socio-Technical Systems', in C. W. Churchman and M. Verhulst (eds), *Management Science, Models and Techniques*, Vol. 2 (Oxford: Pergamon), pp. 83–97.

Emery, F. E. and Trist, E. L. (1965b) 'The Causal Texture of Organisational Environments', *Human Relations*, Vol. 18, pp. 21–31.

The Engineer (1984) Report by Mike Harrison on study by Mark Dodgson now available as: 'Work Organisation and Skills in Small Engineering Firms Using CNC Machines', unpublished PhD thesis, University of London, 1985.

Englestad, P. H. (1972) 'Sociotechnical Approach to Problems of Process Control', in L. Davis and J. Taylor (eds), *The Design of Jobs* (Santa Monica, CA: Goodyear).

Etzioni, A. (1973) 'Mixed Scanning: A "Third" Approach to Decision Making', in A. Faludi (ed.), *A Reader in Planning Theory* (Oxford: Pergamon).

Evan, W. H. (1966) 'The Organisation Set: Toward A Theory of Interorganisational Relations', in J. D. Thompson (ed.), *Approaches to Organisational Design* (University of Pittsburgh Press).

Evan, W. H. (1972) 'An Organisation-Set Model of Interorganisational Relations', in M. Tuite, M. Radnor and R. Chisholm (eds), *Interorganisational Decision Making* (Chicago: Aldine).

Fayol, H. (1916) 'Administration Industrielle et Générale', translated by C. Storrs into *General and Industrial Management* (London: Pitman, 1949).

Fein, M. (1974) 'Job Enrichment: A Re-evaluation', *Sloan Management Review*, Vol. 15, pp. 69–88.

Fellmeth, R. C. (1970) *The Interstate Commerce Commission* (New York: Grossman).

Festinger, L. (1957) *A Theory of Cognitive Dissonance* (Evanston, Ill.: Row Petersen).

Finniston, Sir M. (1980) *Engineering our Future*, Report of the Committee of Inquiry into the Engineering Profession (London: HMSO).

Fiol, C. M. and Lyles, M. A. (1985) 'Organisational Learning', in *Academy of Management Review*, Vol. 10, No. 4, pp. 803–13.

Flamholtz, E. (1979) 'Behavioral Aspects of Accounting Control Systems', in S. Kerr (ed.), *Organizational Behavior* (New York: Wiley).

Fombrun, C. J. (1986) 'Structural Dynamisms within and between organisations', *Administrative Science Quarterly*, 31, pp. 383–417.

Fombrun, C. J. and Shanley, M. (1990) 'What's in a Name? Reputation Building and Corporate Strategy', *Academy of Management Journal*, Vol. 33, No. 2, pp. 233–58.

Ford, R. N. (1973) 'Job Enrichment: Lessons from AT & T', *Harvard Business Review*, Vol. 51, (January–February), pp. 96–106.

Fox, A. (1966) 'Industrial Sociology and Industrial Relations', Research Paper 3, Royal Commission on Trade Unions and Employers' Associations (London: HMSO).

Fox, A. (1973) 'Industrial Relations : A Social Critique of Pluralist Ideology', in J. Child (ed.), *Man and Organisation* (London: Allen & Unwin).

Fox, A. (1974) *Beyond Contract: Work, Power and Trust Relations* (London: Faber & Faber).

Francis A., (1990) 'The Competitive Position of British Industry: Are Non-Price factors a problem and is X-Inefficiency the Cause?', in K. Weiermair and M. Perlman (eds), *Studies in Economic Rationality, X-Efficiency Examined and Extolled* (Ann Arbor: The University of Michigan Press) pp. 277–93.

Francis, A., Turk, J. and Willman, P. (eds) (1983) *Power, Efficiency and Institutions* (London: Heinemann).

Freeman, R. E. (1984) *Strategic Management: A Stakeholder Approach* (Boston, Mass.: Pitman Press).

French , J. R. P. and Raven, B. H. (1959) 'The Bases of Social Power', in D. Cartwright (ed.), *Studies in Social Power* (Ann Arbor: University of Michigan Press), pp. 150–67.

Friedman, D. (1989) *The Misunderstood Miracle: Industrial Development and Political Change in Japan* (Cornell University Press).

Galbraith, J. (1973) *Designing Complex Organisations* (Reading, Mass.: Addison-Wesley).

Galbraith, J. (1977) *Organisation Design* (Reading, Mass.: Addison-Wesley).

Galbraith, J. K. (1967) *The New Industrial State* (London: Hamish Hamilton).

Gallie, D. (1978) *In Search of the New Working Class* (Cambridge University Press).

Garscombke, D. J. (1988) 'Organisational Culture dons the Mantle of Militarism' in *Organisational Dynamics* (Summer), pp. 46–56.

Giddens, A. (1984) *The Constitution of Society: Outline of the Theory of Structuration* (Oxford: Polity Press).

Goldner, F. H. and Ritti, R. R. (1967) 'Professionalisation as Career Immobility', *American Journal of Sociology*, Vol. 72, pp. 489–502.

Goldthorpe, J. H., Lockwood, D., Bechofer, F. and Platt, J. (1968) *The Affluent Worker: Industrial Attitudes and Behaviour* (Cambridge University Press).

Goodman, P. S. and Pennings, J. M. (eds) (1977) *New Perspectives on Organizational Effectiveness* (San Francisco: Jossey Bass).

Gouldner, A. W. (1954) *Patterns of Industrial Bureaucracy* (New York: Free Press).

Gouldner, A. W. (1957) 'Cosmopolitans and Locals: Towards an Analysis of Latent Social Roles', *Administrative Science Quarterly*, Vol. 2, pp. 281–306.

Gow, I. (1986) 'Japanese business in Britain: Raiders, Invaders or simply Good Traders?', *Accountancy* (UK) Vol. 97, No. 1111, March, pp. 66–73

Gregory, D. (ed.) (1978) *Work Organisation, Swedish Experience and British Context* (London: Social Science Research Council).

Gunz, H. P. (1978) 'White Collar Unions in R & D: Some U.K. Experience', *R & D Management*, Vol. 9, No. 1, pp. 29–32.

Gunz, H. P. (1980) 'Dual Ladders in Research: A Paradoxical Organizational Fix', *R & D Management*, Vol. 10, No. 3, pp. 113–18.

Gunz, H. and Pearson, A. W. (1977) 'Matrix Organisation in Research and Development', in Knight (1977), Ch. 2.

Hackman, J. R. and Oldham, G. R. (1980) *Work Redesign* (Reading, Mass.: Addison-Wesley).

Hage, J. and Aiken, M. (1967) 'Program Change and Organization Properties: A Comparative Analysis', *American Journal of Sociology*, 72, pp. 503–19.

Hage, J. and Aiken, M. (1969) 'Routine Technology, Social Structure and Organizational Goals', *Administrative Science Quarterly*, Vol. 14, pp. 366–76.

Hall, R. H. (1962) 'Intraorganizational Structural Variation: application of the bureaucratic model', *Administrative Science Quarterly*, Vol. 7, No. 3 (December), pp. 295–308.

Hall, R. H., Clark, J., Giordano, P., Johnson, P. and van Rockell (1977) 'Patterns of Interorganisational Relationships', *Administrative Science Quarterly*, Vol. 22 (September), pp. 229–49.

Halpin, A. W. and Winer, B. J. (1957) 'A Factorial Study of the Leader Behaviour Descriptions', in R. M. Stogdill and A. E. Loons (eds), *Leader Behaviour: Its Description and Measurement*, research monograph No. 88 (Columbus: Ohio State University, Bureau of Business Research), pp. 39–51.

Handy, C. (1985) *Understanding Organisations*, 3rd edn (Harmondsworth: Penguin).

Handy, C. (1989) *The Age of Unreason* (London: Business Books).

Hastings, A. and Hinings, C. R. (1970) 'Role Relations and Value Adaptation: A Study of the Professional Accountant in Industry', *Sociology*, Vol. 4, pp. 353–65.

Hedberg, B. L. T. (1977) 'Information Systems for Alternative Organisations. Using Information Technology to Facilitate Industrial Democracy and Organisational Learning', *CREST Conference*, Stoke on Trent.

Hedberg, B. L. T. and Mumford, E. (1975) 'The Design of Computer Systems: A Man's Vision of Man as an Integral Part of the Systems Design Process', in E. Mumford and H. Sackman (eds), *Human Choice and Computers* (Amsterdam: North-Holland).

Hedberg, B. L. T., Nystrom, P. C. and Starbuck, W. H. (1976) 'Camping on Seesaws: Prescriptions for a Self-designing Organization', *Administrative Science Quarterly*, Vol. 21, March, pp. 41–65.

Hedberg, B. L. T. (1981) 'How Organisations Learn and Unlearn', in P. L. Nystrom and W. H. Starbuck (eds), *Handbook of Organisational Design* (Oxford University Press).

Herzberg, F. (1966) *Work and the Nature of Man* (Cleveland: World Publishing).

Herzberg, F., Mausner, B. and Snyderman, B. (1959) *The Motivation to Work*, 2nd edn (New York: Wiley).

Hickson, D. J., Hinings C. R., Lee, C. A., Schneck, R. E. and Pennings, J. M. (1971) 'A Strategic Contingencies Theory of Intra-organisational Power', *Administrative Science Quarterly*, Vol. 16, pp. 216–29.

Hickson, D. J., Pugh, D. S. and Pheysey, C. D. (1969) 'Operations Technology and Organization Structure: An Empirical Appraisal', *Administrative Science Quarterly*, Vol. 14, pp. 378–97.

Hirsch, P. M. (1972) 'Processing Fads and Fashions: An Organization-set Analysis of Cultural Industry Products', *American Journal of Sociology*, Vol. 77, No. 4 (January) pp. 639–59.

Hirsch, P. M. (1975) 'Organizational Effectiveness and the Institutional Environment', *Administrative Science Quarterly*, Vol. 20, No. 4 (September), pp. 327–44.

Hirschleifer, J. and Riley, J. G. (1979) 'The Analysis of Uncertainty and Information – An Expository Survey', *Journal of Economic Literature*, Vol. 17, pp. 1375–421.

Hirschman, A. O. (1972) *Exit Voice and Loyalty* (Cambridge, Mass.: Harvard University Press).

Hofstede, G. (1980) *Culture's Consequences: International Differences in Work Related Values* (Beverly Hills, CA: Sage).

Hofstede, G. (1985) 'The Interaction between National and Organisational Value Systems', *Journal of Management Studies*, Vol. 22, No. 4, pp. 347–57.

Hofstede, G. (1990) *Cultures and Organisations: Software of the Mind* (London: McGraw-Hill).

Hopper, T. M. (1978) 'Role Conflicts of Management Accounts in the Context of their Structural Relationship to Production', unpublished M.Phil thesis, University of Aston, Birmingham, cited in Child (1982).

IDE (1981) *International Research Group, Industrial Democracy in Europe* (Oxford University Press).

Janis, I. L. (1972) *Victims of Group Think: A Psychological Study of Foreign Policy Decisions and Fiascos* (New York: Houghton Mifflin).

Jaques, E. (1951) *The Changing Culture of a Factory* (London: Tavistock).

Jaques, E. (1967) *Equitable Payment* (Harmondsworth: Penguin).

Johnson, G. (1987) *Strategic Change and the Management Process* (Oxford: Blackwell).

Kanter, R. M. (1983) *The Change Masters: Corporate Entrepreneurs at Work* (New York: Simon & Schuster).

Kanter, R. M. (1989) *When Giants Learn to Dance* (New York: Simon & Schuster).

Kar, L. (1972) *Business Communication: Theory and Practice* (Homewood, Ill.: Irwin).

Karpik, L. (1978a) 'Organizations, Institutions and History', in Karpik (1978b) first delivered to the 8th World Congress of Sociology, 1974, Toronto, Canada.

Karpik, L. (ed.) (1978b) *Organization and Environment* (London: Sage).

Katz, D. and Kahn, R. L. (1966) *The Social Psychology of Organisations* (New York: John Wiley; 2nd edn, 1978).

Kelly, J. (1980) 'The Costs of Job Design', *Industrial Relations Journal*, Vol. 11, No. 3 (July–August), pp. 22–34.

Khandwalla, P. N. (1973) 'Viable and Effective Organizational Design of Firms', *Academy of Management Journal* (September), 16(3) pp. 481–95.

Khandwalla, P. N. (1974) 'Mass Output Orientation of Operations, Technology and Organizational Structure', *Administrative Science Quarterly*, Vol. 19 (March), pp. 74–97.

Khandwalla, P. N. (1977) *The Design of Organizations* (New York: Harcourt Brace Jovanovich).

Kilmann, R. H., Covin, T. J. *et al.* (1988) *Corporate Transformations* (San Francisco: Jossey Bass).

Kimberly, J. R., Miles, R. H. *et al.* (1980) *The Organizational Life Cycle* (London: Jossey Bass).

Kimberly, J. R. and Quinn, R. E. (1984) 'The Challenge of Transition Management', in J. R. Kimberly and R. E. Quinn (eds), *Managing Organisational Transitions* (Homewood, Ill.: Irwin).

Kingdon, D. R. (1973) *Matrix Organization* (London: Tavistock).

Knight, K. (ed.) (1977) *Matrix Management: A Cross-functional Approach to Organisation* (Aldershot: Gower).

Kornhauser, W. (1962) *Scientists in Industry* (University of California Press).

Kotler, P. (1989) *Principles of Marketing* (Englewood Cliffs, NJ: Prentice-Hall).

Kotter, J. P. and Schlesinger, L. A. (1979) 'Choosing Strategies for Change', *Harvard Business Review* (March–April) Vol. 57, No. 2, pp. 106–14.

Lambert, P. (1982) 'Selecting Japanese Management Practices for Import', *Personnel Management* (January) Vol 14, No. 1, pp. 38–41.

Lawrence, P. (1981) 'The Harvard Organisation and Environment Research Programme', in A. H. Van de Ven and W. T Joyce (eds), *Perspectives on Organisation Design and Behaviour* (New York: Wiley).

Lawrence, P. R. and Lorsch, J. W. (1967) *Organisation and Environment* (Boston, Mass.: Graduate School of Business Administration, Harvard University).

Leavitt, H. J. (1964) 'Applied Organizational Change in Industry', in W. W. Cooper, H. J. Leavitt and M. W. Shelly (eds), *New Perspectives in Organization Research* (New York: Wiley).

Legge, K. (1984) *Evaluating Planned Organisational Change* (London: Academic Press).

Lewin, K. (1948) *Resolving Social Conflicts* (New York: Harper & Row).

Likert, R. (1961) *New Patterns of Management* (New York: McGraw-Hill).

Lindblom, C. E. (1959) 'The Science of "Muddling Through"', *Public Administration Review*, Vol. 19, pp. 79–88.

Littler, C. (1982) *The Development of the Labour Process in Capitalist Societies* (London: Heinemann).

Littler, C. and Salaman, G. (1982) 'Bravermania and Beyond', *Sociology*, Vol. 16, pp. 251–69.

Locke, E. A. and Schweiger, D. M. (1979) 'Participation in Decision Making: One More Look', in B. M. Staw (ed.), *Research in Organizational Behaviour*, Vol. 1 (Greenwich, CT: JAI Press).

Lorsch, J. W. and Matthias, P. E. (1987) 'When Professionals have to Manage', *Harvard Business Review*, Vol. 65, No. 4, pp. 78–83.

Lorsch, J. W. and Morse, J. J. (1974) *Organizations and Their Members: A Contingency Approach* (New York: Harper & Row).

Lukes, S. (1974) *Power: A Radical View* (London: Macmillan).

Lupton, T. and Gowler, D. (1969) 'Selecting a Wage Payment System', Research Paper No. 3 (London: Engineering Employers Federation).

Maister, D. H. (1985) 'The "one-firm" Firm: What makes it Successful?' *Sloan Management Review* (Fall), pp. 3–14.

Maister, D. H. (1989) *Professional Service Firm Management*, Monograph (New York: Maister Associates Inc.).

Mallet, S. (1969) *La nouvelle classe ouvrière* (Paris) cited in Gallie (1978) pp. 16–21.

Mandel, E. (1975) *Late Capitalism* (London: New Left Books).

March, J. G. (1974) 'The Technology of Foolishness', in H. Leavitt, L. Pinfield and E. Webb (eds), *Organizations of the Future: Interaction with External Environment* (New York: Praeger).

March, J. G. (1981) 'Footnotes to Organisational Change', *Administrative Science Quarterly*, Vol. 26, No. 4 (December), pp. 563–77.

March, J. G. and Simon, H. A. (1958) *Organisations* (New York: Wiley).

Marchington, M. and Armstrong, P. (1982) 'A Comparison Between Shop Steward Activity in Local Government and the Private Sector', in *Local Government Studies*, Vol. 8, No. 6, pp. 33–48.

Marchington, M. and Armstrong, P. (1983) 'Shop Steward Organization and Joint Consultation', in *Personnel Review*, Vol. 12, No. 1, pp. 24–31.

Marglin, S. (1974) '"What Do Bosses Do?" The Origins and Functions of Hierarchy in Capitalist Production', *Review of Radical Political Economics*, Vol. 6, pp. 60–112.

Martin, J. (1982) 'Stories and Scripts in Organisational Settings', in A. Hastorf and A. Isen (eds), *Cognitive Social Psychology* (New York: Elsevier), pp. 225–305.

Maslow, A. H. (1943) 'A Theory of Human Motivation', *Psychological Review*, Vol. 50, pp. 370–96.

Maslow, A. H. (1954) *Motivation and Personality* (New York: Harper & Row).

McGregor, D. (1960) *The Human Side of Enterprise* (New York: Harper & Row).

Mechanic, D. (1962) 'Sources of Power of Lower Participants in Complex Organisations', *Administrative Science Quarterly*, Vol. 7, pp. 349–64.

Merton, R. K. (1940) 'Bureaucratic Structure and Personality', *Social Forces*, Vol 18, pp. 560–8.

Merton, R. K. (1957) *Social Theory and Social Structure*, rev. edn (Chicago: Free Press).

Miller, D. (1990) *The Icarus Paradox* (New York: Harper Business)

Millerson, G. (1964) *The Qualifying Associations: A Study in Professionalisation* (London: Routledge).

Mills, C. Wright (1965) *The Power Elite* (New York: Oxford University Press).

Mindlin, S. E. and Aldrich, H. (1975) 'Interorganizational Dependence: a review of the concept and a reexamination of the findings of the Aston group', *Administrative Science Quarterly*, Vol. 20, September, pp. 382–92.

Mintzberg, H. (1978) 'Patterns in Strategy Formation', in *Management Science*, Vol. 24, pp. 934–48.

Mintzberg, H. (1979) *The Structuring of Organizations* (Englewood Cliffs, NJ: Prentice-Hall).

Mintzberg, H. (1989) *Mintzberg on Management: Inside our Strange World of Organisations* (Chicago: Free Press).

Mohr, L. B. (1971) 'Organizational Technology and Organization Structure', *Administrative Science Quarterly*, Vol. 16, No. 3, pp. 444–59.

Mohr, L. B. (1982) *Explaining Organizational Behaviour* (San Francisco: Jossey Bass).

Moore, D. C. and Davies, D. S. (1977) 'The Dual Ladder – Establishing and Operating', in *Research Management* (July), pp. 14–19.

Morgan, G. (1986) *Images of Organisation* (London: Sage).

Morgan, G. (1989) *Riding The Waves of Change: Developing Managerial Competencies for a Turbulent World* (San Francisco: Jossey Bass).

Morgan, G. and Ramirez, K. (1984), 'Action Learning: a holographic metaphor for guiding social change', in *Human Relations*, Vol. 37, No. 1, pp. 1–28.

Mumford, E. and Pettigrew, A. (1975) *Implementing Strategic Decisions* (London: Longman).

Nash, M. (1983) *Managing Organizational Performance* (San Francisco: Jossey Bass).

Noble, D. F. (1977) *America by Design: Science, Technology and the Rise of Corporate Capitalism* (New York: Knopf).

Noble, D. F. (1984) *Forces of Production: A Social History of Industrial Automation* (New York: Knopf).

Okimoto, D. I. (1989) *Between MITI and the Market: Japanese Industrial Policy and High Technology* (Stanford University Press).

Olins, W. (1989) *Corporate Identity, Making Business Strategy Visible* (London: Thames & Hudson).

Oppenheimer, M. (1973) 'The Proletarianisation of the Professional', in P. Halmos (ed.), *Professionalisation and Social Change*, Sociological Review Monograph, No. 20 (University of Keele) pp. 213–27.

Ouchi, W. G. (1981) *Theory Z* (Reading, Mass.: Addison-Wesley).

Ouchi, W. G. and Price, R. L. (1978) 'Hierarchies, Clans and Theory Z: a New Perspective on Organization Development', *Organizational Dynamics*, Vol. 7, pp. 25–44.

Pascale, R. T. (1990) *Managing on the Edge: The Learning Organisation* (New York: Simon & Schuster).

Pascale, R. T. and Athos, A. G. (1981) *The Art of Japanese Management* (New York: Werner).

Payne, R. L, Pheysey, D. and Pugh, D. (1971) 'Organisational Structure, Organisational Climate and Group Structure', in *Occupational Psychology*, Vol. 45, pp. 45–55.

Pennings, J. (1973) 'Measures of Organizational Structure: a Methodological Note', *American Journal of Sociology*, Vol. 79, No. 3, pp. 686–704.

Perrow, C. (1961) 'The Analysis of Goals in Complex Organizations', *American Sociological Review*, Vol. 26, pp. 854–66.

Perrow, C. (1967) 'A Framework for the Comparative Analysis of Organisations', *American Sociological Review*, Vol. 32, pp. 194–208.

Perrow, C. (1970) *Organizational Analysis: A Sociological View* (London: Tavistock).

Perrow, C. (1979) *Complex Organizations: A Critical Essay* (Dallas: Scott Foresman)

Perrow, C. (1981) 'Markets Hierarchies and Hegemony', in A. H. Van de Ven and W. F. Joyce (eds), *Perspectives on Organisation Design and Behaviour* (New York: Wiley).

Perrow, C. (1984) *Normal Accidents, Living with High Risk Technologies* (New York: Basic Books).

Peters, T. J., (1987) *Thriving on Chaos* (London: Pan).

Peters, T. J. and Waterman, R. H. (1982) *In Search of Excellence* (New York: Harper & Row).

Peterson, R. A. and Berger, D. G. (1971) 'Entrepreneurship in Organizations: Evidence from the Popular Music Industry', *Administrative Science Quarterly*, Vol. 16, No. 1, pp. 97–106.

Pettigrew, A. (1973) *The Politics of Organizational Decision-Making* (London: Tavistock).

Pettigrew, A. and Whipp, R. (1991) *Managing Change for Competitive Success* (Oxford: Blackell).

Pfeffer, J. (1978) 'The Micropolitics of Organisations', in Marshall W. Meyer and associates (eds), *Environments and Organisations* (San Francisco: Jossey Bass), pp. 29–50.

Pfeffer, J. (1981a) 'Bringing the Environment back in: The Social Context of Business Strategy', in D. J. Teece (ed.), *The Competitive Challenge: Strategies for Industrial Innovation and Revitalisation* (Cambridge, Mass.: Ballinger).

Pfeffer, J. (1981b) *Power in Organizations* (London: Pitman).

Pfeffer, J. and Salancik, R. (1978) *The External Control of Organizations: A Resource Dependence Perspective* (New York: Harper & Row).

Porter, L. W. and Lawler, E. E. (1968) *Managerial Attitudes and Performance* (Homewood, Ill.: Dorsey Press).

Porter, M. (1985) *Competitive Advantage: Creating and Sustaining Superior Performance* (New York: The Free Press).

Powell, A. G. (1981) *The Changing Roles of Accountants in Industry: Initial Research Findings* (London: Ealing College of Higher Education), January.

Pressman, J. L. and Wildavsky, A. B. (1973) *Implementation* (Berkeley: University of California Press).

Pritchard, R. D. (1969) 'Equity Theory: A Review and Critique', *Organizational Behaviour and Human Performance*, Vol. 4, pp. 176–211.

Project Sappho (1972) *Success and Failure in Industrial Innovation* (London: Centre for the Study of Industrial Innovation).

Pugh, D. S., Hickson, D. J., Hinings, C. R., MacDonald, K. M., Turner, C. and Lupton, T. (1963) 'A Conceptual Scheme for Organizational Analysis', *Administrative Science Quarterly*, Vol. 8, pp. 289–315.

Pugh, D. S., Hickson, D. J. and Hinings, C. R. (1969a) 'The Context of Organization Structures', *Administrative Science Quarterly*, Vol. 14 (March), pp. 91–114.

Pugh, D. S., Hickson, D. J. and Hinings, C. R. (1969b) 'An Empirical Taxonomy of Structures of Work Organizations', *Administrative Science Quarterly*, Vol. 14 (March), pp. 115–26.

Pugh, D. S. and Hickson, D. J. (1976) *Organizational Structure in its Context*, The Aston Programme, Vol. 1 (Farnborough: Saxon).

Pugh, D. S. and Hinings, C. R. (1976) *Organization Structure: Extensions and Replication*, The Aston Programme, Vol. 2 (Farnborough: Saxon).

Quinn, J. B. (1980a) *Strategies for Change: Logical Incrementalism*, (Homewood, Ill.: Dow Jones, Irwin).

Quinn, J. B. (1980b) 'Managing Strategic Change', *Sloan Management Review* (Summer).

Quinn, R. E. (1988) *Beyond Rational Management: Mastering the Paradoxes and Competing Demands of High Performance* (San Francisco: Jossey Bass).

Quinn, R. E. and Cameron, K. S. (ed.) (1988) *Paradox and Transformation: Towards a Theory of Change in Organisation and Management* (Cambridge, Mass.: Ballinger).

Randall, R. (1973) 'Influence of Environmental Support and Policy Space on Organizational Behaviour', *Administrative Science Quarterly*, Vol. 18, No. 2, pp. 236–47.

Reed, M. (1985) *Redirections in Organizational Analysis* (London: Tavistock).

Reeves, T. K. and Turner, B. A. (1972) 'A Theory of Organization and Behaviour in Batch Production Factories', *Administrative Science Quarterly* (March).

Reeves, T. K. and Woodward, J. (1970) 'The Study of Managerial Control', in J. Woodward (ed.), *Industrial Organisation: Theory and Practice* (Oxford University Press) pp. 81–98.

Rice, A. K. (1963) *The Enterprise and its Environment* (London: Tavistock).

Robens, Lord (1972) *Safety and Health at Work: Report of the Committee of Inquiry*, 1970–72, Cmnd 5034 (London: HMSO).

Roethlisberger, F. G. and Dickson, W. J. (1939) *Management and the Worker* (Cambridge, Mass.: Harvard University Press).

Rorty, R. (1989) *Contingency, Irony and Solidarity* (Cambridge University Press).

Rose, M. (1975) *Industrial Behaviour* (Hardmondsworth: Penguin).

Rose, M. and Jones, B. (1984) 'Managerial Strategy and Trade Union Response in Plant-level Reorganisation at Work', in D. Knights, D. Collison and H. Willmott (eds), *Job Redesign: The Organisation and Control of Work* (London: Heinemann).

Sabel, C. F. (1982) *Work and Politics and the Division of Labour in Industry* (Cambridge University Press).

Salaman, G. (1979) *Work Organisation: Resistance and Control* (London: Longman).

Salancik, G. R. and Meindl, J. (1984) 'Corporate Attributions as Strategic Illusions of Management Control', *Administrative Science Quarterly*, Vol. 29, pp. 238–54.

Salancik, G. R. and Pfeffer, J. (1974) 'The Bases and Use of Power in Organizational Decision Making: The Case of a University', *Administrative Science Quarterly*, Vol. 29, pp. 453–73.

Sampson, A. (1973) *The Sovereign State* (London: Hodder & Stoughton).

Saythe, (1985) *Culture and Related Corporate Realities* (Homewood, Ill.: Irwin).

Schattschneider, E. E. (1960) *The Sovereign People* (New York: Holt, Rinehart & Winston).

Schien, E. H. (1985) 'Organisational Culture', *Organisational Dynamics*, Vol. 12, pp. 13–28.

Schien, E. H. (1986) *Organisational Culture and Leadership* (San Francisco: Jossey Bass).

Schmenner, R. W. (1988) 'How can Service Businesses Survive and Prosper', in C. H. Lovelock (ed.), *Managing Services, Marketing, Operations and Human Resources* (Englewood Cliffs, NJ: Prentice-Hall).

Schwab, D. P. and Cummings, L. L. (1970) 'Theories of Performance and Satisfaction: A Review', *Industrial Relations*, Vol. 10, No. 4, pp. 408–30.

Scott, R. A. (1967) 'The Factory as a Social Service Organisation: Goal Displacement in Workshops for the Blind', *Social Problems*, Vol. 15, No. 2, pp. 160–75.

Selznick, P. (1949) *TVA and the Grass Roots* (Berkeley: University of California Press).

Senge, P. (1990) *The Fifth Discipline: The Art and Practice of the Learning Organisation* (New York: Doubleday/Currency).

Shrum, W. and Wuthnow, R. (1988) 'Reputational Status of Organisations in Technical Systems', *American Journal of Sociology*, Vol. 93, pp. 623–58.

Sills, D. L. (1957) *The Volunteers: Means and Ends in a National Organization* (Chicago: Free Press).

Silverman, D. (1970) *The Theory of Organisations* (London: Heinemann).

Simon, A. (1957) *Models of Man* (New York: Wiley).

Smircich, L. (1983) 'Concepts of Culture and Organizational Analysis', *Administrative Science Quarterly*, Vol 28, September, pp. 339–58.

Smircich, L. and Stubbart, C. (1985) 'Strategic Management in an Enacted World', *Academy of Management Review*, Vol. 10, No. 4, pp. 724–36.

Smith, J. (1983) *The Management of Remuneration* (London: Institute of Personnel Management).

Sorge, A., Hartmann, G., Warner, M. and Nicholas, L. (1983) *Microelectronics and Manpower in Manufacturing* (Aldershot: Gower).

Spradley, J. P. and Mann, B. J. (1975) *The Cocktail Waitress* (New York: Wiley).

Spriano, G. (1989) 'R & D Networks: The Emerging Market for Technological and Scientific Services';, in A. Bressand (ed.) *Strategic Trends in Services* (New York: Harper & Row).

Starbuck, W. H. (1965) 'Organizational Growth and Development', in J. G. March (ed.) *Handbook of Organisations* (Chicago: Rand McNally).

Starbuck, W. H. (1976) 'Organizations and their environments', in M. D. Dunnette (ed.), *Handbook of Industrial and Organizational Psychology*, (Chicago: Rand McNally) pp. 1069–123.

Staw, B. M., Sandelands, L. E. and Dutton, J. E. (1981) 'Threat Rigidity Effects in Organizational Behaviour: A Multilevel Analysis', *Administrative Science Quarterly*, Vol. 26, No. 4, pp. 501–24.

Staw, B. M. and Szwajkowski, E. (1975) 'The Scarcity-Munificence Component of Organizational Environments and the Commission of Illegal Acts', *Administrative Science Quarterly*, Vol. 20, pp. 345–54.

Steers, R. M. (1977) *Organizational Effectiveness: A Behavioural View* (Santa Monica: Goodyear).

Steward, K. and Dawson, S. (1991) 'Pan European Annual Reports', *Investor Relations* (August) pp. 37–9.

Stewart, V. (1983) *Change, the Challenge for Management* (London: McGraw-Hill).

Tannenbaum, A. S. (1966) *Social Psychology of the Work Organization* (London: Tavistock).

Tannenbaum, A. S. (1968) *Control in Organizations* (New York: McGraw-Hill).

Taylor, F. W. (1911) *The Principles of Scientific Management* (New York: McGraw-Hill).

Terreberry, S. (1968) 'The Evolution of Organizational Environments', *Administrative Science Quarterly*, Vol. 12, No. 4, pp. 590–612.

Thompson, J. D. (1967) *Organizations in Action* (New York: McGraw-Hill).

Thompson, J. D. and Bates, F. L. (1957) 'Technology, Organization and Administration', *Administrative Science Quarterly*, Vol. 2, pp. 325–43.

Thompson, J. D. and McEwen, W. J. (1958) 'Organizational Goals and Environments: Goal Setting as an Interaction Process', *American Sociological Review*, Vol. 23, pp. 23–31.

Thompson, J. D. and Tuden, A. (1959) 'Strategies, Structures and Processes of Organizational Decision', in J. D. Thompson *et al.* (eds), *Comparative Studies in*

Administration (University of Pittsburgh Press), pp. 195–216.

Thompson, M. and Wildavsky, A. (1986) 'A Cultural Theory of Information Bias in Organizations', *Journal of Management Studies*, Vol. 23, pp. 273–86.

Thurley, K. (1981) 'The British Worker and the Japanese Way of Work', *New Society*, 9 July.

Thurley, K. (1984) 'A Touch of Genius or Purely Indigenous?' *Europe-Asia Business Review* (April).

Tichy, N. (1983) *Managing Strategic Change: Technical, Political and Cultural Dynamics* (New York: Wiley).

Tichy, N. M. and Devanna, M. A. (1986) *The Transformational Leader* (New York: Wiley).

Tosi, H., Aldag, R. and Storey, R. (1973) 'On the Measurement of the Environment: an Assessment of the Lawrence and Lorsch Environmental Uncertainty Scale', *Administrative Science Quarterly*, Vol. 18 (March), pp. 27–36.

Trist, E. L. (1981) 'The Evolution of Sociotechnical Systems as a Conceptual Framework and as an Action Research Programme', in A. H. Van de Ven and W. F. Joyce (eds), *Perspectives on Organizational Design and Behaviour* (New York: Wiley).

Trist, E. L. and Bamforth, K. (1951) 'Some Social and Psychological Consequences of the Longwall Method of Coal-Getting', *Human Relations*, Vol. 4, pp. 3–38.

Trist, E. L., Higgin, G., Murray, H. and Pollock, A. (1963) *Organisational Choice* (London: Tavistock).

Turner, B. (ed.) (1990) *Organisational Symbolism* (Berlin: de Gruyter).

Tushman, M. L. (1977) 'A Political Approach to Organizations: A Review and Rationale', *Academy of Management Review*, Vol. 2, pp. 206–16.

Urwick, L. (1929) *The Meaning of Rationalisation* (London: Nisbet).

Van de Ven, A. H. (1981) 'The Organisation Assessment Programme', in A. H. Van de Ven and W. F. Joyce (eds), *Perspectives on Organisation Design and Behaviour* (New York: Wiley).

Vernon, R. (1971) *Sovereignty at Bay* (New York: Basic Books).

Vroom, H. (1964) *Work and Motivation* (New York: Wiley).

Vroom, H. and Yetton, P. W. (1973) *Leadership and Decision-Making* (University of Pittsburgh Press).

Wall, T. D. and Lischeron, J. A. (1977) *Worker Participation: A Critique of the Literature and Some Fresh Evidence* (London: McGraw-Hill).

Weber, M. (1947) *The Theory of Social and Economic Organisation*, translated by T. Parsons and A. M. Henderson, with an introduction by T. Parsons (New York: Free Press).

Weber, M. (1948) *From Max Weber: Essays in Sociology*, translated, edited and with an introduction by H. C. Gerth and C. Wright Mills (London: Routledge & Kegan Paul).

Wedderburn, D. E. C. and Crompton, R. (1972) *Workers' Attitudes and Technology* (Cambridge University Press).

Weick, K. E. (1969) *The Social Psychology of Organising* (Reading, Mass.: Addison-Wesley).

Weick, K. E. (1987) 'Substitutes for Corporate Strategy', in D. J. Teece (ed.), *The Competitive Challenge: Strategies for Industrial Innovation and Revitalisation* (Cambridge, Mass.: Ballinger).

Wheelwright, S. C. (1987) 'Restoring Competitiveness in US Manufacturing' in D. J. Teece (ed.), *The Competitive Challenge: Strategies for Industrial Innovation and Revitalisation*, (Cambridge, Mass: Ballinger).

White, M. (1981) *Payment Systems in Britain* (Aldershot: Gower).

Wickens, P. (1987) *The Road to Nissan* (London: Macmillan).

Wildavsky, A. (1983) 'Information as an Organizational Problem', *Journal of Management Studies*, Vol. 20, No. 1, pp. 29–40.

Wilensky, H. (1967) *Organizational Intelligence, Knowledge and Policy in Government and Industry* (New York: Basic Books).

Wilkinson, B. (1983) *The Shopfloor Politics of New Technology* (London: Heinemann).

Williamson, O. E. (1975) *Market and Hierarchies: Analysis and Antitrust Implications* (New York: Free Press).

Williamson, O. E. (1985) *The Economic Institutions of Capitalism* (New York: Free Press).

Wilson, J. Q. (1966) 'Innovation in Organization: Notes Towards a Theory', in J. D. Thompson (ed.), *Approaches to Organizational Design* (University of Pittsburgh Press) pp. 195–218.

Womack, J. P., Jones, D. T. and Roos, D. (1990) *The Machine that changed the World* (New York: Ranson Associates).

Wood, S. (1979) 'A Reappraisal of the Contingency Approach to Organisation', *Journal of Management Studies*, Vol. 16, No. 3, pp. 334–54.

Woodward, J. (1958) *Management and Technology* (London: HMSO).

Woodward, J. (1965) *Industrial Organisation: Theory and Practice* (Oxford University Press).

Woodward, J. (1970) *Industrial Organisation: Behaviour and Control* (Oxford University Press).

Woot, P. de (1984) 'Le Management Stratégique des Groupes Industriels', reference in the *Financial Times*, 26 November 1984.

Yutchman, E. and Seashore, S. (1967) 'A System Resource Approach to Organizational Effectiveness', *American Sociological Review*, Vol. 32, pp. 891–903.

Zald, M. (ed.) (1970) *Power in Organisations* (Nashville, Tenn.: Vanderbilt University Press).

Name Index

Note: where multiple authors are given in the text, the index may only list the name of the first author.

Subject Index